The Parish Churches of Medieval England

By the same author

The Monastic Grange in Medieval England
Medieval Archaeology in England. A Guide to the Historical Sources
Medieval Southampton. The Port and Trading Community, A.D. 1000–1600
Excavations in Medieval Southampton 1953–1969
The English Medieval Town
Medieval England. A Social history and archaeology from the Conquest to A.D. 1600
The Atlas of Medieval Man

The Parish Churches of Medieval England

COLIN PLATT

Secker & Warburg
London

First published in England 1981 by
Martin Secker & Warburg Limited
54 Poland Street, London W1V 3DF

Copyright © Colin Platt 1981

ISBN 0–436–37553–2 (Cased Edition)
ISBN 0–436–37554–0 (Paperback Edition)

Filmset in Great Britain by BAS Printers Limited,
Over Wallop, Hampshire
Printed in Hong Kong by Wing King Tong Co Ltd

Contents

List of Illustrations

Preface and Acknowledgements

For centuries, the parish churches of medieval England have been among its best-loved antiquities, and there has been no shortage of books to celebrate them. However, almost all of these, whatever their date, have been primarily descriptive. What they have set out to do, frequently achieving this very well, has been to establish sequences in building styles and to record peculiarities of structure. They have discussed the fabric of our churches and their furnishings, but they have said comparatively little about the role of the parish church in contemporary society and have seldom dwelt long on its priests. Yet the buildings of a church, as it must be obvious to all, reflect more than changes in techniques and in fashion. It has been my purpose in this book to write a social history of the parish church which may also do service in the interpretation of its surviving remains. Of course, I have illustrated my book from the great stock of church buildings that has been preserved for us by centuries of continuous worship. But this is not a study of parish church architecture in the conventional sense, nor has it been my intention to pre-empt the discussion of the archaeology of the parish church in which others have made themselves more expert. In short, my concern here has always been more with the reasons for a parish church rebuilding or refurnishing than with the material characteristics of either. It is in this primary emphasis on historical explanation that my book sets out to say something new.

We may want to know *why* a parish church came to look like it did, but we must also, to appreciate this, have some understanding of *what* happened to its fabric and its furnishings in the process. Accordingly, I have tried wherever possible to illustrate the buildings and the individual church furnishings I have discussed, counting such illustration not just as ornament to my text but as an essential adjunct to it. In assembling the illustrations, I have become indebted to many individual authors and photographers, and I am happy to place this now on record. As always, I have owed much to the skill of Alan Burn and his staff, of the Southampton University Cartographic Unit, in the preparation for this book of each of the maps and other line-drawings in it, with a special debt to Alan Burn himself for his redrawing of the Pounder brass (Fig. 120). For permission to work from their originals, freely and generously given, I am grateful to Professor Frank Barlow for Fig. 3 (*The English Church 1000–1066*, p. 181); to Dr Harold Taylor for Fig. 7 (*Anglo-Saxon Architecture*, vol. 3, figs 720, 731 and 746); to Dr Warwick Rodwell for Fig. 16 (*Antiq. J.*, 58 (1978), p. 144); to Dr Lawrence Butler for Fig. 42 (*Proc. Cambridge Antiq. Soc.*, 50 (1956), pp. 91 and 95); to the executors of the late Dr W. A. Pantin for Fig. 49 (*Med. Arch.*, 1 (1957), p. 123); and to Professor Barrie Dobson for Fig. 59 (*Durham Priory 1400–1450*, pp. 147, 150 and 154).

For the plates, copyright of which remains with the original photographers, I am indebted to Professor Martin Biddle and the Winchester Excavation Committee for Fig. 13; to Alan Hannan and the Northamptonshire Archaeology Unit for Fig. 14; to Brian Spencer, the Rev. G. Humphriss (rector of St Martin's, Canterbury) and the Warden and Fellows of New College, Oxford, for Figs 22, 53 and 72; to Canon Maurice Ridgway, literary executor of Fred H. Crossley, and to the Courtauld Institute of Art for Figs 40, 47, 60, 77, 101, 114, 124, 126 and 134; to Mrs Olive Smith, widow of the late Edwin Smith, for Figs 1, 2, 19, 31, 36, 43, 44, 45, 50, 86, 87, 104, 105, 111, 112, 113, 115, 116, 122, 125, 128 and 135; to Hallam Ashley for Figs 8, 9, 10, 12, 15, 20, 23, 30, 61, 62, 65, 67, 69, 75, 100, 102, 106, 107, 110, 133 and 138; and to the National Monuments Record for Figs 4, 5, 6, 11, 17, 18, 21, 24–9, 32, 33, 34, 35, 37–41, 46, 48, 51, 52, 54–8, 63, 64, 66, 68, 70, 71, 73, 74, 76, 78–82, 84, 85, 88–89, 103, 108, 109, 117–9, 121, 123, 127, 129–32, 136 and 137.

For permission to quote passages from their volumes in the *English Historical Documents* series, I am much obliged to the late Professor Harry Rothwell, with whom I was in correspondence shortly before his death, to Professor A. R. Myers, and to Professor C. H. Williams, as I am again to the executors of the late Dr W. A. Pantin for the quotations from parish priests' manuals, originally published in Dr Pantin's *The English Church in the Fourteenth Century* (1955).

I dedicate this book to my wife, Valerie, and to our children, Emma, Miles, Tabitha and Theo. 'Full woeful is the household that lacks a woman.'

Glossary

Acolyte   a clerk in minor orders whose particular duty was the service of the altar

Advowson   the patronage of a church; the right of presentation to a benefice

Agistment   a Church rate, or tithe, charged on pasture lands

Alb   a full-length white linen garment, with sleeves and girdle, worn by the celebrant at mass under a chasuble

Antiphon   a sentence, or versicle, from Scripture, sung as an introduction to a psalm or canticle

Apparitor   a summoner; an officer of an ecclesiastical court whose duty it was to cite persons to appear before it

Appropriation   the formal transfer to a monastic house of the tithes and other endowments of a parish church, agreed usually in return for the promise to keep a vicar on the proceeds

Apse   the semicircular termination of the chancel at its eastern end

Aquebajulus   a holy-water clerk

Aumbry   a locker or cupboard of some kind, usually placed in the north chancel wall, for the safe-keeping of service-books and sacramental vessels

Avoidance   the vacating of a benefice

Benefice   an ecclesiastical living; an office held in return for duties and to which an income attaches

Breviary   a book containing the Divine Office (lessons, psalms, hymns etc.) for each day

Canonist   a lawyer trained in canon law (the law of the Church)

Capitulary   a compilation of episcopal or other statutes

Catechumens   members of a Christian congregation being prepared for baptism or confirmation

Chapter   the body of canons, presided over by a dean, responsible for the administration of a cathedral and its endowments

Chasuble   the top garment (a sleeveless mantle) worn by the celebrant at mass over the alb and stole

Chrism   holy oil; a mixture of olive oil and balsam used in Christian ritual

Chrismatory   a small box or other vessel, usually of metal but sometimes also of a cheaper material like pottery, for keeping the holy oils

Ciborium   a chalice-shaped vessel, with a lid, for the consecrated bread (the reserved Host)

Clerestory   the upper part of the main walls of a church, above the line of the aisle roofs, pierced by windows to help light the church interior

Collect   a short prayer appointed for a particular day (hence 'collect-books')

Commissary   an officer representing the bishop in a part of his diocese and exercising jurisdiction there in his name

Compline   the last service of the day, being the final canonical hour

Convocation   the provincial assembly of the clergy

Corporal   a linen square on which the consecrated elements are placed during the celebration of the Eucharist

Coucher   a large book (hence 'coucher-book', a large cartulary)

Cruet   a vessel, usually one of a pair, for holding the wine or the water at the Eucharist

Cure   cure of souls; the spiritual charge of parishioners (hence 'curate')

Deacon   assistant to the priest and next under him in rank, being a member of the third order of the ministry

Dilapidations   payments due on the vacating of a benefice to make good any damage sustained by Church property during the previous incumbency

Enterclose   a partition

Eucharist   the Communion, or Sacrament of the Lord's Supper: the central ceremony of the mass

Free chapel   a chapel founded by the king (often developing into a wealthy church), not subject to the jurisdiction of the bishop

Freestone   any easily carved fine-grained stone (e.g. a limestone or a sandstone)

Frontal   an embroidered covering for the front of the altar

Glebe   land attaching to a church and intended to supplement the incumbent's income

Gradual   a book of antiphons

Hymnary   a hymn-book, or hymnal

Legenda   a legendary, or book of legends, concerning the lives of saints

Lenten veil   a veil used for veiling pictures and crucifixes during Lent

Maniple   a strip of silk, or other fine-stuff, worn over the left arm of the celebrant at mass

Manual   a handbook of directions to the celebrant for the administration of the sacraments

Mazer   a bowl or drinking-cup

Missal   a mass-book, giving the words of, and directions for, the mass

Mortuary   a customary levy, claimed by the priest, on the estate of a deceased parishioner

Notary public   a lawyer or other person authorized to draft and attest contracts etc.

Obit   a memorial mass celebrated annually on the mind-day of a deceased person, usually the anniversary of his death

Oblation   an offering to Church funds

Ordinal   a service-book, with instructions to the priest on the order of services through the ecclesiastical year

Ordinary   a high ecclesiastic, usually the bishop, entitled to exercise jurisdiction in his own right

Orphrey   an embroidered strip, or band, on a vestment

Paten   a shallow circular dish, usually of silver, on which the consecrated bread is placed during the celebration of the Eucharist

Pardoner   a person holding a papal licence to sell indulgences or pardons

Pax brede   a small plate or tablet (also known as an 'osculatory'), with a handle on the back and with the image of Christ or of the Virgin on the front, to be kissed at mass by priest and congregation

Penitential   a book listing sins and the appropriate penances

Penitentiary   an ecclesiastical officer concerned with the administration of penance in the diocese

Piscina   a basin, usually set in the south chancel wall, for washing the chalice and paten at mass

Porticus (pl.)   the side-chapels common at Anglo-Saxon minster churches, frequently used for the more important burials

Prebend   the revenues, whether from land or tithes, granted to an ecclesiastic as his stipend

Processional   an office-book, giving the text of the hymns, psalms, and litanies used in ecclesiastical processions

Proctor   an officer, or other agent, appointed to collect Church dues

Procuration   a customary payment extracted from incumbents in lieu of their obligation to entertain a visiting bishop, archdeacon, or other high ecclesiastic

Pyx   a vessel, usually a box, for holding the consecrated bread (the reserved Host)

Quatrefoil   a very common Gothic architectural ornament in which four arcs are divided by cusps, rather in the form of a four-leafed clover

Reliquary   a casket, often richly decorated, in which relics are kept

Reredos   a screen, usually carved and painted, behind and above the altar

Retable   an altar-piece; a painting, or frame holding sculptures, fixed to the back of an altar

Rochet   a white-linen vestment, similar to a surplice

Rood   the great cross, or crucifix, placed on the rood-beam in the chancel arch

Sacring   the consecration of the elements (hence 'sacring bell' and 'sacring torch')

Sedilia   the seats, usually three and set in the south chancel wall with the piscina, of the priest, deacon, and subdeacon

Sepulchre   a tomb or tomb-like structure (hence 'Easter Sepulchre')

Sequestrator   the diocesan official appointed to take charge of estates or other property on which dues are owing to the bishop

Server   the celebrant's assistant at the altar during mass

Soul-scot   a mortuary, or offering made to the priest on behalf of a deceased parishioner

Stole   a narrow strip of embroidered silk or linen, worn over other vestments to hang round the neck and down the front of the celebrant at mass

Stoup   a stone basin for holy water, usually placed near the main entrance of the church

Suffragan   assistant (hence 'suffragan bishop')

Surplice   a loosely fitting white linen vestment, with wide sleeves

Synod   a council, or assembly, of the clergy

Synodal   a customary payment made to the bishop by his lower clergy on the occasion of a visitation or a synod

Tenebrae   the office of Matins and Lauds in the special form sung during the Wednesday, Thursday, and Friday of Holy Week, at which candles are extinguished one by one following each psalm

Thurible   a censer; a vessel, usually of metal, for the burning of incense

Tithe (praedial)   a tax, payable to the rector, of the tenth part of all agrarian produce

Transepts   the two arms, to north and south, of a cruciform church

Troper   a book of tropes, being the phrases or sentences added by a choir to embellish the mass

Vicar General   an ecclesiastical officer appointed by the bishop as his deputy in matters jurisdictional and administrative

Weeper   a sculptured mourning figure, often shown hooded, set against the side of a tomb-chest

Chapter 1

Origins

The more apples the tree beareth, the
more she boweth to the folk[1]

The division of medieval England into the ecclesiastical parishes that have retained
their identity to this day was already far advanced in 1086–7 when first recorded in
Domesday Book. Yet the circumstances of this pre-Conquest reordering of the Church
are obscure still and highly debatable, and the Domesday survey itself, for our
purposes at least, was not very happily timed. England at the end of William the
Conqueror's reign was very much in a condition of flux. Where the emergence of the
parish is concerned, as in much else, Domesday Book shows us a process in action. It
gives us some hint of what had gone before and helps us towards an understanding of
what followed. It denies us the certainties we might have enjoyed had it been
compiled either a century later or earlier.

Where Domesday looks both forward and back is in its portrayal of a Church that
was shedding at an increasing rate its original missionary organization. We cannot
now hope for a complete view of the minster system of Anglo-Saxon England, with its
large collegiate churches answerable, if only loosely, to the bishop. Nevertheless, it is
plain that, during the seventh-century conversion of England, the minster became
the focus of missionary activity in the countryside, much as the baptistery had been
in Italy before, or the great 'country church' in Gaul. Under the patronage of king and
bishop, the minster clergy carried the word of God out into the estates and villages,
offering the facilities of a central church for baptism and burial or for the observance
by a large congregation of the more important of the Christian festivals.

No system such as this, being designed to economize both in buildings and in
clergy, could hope to meet the needs of every Christian believer. And it was
inevitable that, alongside these centres, a network of private chapels, or oratories,
should very quickly have developed. By the early eighth century already, the
private estate church had become, indeed, quite common. But there is little as yet, in
churches such as these, to do more than hint at the much later emergence of the
village church and parish as these would come to be understood in the tenth century.
Priests themselves continued to be in short supply, and the rights and interests of the
established minsters stood in the way of that village-based ministry for which Bede,
the historian, was among the first to call, as early as the first decades of the eighth
century. A comprehensive and effective organization of the parishes had in practice
to await the erosion by impoverishment of the minsters. When at last the village
church multiplied, bending the boughs of the Church to the folk, it did so on the
initiative of the private proprietor, as much in despite of the Church as because of it.

Very probably, it was the weakening of the existing institutions of the Church,

1 *Left* Brixworth, Northamptonshire: a former minster and now
the largest surviving Anglo-Saxon
church in England

2 The double-headed Anglo-Saxon
window on the inside wall of the
tower, formerly a porch, of Deer-
hurst Church, Gloucestershire

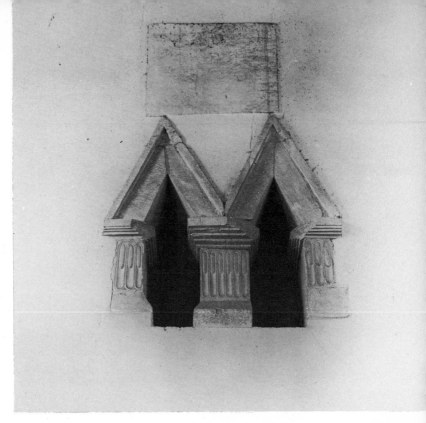

brought about during the ninth-century Viking invasions, that set the scene for fresh developments in the villages. Many minsters were plundered beyond hope of recovery, and others entered a steady decline. Nevertheless, there were other pressures in the localities at work as well, both social and (still more obviously) economic. It is clear that, by comparatively early in the tenth century, the presence of a priest in every village community, at least in Wessex, had come to be assumed by the legislators.[2] Similarly, before the reign of Athelstan (925–40), the manorial church—sometimes called an 'inferior' church or a church 'of the second foundation'—had recognizably become a badge of thegnly status. Athelstan himself might raise a ceorl to the rank of thegn if he had accumulated an estate of four hides and a church,[3] while in an eleventh-century text, *Of People's Ranks and Law*, the ownership of the manorial church was among the conditions for promotion.[4] Moreover, ownership of the church, as it was then understood, carried with it substantial advantages. Not only did the builder of the church and his heirs retain the right to appoint the priest who would serve it—as patrons they preserved what is still called the 'advowson'—but they acquired an interest in the tithes and offerings (the 'oblations') which, although it continued to be disputed by the minster clergy and the bishop, was very difficult to shake. In effect, the village church was both essential to the status of the Late Saxon thegn and a part of his capital worth. Like his estate, his hall, and his weapons of war, it was a necessary element in his equipment.

Plainly, what gave the parish church its widening advantage over the much longer-established minster was the financial definition that tithes and other revenues increasingly came to bestow on it. Tithe payments, although recommended and well understood before the tenth century, did not become compulsory in England until the enactments of Edmund (939–46) and Edgar (959–75), the one imposing ecclesiastical penalties on tithe-evaders, the other writing payment into the law of the land.[5] As soon as they did so, they forced some definition of the limits of personal responsibility, with the agreement in many cases of parish boundaries. Regular patterns in parish boundaries are discernible still in counties as far apart as Yorkshire and Berkshire, Lincolnshire and Wiltshire.[6] And whether these are owed chiefly to some dominant natural feature or to a need, much earlier recognized, to share out resources between estates, they underline the force of the financial incentive in bringing order (of a kind) out of anarchy. Such definitions as these were characteristic of tenth-century English society, being among the more significant consequences of unification under the Wessex line of kings. Before the end of the century, every man in England, for purposes of geld and tithing (taxation and policing), belonged to a vill; he was a member of a parish with a tithe liability; he had identifiable duties and rights.

How far the individual church of the vill had advanced by the Conquest is recorded, if unevenly, in Domesday. In different parts of the country, different methods of listing were adopted, with the result that the picture Domesday gives us of church-provision in late-eleventh-century England is nothing like complete. Nevertheless, where the recording of churches was at its most systematic, as it was in the counties of Suffolk and Huntingdonshire, over 50 per cent of the vills named in the survey already had churches of their own. And if the national total is less impressive, with a total of just over 2,000 churches shared among no fewer than 13,400 places, the under-recording that resulted in these figures has been established time and again.[7] Among the more interesting products of recent church archaeology (below, p. 17) has been the demonstration of a degree of pre-Conquest village-church building altogether unexpected in its scale. But even without the evidence of material remains, the thickly-churched aspect of the Late Saxon landscape is no longer reasonably in doubt. In some counties, especially in the west and north, the old minsters co-existed with village churches and may even have continued to dominate them. However, the crowding-out of the old system by the new was everywhere evident, and was probably gathering pace. Our most precious evidence both of the character of Late Saxon church organization and of the development of a parish-church system alongside it, has been preserved in a document slightly later than Domesday—the so-called *Domesday Monachorum* of Christ Church Cathedral Priory. This Canterbury survey, although of early-twelfth-century date, was evidently based on much earlier material, originating before the Conquest. It records still the dominance of the twelve central churches, or minsters, in Kent, listing the groups of 'inferior' churches by now considered to be dependent upon them (Fig. 3). Yet it was these latter, of course, some of them bearing the names of their founders or current lay owners, that were just then in process of breaking away from the baptismal churches of the first missionary-based partition of the county. Like Domesday Book itself, the *Domesday Monachorum* of Christ Church, Canterbury, freezes the movement from minster to parish at a point mid-way towards completion. It lays out for us both the framework of the old organization and the individual elements, still traditionally related to that frame, of the parish-church system which displaced it.[8]

3 *Right* Some East Kent mother churches and their dependants in *c*. 1100 (Frank Barlow)

EAST KENT

Minster

East Church

Leysdown

Iwade

Upchurch

Lower
Halstow

Rainham

Milton

Newington

Bobbing

Tonge

Teynham

Hartlip

Bapchild

Borden

Stone

Stockbury

Tunstall

Rodmersham

Bredgar

Milsted

Boxley

Detling

Allington

Thornham

Frinsted

Doddington

Selling

Maidstone

Hollingbourne

Leeds

Lenham

Langley

Chart Sutton

Ulcombe

Boughton

Sutton Valence

Headcorn

Marden

Goudhurst

N

Mother church

Dependency

Grouping

0   km   10

Evidently, a reorganization by parish of the Anglo-Saxon Church had got under way well before the Norman invasion. In the century and more of its initial emergence, the village church had collected an endowment in lands (its 'glebe'); it had established a claim to the usual oblations, was maintained on such payments as plough-scot (a penny levied on each plough team) and soul-scot (a mortuary or 'corpse-present'), and could look to tithes for the bulk of its income. Moreover, in acquiring these rights, it had contributed to an elevation in standing of the parish priest, diligently urged by the reformers—he might rank with a thegn if unmarried and chaste, and was rarely less than a freeman.[9]

Yet if there is one principal lesson to be drawn from Domesday, it is, quite simply, that these processes were far from complete. Over-large parishes, some of them the traditional territories of minsters, had still to be divided. There were new towns to be provided with churches, and regions which, as they attracted settlement, would require the services of more priests. In a village church system that had grown up haphazardly, at the whim of the estate owner, or lay proprietor, there were many anomalies to be ironed out, including the phenomenon of the partitioned church, divided in fractions of a quarter, a third, a sixth, or even a twelfth between founders, their heirs and successors.[10] Church-building had been active before the Conquest, but there is much evidence to suggest—in re-dedications, in the claims of near-contemporary chroniclers like Orderic Vitalis and William of Malmesbury, and in the fabric of the churches themselves—that the pace quickened as Norman government took hold.[11] In Sussex alone, church provision is thought to have doubled in the two centuries following the Domesday listing.[12] And although, of course, there are all sorts of difficulties in determining exactly where the Anglo-Saxon contribution to this process ended and where the Norman subsequently began, individual studies have suggested a similar post-Conquest multiplication of the churches in Lancashire, Staffordshire, and Cheshire, while London, for all its growth in the pre-Conquest period, is known to have collected a great number of its churches in the next hundred and fifty years.[13]

In part, the surge in Norman church-building resulted from the windfall of the Conquest. The new wealth of many alien landowners encouraged them to put money into church-building programmes which further manorialization and the re-grouping of estates would probably in any event have made necessary. Nevertheless, it would be a mistake to see the Normans as alone responsible for a transformation of the Church which had many other pressures to promote it. A major campaign for reform in the Western Church was to begin, within scarcely a decade of the Norman Conquest of England, during the pontificate of Gregory VII (1073–85), also known as Hildebrand. And although the principal drive of the Hildebrandine reformers was towards a reorganization of the upper reaches of the Church, securing the independence of the bishops from the king, their fundamentalist position on the separation of Church and State (of the ecclesiastical and the lay power) inevitably found its echoes lower down. The proprietorial church had had its critics before the elevation of the monk Hildebrand to the papacy. The marriage of clergy, with its implied threat to the property of the Church, had been discouraged where possible by Anglo-Saxon reforming bishops, and the transfer of individual parish churches to the care and ownership of monastic institutions had begun some decades before the

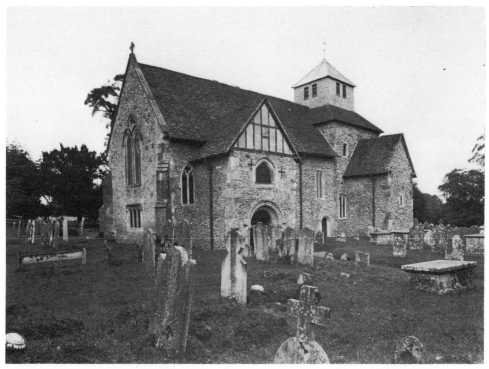

4 Breamore, Hampshire: an Anglo-Saxon minster of *c*. 1000, with post-Conquest additions

Conquest, as a list of such donations to Christ Church, Canterbury, makes clear.[14] Nevertheless, the trickle of such gifts, already seen before Gregory's reforms, became a flood during the course of the next century as many factors combined to encourage them. It was in Lincoln that a thirteenth-century jury would recall the time when Lincoln citizens like themselves had owned many churches, with their advowsons or right to appoint priests. Since then the bishop, over the course of the years, had successfully gained control of those churches, the majority coming to him (or so it was thought) by neglect of their original possessors.[15]

By that time, a powerful reason for such neglect had become the difficulty experienced by many lay patrons in getting much of a profit out of their churches. Over the years, the belief that the Church's property should belong only to God had strengthened. The lay proprietor who had considered it his right to derive rents and services from the parish church traditionally bound to his family, now found these ever harder to collect or exact, so that what he was left with was seldom more than the patronage—the right to select a priest and to present him to the bishop for formal institution, or admission, to the spiritual care (the 'cure of souls') of the parish. However, it would surely be wrong to emphasize profitability alone as the motive for a transfer of rights in the parish churches. The late-eleventh-century reforms had been both accompanied and succeeded by a deep surge of popular feeling and by a return to a more broadly based faith. To many, the millennial year, now almost three generations away, had implied a re-awakening in religion. It was after this, Raul

Glaber wrote, that great campaigns of church-building and improvement seemed to clothe the earth 'in the white robe of the Church'.[16] But later events, including the launching of an immensely influential monastic reform and the apparent miracle of the First Crusade, did much to confirm and extend the revival. One of the more attractive characteristics of the popularization of religion in the period was the mounting appeal, in the Catholic West as much as in the Orthodox East, of the cults of the Virgin and the saints. Practices varied between the counties of England, but overwhelmingly the preference in parish-church dedications came to be for the Virgin Mary, far in the lead, with All Saints second, and St Peter a very close third.[17] Not uncommonly, the more cautious parishioners would hedge their bets with a dedication to the Blessed Virgin (St Mary) and All Saints (All Hallows) together. Or they might, on the recognition of a new saint in their own times, select him to serve as their intercessor. St Thomas of Canterbury, the martyred Thomas Becket (d. 1170), had some eighty dedications to his name, ranking as high as twenty-second in the list of more popular choices. No doubt it was felt that, as a recent messenger to heaven, St Thomas would enjoy a special position in the affections and the counsels of the Almighty.

Church dedications have sometimes been used as a measure of parish-church provision, the obviously twelfth-century dedications to St Mary and St Thomas, with other favourite Norman dedications to St Michael and St John, being set against a characteristically Anglo-Saxon dedication preference, like that to the Holy Rood, to establish a multiplication of village churches in the century following the Conquest. However, dedications can change—the church of St Thomas of Canterbury at Pagham (Sussex), for example, incorporates work that is plainly Saxon.[18] And their

5 A memorial sundial of c. 1060 over the south door at Kirkdale Church, Yorkshire. The inscription begins: 'Orm son of Gamal bought St Gregory's minster when it was all ruined and fallen down, and he caused it to be built afresh from the foundation'

evidence is of less value in the counting of churches than as a measure of new fashions in the faith. The cult of the Virgin, they certainly spell out for us, had taken a hold in twelfth-century England right down through the Church and lay hierarchy to the folk. Arising from this climate of popular devotion, the contribution of peasants and craftsmen to the rebuilding of Chartres and other French cathedrals is documented and has frequently been cited. Less well known is the part that the peasants played— the *rustici* or *homines* of the vill—in the erection and the endowment in perpetuity of their own churches. Yet it is clear that the peasants, villeins as well as freemen, were not infrequently associated with their lords in works of such cooperative piety. At Keddington, for example, a Lincolnshire parish, the men of the vill are known to have contributed an agreed proportion of their lands (a tenth or slightly less) to augment the glebe of their church, while similar gifts, whatever the story that lies behind them, seem also to have been made by the *rustici* of Great Sturton in the same county, endowing their chapel with eight acres of arable, as by the peasant parishioners of Badby and Newnham (Northamptonshire) and Norton and Lenchwick (Worcestershire), all probably within the twelfth century.[19]

Certainly, it was during the course of the twelfth century in particular that the bishops took a grip on the parish churches which they were never thereafter to loosen. The proprietorial church was not wholly to disappear, the king and other great landowners continuing to make claims, denied to lesser men, to the advowsons and even to the profits of their churches.[20] Yet the king himself, during that century, had granted away many of his free chapels in perpetuity, and the moral and other pressures that he found himself exposed to were obviously still more powerful lower down. By the end of the twelfth century, the privately owned church had become a rarity. Something like a quarter of the parish churches of England were now in the hands of the religious houses, with most of the remainder answering directly to the bishops. A revolution in land-holding had occurred.

It is perhaps true to say that no such revolution could ever have happened if the landowners had not, over the period as a whole, enjoyed considerable (and mounting) prosperity. Population was rising, harvests were good, epidemics were rare, and markets were everywhere proliferating. Nevertheless, most parish revenues were going up as well, and their loss to the lay owners, for all the new difficulties in collecting them, must often have been judged a real sacrifice.

Indeed, nowhere is the true worth of the freshly transferred churches better illustrated than in the disputes that frequently arose, within a few years of the transfer, between those who might claim to be the beneficiaries. For many monastic houses, and in particular for the smaller Augustinian foundations that had proliferated in twelfth-century England, the ownership of a parish church, or of a group of such churches, constituted the greater part of their original endowment, without which they could scarcely have hoped to survive. Yet inevitably the speed with which the transfer of parish-church rights had occurred, accompanied by the ambiguities of badly drafted charters, left claims in doubt, whether as to the entitlement of the original owner to give away the church or as to who he truly intended to receive it. One of the more straightforward of these disputes concerned the church of Babraham, in Cambridgeshire, claimed equally by the Augustinian canons of Waltham (Essex) and by the Huntingdonshire Cistercians of Sawtry. Geoffrey de Scalers's gift to Waltham of the patronage of Babraham, together with tithes from his demesne and rights of common in the vill, was an act of conventional piety, characteristic of his times and agreed without difficulty by his overlord, Geoffrey Plantagenet. Yet what he had neglected to establish before making his donation was whether or not any similar transfer of rights had been made by his father before him. Again very much in harmony with his period, Geoffrey's father had chosen to round off his life by seeking admission to the Cistercian community at Sawtry, and among the assets he seems to have taken to Sawtry was the gift of the patronage of the church at Babraham, in which parish the monks had already established a grange. By the end of the century, both Waltham and Sawtry could exhibit a charter of gift and a right to Babraham which, in a perhaps not untypical example of confusion at Rome, would be confirmed successively in 1193 and 1195 by the same pope, Celestine III.[21] The resolution of the disputed advowson in favour of Waltham, although freely conceded by the abbot and monks of Sawtry just a few years later, could scarcely have been secured without a legacy of bitterness that would continue to divide the two communities.

Another more complex rivalry, although of especial interest as it illustrates a consequence of the separation of the parish churches from their minster, concerned the churches of Berkeley Hernesse, in Gloucestershire, eventually tied up in a triangular dispute between two Benedictine communities, at Gloucester and Reading, and one of the wealthier Augustinian houses, at Bristol. What complicated the distribution of the Berkeley churches was a continuing uncertainty over the degree of authority still attaching to the old minster and mother-church at Berkeley, of which even a list of former dependencies could no longer be agreed by the disputants. Clearly, the old 'parish' of the Anglo-Saxon minster had long since split into its several elements, making it difficult to determine what a gift of the patronage of the church at Berkeley truly conferred on its new owner. The final outcome of the quarrel was that the Benedictines of Gloucester kept the two Berkeley churches they had acquired in 1146, while the canons of Bristol were awarded three churches and the former mother-church at Berkeley itself. Reading was paid off with a pension.[22]

A solution of a kind had been reached at Berkeley, but it had required the good offices of the pope and the king, of the abbot of St Albans, and of the bishops of Hereford, Chichester, and Exeter, and it had not been arrived at without pain. Yet, to us, what the Berkeley quarrel brings together is two of the major problems of organization that haunted the twelfth-century Church. Plainly, there were remnants still of the pre-Conquest minster system to confuse the allegiances of the new parishes. It was far from clear, even within the Church, how one element related to another. But there were difficulties, too, in the definition of patronage, and few were certain whose right it was to alienate properties of this nature. The sad history of the church at Bexley, a Kentish possession of the canons of Holy Trinity, Aldgate, provides convincing demonstration of continuing confusions even where none, in truth, should have arisen. Bexley had belonged to the archbishops of Canterbury since the early ninth century, both as lay and ecclesiastical lords, and William of Corbeil (archbishop 1123–36), a former canon of Holy Trinity, was perfectly within his rights in transferring the ownership of the church there, with all tithes and

6 Babraham, Cambridgeshire: the subject of a late-twelfth-century patronage dispute between the Augustinian canons of Waltham, in Essex, and the Huntingdonshire Cistercians of Sawtry, eventually resolved in favour of Waltham Abbey

customary perquisites, to the house of canons that had given him his beginnings. Yet his successors at Canterbury, who continued to hold the manor at Bexley, repeatedly forgot, or chose to ignore, the rights of the canons in the church there. It was their practice to withdraw when confronted with the documents that gave unequivocal proof of Holy Trinity's long-standing ownership. However, they usually succeeded in exacting a price for what they persisted in regarding as a concession, bringing upon the canons, time and again, the heavy expense of taking their grievances to law.[23]

The disputed advowson of Bexley Church is not the only interest that Holy Trinity's rights in the parish possess for us. During the eleventh- and twelfth-century transfer of churches, many had come to the monastic houses with little more than patronage (the advowson) and with a pension, or fee, payable by the incumbent out of parochial revenues that were otherwise controlled by himself. These were important rights, and they constituted a large part of the annual income of a good number of monastic communities. But they did not amount to formal appropriation *ad proprios usus*, which would have given the new owner the authority to annex to his own use whatever tithes and other endowments of the parish were currently drawn on to support it. Archbishop Corbeil, however, had been quite explicit in granting Holy Trinity not merely the right to present the priest at Bexley, but also 'all tithes of tithe-able things' in the parish, as well as whatever the priory might obtain from 'all right customs belonging to the church'. In effect, the canons were appropriating the church in one of the earliest adequately recorded examples of a practice which, in later generations and as the needs and expectations of the religious houses mounted, became increasingly common.[24]

Holy Trinity, Aldgate, as would be the practice of other monastic appropriators in their turn, took to itself the 'great tithes' (on the main cereal crops and on hay), while assigning what were known as the 'small tithes' of the parish (on minor produce and livestock) to the support of a vicar at Bexley. And plainly such an arrangement as this could become very profitable for the canons. Inevitably, they had their imitators. Whether or not they took their model from Aldgate Priory, the monks of Westminster before the end of the twelfth century were making their first formal appropriations of the tithes and other receipts of the parish churches from which earlier they had been content with a pension.[25] And while Westminster Abbey continued to augment its income with further successful appropriations, other religious houses followed suit. Such a diversion of revenues away from the parishes could scarcely fail to lead to abuses, and the remedying of these, by one method or another, became in due course one of the principal concerns of the more active of the late-medieval bishops (below, p. 74). Nevertheless, it had been a principle of tithe-collection from the beginning that at least part of the tithes—a quarter or some greater fraction than this—should be assigned to purposes outside the parish, normally to the benefit of the bishop. And if the Anglo-Saxon bishops had neglected this right, allowing many lay proprietors to retain the whole tithe for their own purposes, the bishops of the reformed twelfth-century Church, in giving their consent to monastic appropriations of tithes, were perhaps doing no more than restoring the observance of an earlier acceptable practice.

Indeed, formal appropriation of the parish churches, although it would later have many critics, should surely be seen, in the twelfth century at least, as a part of that process of rationalization of rights to which, after centuries of subjection to over-powerful laymen, the Church was at last in the position to give full attention. Everywhere, both on Church and lay estates, boundaries were in dispute, jurisdictions were questioned, and rights remained very uncertain. Many must have felt that a clear definition of the ownership of church and tithes, even if it seemed to give too much to the new monastic appropriator, was preferable to the doubts they had hitherto been troubled by. In part at least, the monks had been driven to establish their rights in the parish churches by the pressure put upon them by reforming bishops to justify whatever they might claim there. Such zeal was not without promise.

Chapter 2

Buildings and Church Furnishings before 1350

> He that will not willingly go into the church door
> shall unwillingly be led into hell door.

The parish church, like any other building, is designed for a very clear purpose. It must accommodate a congregation, which may enlarge or contract according to the fortunes of the settlement, and it must make some provision for liturgical space—for the unencumbered celebration of the mass. Inevitably, the needs of such a building are different from those of a great cathedral or monastic church, although some parish churches in the course of time grew almost to cathedral proportions. A village congregation is predictable and reasonably stable: it does not swell exceptionally, even at the greater Church festivals. There are no relics, icons, effigies, or the tombs of saints for the pilgrim to visit and adore. At the same time, ritual is limited by the paucity of clergy, and if space is still needed for liturgical purposes, it need not usually be very great. The early monastic churches and cathedrals, and even the collegiate minster, display a characteristic elaboration of plan, with side-chapels (porticus), crypts, porches, and apsidal chancels, unknown in the pre-Conquest parish church. In Anglo-Saxon England, the parish church, at the beginning of its development, was of the simple cellular type. It might be no more than a single rectangular chamber, and churches (or chapels) of this single-cell plan were of course to remain common throughout the Middle Ages in the rural areas of England.[1] Yet at the larger settlements, the dual needs of the building (for congregation and liturgical space) were reflected more usually in a two-cell arrangement, with nave and chancel annexed to each other in what is now called the 'cellular linear' plan.

It is to this class overwhelmingly—the cellular linear type—that the surviving Anglo-Saxon parish churches belong. And the clustering of the village churches within this category is all the more striking because it seems to reflect a clear differentiation by status. Determining the rank of an individual Anglo-Saxon church is not always easy: we know too little about the minsters and their earliest dependencies except in the occasional region like Kent.[2] Nevertheless, it is surely significant that in the next most frequently found category of churches—those of cellular transverse type (Fig. 7)—there is scarcely a building in the known group of twenty-four that is not of minster status or above.[3] Lateral chapels (porticus) are the distinguishing feature of churches of cellular transverse plan, and it is not uncommon for churches within this class to have been equipped with apsidal (semicircular) chancels. Side chapels of this kind were used for burials, or for additional altars dedicated to saints and their relics. Like the apsidal chancel, which is comparatively

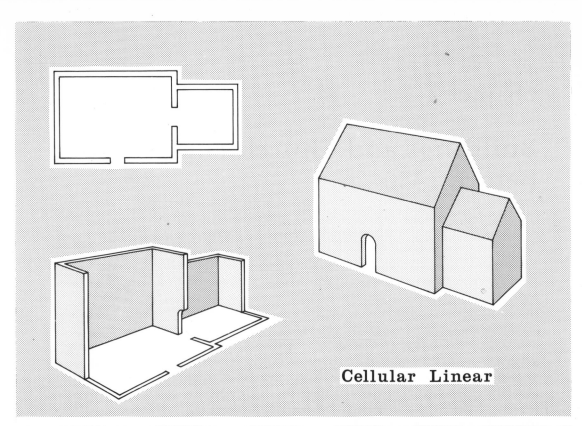

Cellular Linear

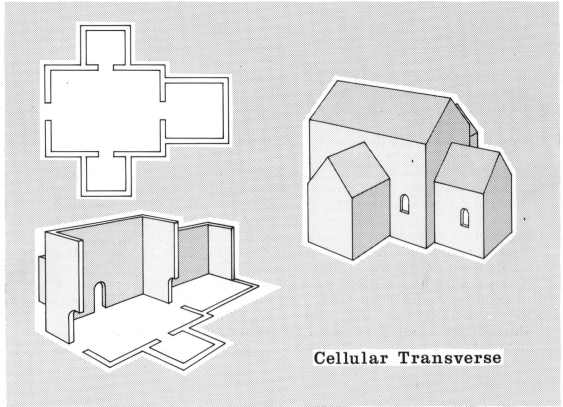

Cellular Transverse

7 Anglo-Saxon churches of cellular linear and cellular transverse type, the former more characteristic of the parish church, the latter of the larger minster (Harold Taylor)

rare in Anglo-Saxon churches of the simpler 'cellular linear' plan, the chapels suggest an emphasis on the provision and embellishment of liturgical space more likely to have occurred in a minster or a monastic church than in their humbler village equivalents.

It is very likely that the basic cellular linear plan, being the most common church arrangement throughout north-west Europe as well,[4] is as old as the English parish church itself. However, the west tower which is also characteristic of many pre-Conquest village churches, especially in Danelaw areas (Northumbria, Lincolnshire, and East Anglia), is quite certainly a later development, perhaps of the tenth but more usually the eleventh century. The purpose of these towers has been hotly debated. Some were certainly belfries, while at others there is evidence for the use of the lower chambers as private galleries for the founder and his kin, as chapels, and even as treasuries. More problematic is their defensive role, and it is perhaps reasonable to conclude that this was no more the primary purpose of the Anglo-Saxon tower than of those of the later Middle Ages. A church is built to the glory of God and for the prestige, as well as the convenience, of a community. Many Anglo-Saxon towers, both western towers and towers over the central crossing, are thought to have been crowned with timber upper-works. These may have taken the form, as in surviving medieval Scandinavian churches, of a belfry and pyramidal steeple, rising in diminishing tiers. Whatever the solution, the tower of the church would have given it then, as it still does today, an unchallenged dominance in the village, to be a landmark for the parish as a whole.

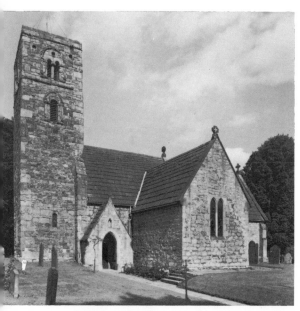

8 *Above* An Anglo-Saxon west tower of *c*. 1000 on a possibly earlier base at Bywell Church, Northumberland

9 *Right* Thorpe-next-Haddiscoe, Norfolk: an Anglo-Saxon west tower rebuilt, above its characteristic but much-worn blank arcading, in the post-Conquest period

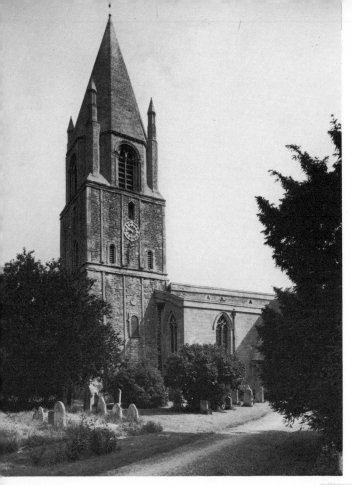

10 The early-eleventh-century west tower, with decorative pilaster strips in the Anglo-Saxon manner, at Barnack Church, in the Soke of Peterborough; the steeple was added in the thirteenth century

11 Decorative blank arcading, possibly a reflection of the more usual timberwork construction of Anglo-Saxon church towers, at Earls Barton Church, Northamptonshire

The very common rebuilding in stone of the upper storeys of Saxon towers is the best evidence we possess for their original part-timber character. However, it was rebuildings of this kind, shortly following the Conquest and then later, that so frequently destroyed altogether the earliest parish churches, seriously distorting our view today of Anglo-Saxon church provision in the countryside. Indeed, it has only been recently, as a result of the sudden accumulation of new archaeological evidence, that the balance has been somewhat restored. In one church excavation after another, traces have been found of an earlier Saxon building, sometimes itself of several phases and almost always virtually completely obscured by the grander building that had later come to replace it. Nor, interestingly, has this grander building always been datable to the post-Conquest Anglo-Norman period of reform and renewal in the Church, not infrequently proving to be much earlier. At Rivenhall, in Essex, and at Wharram Percy, in Yorkshire, fragmentary timber churches on a very small scale were replaced, well within the Late Saxon period, by more substantial buildings in stone, the former probably dating to the late tenth century, while the latter—with an extension and subsequent total rebuilding both to be fitted in before the Conquest—may go back very much further.[5] The more important minster church at Hadstock (Essex) was already demonstrably an impressive stone building in the Middle Saxon period, with a sophisticated cruciform plan perhaps crowned at the east end with an apse. Its first rebuilding seems to have been a repair following a fire that could possibly be attributed to the Danes. However, still within the Late Saxon period, it was to be rebuilt yet again on an altogether more generous scale, the half-timber structure of the earlier phases being replaced entirely by masonry. It was this form, substantially, that Hadstock retained well into the fourteenth century.[6]

12 Greenstead, Essex: the only surviving example (centre) of an Anglo-Saxon timber-built nave, datable to c. 1013; the brick chancel is early sixteenth century, the dormers also being Tudor

13 St Mary, Tanner Street, Winchester: the excavated remains—apsidal chancel and rectangular nave—
of the diminutive tenth-century church, subsequently given a much enlarged square-ended chancel
in the post-Conquest period

The lesson of Hadstock, of Rivenhall, and of Wharram is that our view of the wealth and resources of the Anglo-Saxon rural church is likely to change dramatically as the study by excavation of the English village churches gathers momentum. In the urban church, the picture will probably be the same. Simple two-cell churches of the familiar cellular linear plan have been excavated at Winchester, at Lincoln, and in London, with convincing evidence of building or extension either within the tenth century or earlier.[7] And there is no reason to suppose that these are in any way unique. Nevertheless, there are probably useful distinctions still to be made between the church of the tenth century—the frequently diminutive private oratory of the lay proprietor—and its more ambitious replacement, over the two centuries that followed, by the parish church properly so called. This was transparently not the result of the Conquest alone, and no good purpose is served by drawing the line at 1066 too firmly. Rather, it should be seen as a continuing process of development that peculiar circumstances, from the late eleventh century, did much to hasten and to promote. Certainly, the imprint of the Normans on the ecclesiastical map of medieval England was to be one of their more remarkable legacies.

14 The stone foundations and surrounding graveyard of two Anglo-Saxon village churches at Raunds, Northamptonshire, as excavated in 1979. In its second phase the church was much enlarged, to be converted, shortly after the Conquest, into one of the principal buildings of a manor-house

Examples of standing post-Conquest church buildings in what we have come to call the 'Norman' (Romanesque) style are easy enough to find. They scatter and beautify the land. However, more interest attaches, for our immediate purposes, to those few cases where the systematic archaeological investigation of a site has yielded clear evidence of post-Conquest changes, almost certainly attributable to new ownership.

Perhaps the most valuable of these to date has been the excavation of the small parish church of St Lawrence, Asheldham (Essex), now redundant and consequently available for study (Fig. 16). The main part of the present church at Asheldham is fourteenth century in construction, and it was to this period that the building was usually attributed without any further debate. However, what the excavations revealed was a nine-phase sequence, ending with nineteenth-century restorations, which began convincingly with an immediately adjoining Late Saxon two-cell timber church—nave and chancel—with its own associated burials. Furthermore, the first rebuilding of Asheldham Church in stone would seem to have occurred within a few decades of the Conquest, being either the work of the new Norman landowners, Robert and Beatrice, or of the Cluniac monks they rewarded with the church as part of the price of their new-found prosperity. In a gesture very characteristic of their times, Robert and Beatrice transferred the patronage of Asheldham, with sixty acres of glebe, to the priory of Horkesley in their own county as a part of its original endowment. And while we have no record of the date of the actual transaction, we know that it occurred within the reign of the Conqueror's son, Henry I (1100–35).[8]

15 Hales, Norfolk: an unusually perfect twelfth-century two-celled village church, with a fine apsidal chancel and a contemporary round west tower. Although the Norman windows have been blocked and larger window openings inserted in the thirteenth century and later, the main structure of the church remains substantially unchanged since its first building

Late Saxon

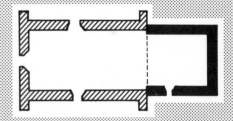

ASHELDHAM
St. Lawrence's Church

11 - 12c

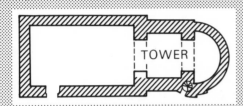

Early 14c

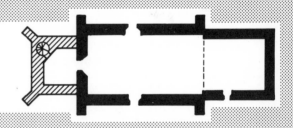

13c

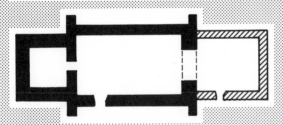

Mid 14c

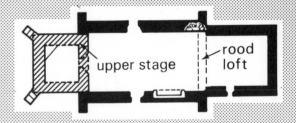

Late 13c to early 14c

Mid to late 14c

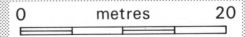

upper stage · rood loft

New in each phase

Retained from previous phase

0   metres   20

16   The plan development of Asheldham Church, Essex, from the tenth until the late fourteenth century (Warwick Rodwell)

The new form that Asheldham took was a stone church of tripartite apsidal plan, making provision, somewhat exceptionally, for a tower, subsequently demolished, over the chancel to the west of the apse. And it is quite clear that the building thus put up was an expensive embellishment of the parish. Over half a century later, although in much the same circumstances, another landowner, William, son of Ernis, would make his intentions explicit in a charter of gift by which he transferred to the Norfolk Cluniacs of Castle Acre Priory his Lincolnshire church of Sutton, with a site for the new building he intended there. He gave them 'three acres of land in Sutton, in the field called Heoldefen next the road, to build a parish church there. And my wish is that the earlier wooden church of the same vill, in place of which the new church will be built, shall be taken away and the bodies buried in it shall be taken to the new church.'[9]

There are two points of great significance in this Castle Acre charter, the first being the unequivocal association of the church rebuilding with a change in ownership, the second being the reconstruction of Sutton within the twelfth century in a new and more expensive material—stone. At Wharram Percy, as we have seen (above, p. 17), the first masonry rebuildings quite certainly pre-date the Conquest. Nevertheless, there is intriguing evidence rather later of a major reconstruction of St Martin's Church, Wharram, approximately contemporary with the rebuilding of Sutton. At Wharram, a grand new manor-house was built in stone a decade or so before the end of the twelfth century, and what is especially interesting about this building is that the fine diagonal tooling of its masonry, and even one of its surviving mason's marks, may be found on the church as well. Here, late in the twelfth century also, the east end of the chancel was rebuilt as an apse, and a long south aisle, almost the full length of the church, extended the accommodation within it.[10] Evidently, the lord of Wharram intended to display his prosperity in a building programme that took in the village church as well as his personal manor-house. He is most likely to have done that when either newly arrived at, or returned to, the parish.

New building, in any event, was in fashion, and it seems usually to have been carried out in stone. It was probably in the twelfth century that the chancel at Rivenhall was rebuilt with an apse,[11] and that other parish churches like St Nicholas, Angmering (Sussex),[12] and St Peter-in-Macellis (Winchester)[13] were very extensively remodelled. St Mark's Church, Lincoln, first built in stone in the eleventh century, was equipped with a substantial west tower during the following century, and then, with this exception, was almost immediately completely rebuilt.[14] The already considerable masonry church at Thurleigh, in Bedfordshire, dated to the early twelfth century, was extended before 1200 by the addition of a north aisle,[15] while progressive extensions in the twelfth and thirteenth centuries characterized the originally diminutive church of St Helen-on-the-Walls, in York.[16]

We do not, of course, know the circumstances of each of these remodellings. Some of them undoubtedly would have followed a change in ownership, and may have reflected too the rising status of the clergy themselves as Church reform everywhere took hold. Others are likely to have been a response to increasing pressure of population. Yet perhaps the most compelling reason for the conversion from timber to stone would have been no more than the sense of what was truly appropriate for such a building. Outside England, this feeling was not always shared, and in

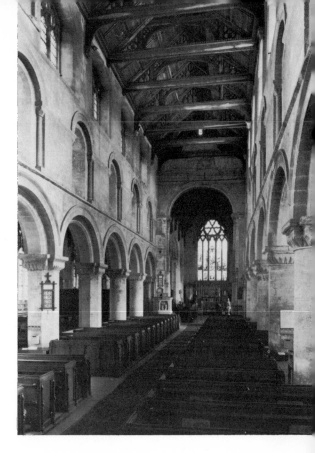

17 *Right* Long Sutton, Lincolnshire: a church rebuilt on a fresh site in the late twelfth century when a change of ownership occurred

18 The remarkable stone crossing and chancel at Devizes Church, Wiltshire, thought to have been built for Roger, bishop of Salisbury (d. 1139), who was also the rebuilder of the castle

Scandinavia, most particularly, the parish churches continued to be built, for many centuries yet and sometimes with great elaboration, in timber. However, what the English landowner or burgess was prepared to do for his own comfort and convenience, he would surely see as still more fitting for the house of the Lord. Just as the builder of the new manor-house at Wharram chose stone as the material most appropriate for the two major structures in his village—for his own dwelling equally with his contemporary extensions to the church—so men of wealth everywhere by the late twelfth century were showing their preference for stone over the timber with which hitherto they seem usually to have been content. It was in this new material, almost exclusively, that the major building enterprises of the period were completed, whether in the tenement of the wealthy burgess in the towns, in the rural manor-house of the nobility and gentry, in the tithe-barn of the monastic appropriator, or inevitably in the parish church itself.[17] Significantly, the three-acre plot given by William, son of Ernis, to Castle Acre Priory in Sutton-in-Holland was for a stone church, not for a wooden one (above, p. 22). By the late twelfth century, when he made the gift, he would not have seen it as a matter for debate.

19 The fine chancel arch, decorated with stone-carving of high quality, at Kilpeck Church, Herefordshire, datable to c. 1135

20 Wyberton, Lincolnshire: a parish church rebuilt in the early thirteenth century and then again reconstructed two centuries later, following the collapse of the tower; the chancel is Georgian and must itself replace an earlier building

Everywhere in England, the pattern of church building and extension that had been established in the twelfth century was continued through the thirteenth century as well, to change direction only in the later fourteenth century as one of the more obvious of the many responses to the demographic catastrophe of the plague. Some of the building was clearly over-hasty, or it took too little notice of the condition of the fabric already there. We know of later collapses, for example, at Hadstock, in Essex, and at the parish churches of St Paul-in-the-Bail and Wyberton, in the city and county of Lincoln.[18] Nevertheless, in each case these disasters were to be taken as the occasion for a still more ambitious reconstruction, very much in line with what was happening elsewhere. It was in the thirteenth century that the church at Cricklade (Wiltshire), having started its life as a Late Saxon chapel subsequently rebuilt in the twelfth century as a two-cell church of conventional plan, acquired first a south aisle and western tower, and then was given a north aisle as well; in the next century, Cricklade's chancel was substantially enlarged.[19] Angmering (Sussex) had got its south aisle before 1250, by which time also Wharram Percy (Yorkshire) had been equipped with another aisle on the north.[20] At Thurleigh (Bedfordshire), successive rebuildings of the nave and aisles, beginning in the late thirteenth century, followed a two-phase development of the church, already considerable, no earlier than the century before (above, p. 22); while at Asheldham (Essex), two rebuildings of the chancel, from foundation-level up, were to be undertaken in the thirteenth and early fourteenth centuries, with only a handful of decades to separate them.[21]

By a happy chance, the earliest church-building contract that survives to us today refers to just such a rebuilding of the chancel at the parish church of Sandon, in Hertfordshire, one of the churches of the dean and chapter of St Paul's. The contract, which is dated 1348, included demolition of the old chancel (noted as being in bad repair at a visitation of 1297) and its reconstruction on the former foundations. The mason, Thomas Rykeling, was to build up the side walls again to a height of seventeen feet, with substantial angle-buttresses at the east end and another buttress on each side as well. He was to improve the lighting of the chancel, formerly one of its deficiencies, by supplying a great three-light window for the east end, over the altar, with pairs of two-light windows on each side, finished in an identical style. He was to make provision for a door on the south side of the chancel, and would be paid twenty marks and the old stonework for his labour.[22] The outcome was clearly satisfactory. Just over a century later, in 1458, another visitation of the church at Sandon found it to be in very good repair.[23]

21 The chancel, rebuilt in the mid-fourteenth century and subsequently restored in the nineteenth, of Sandon Church, Hertfordshire

22 A brass chrismatory of mid-fourteenth-century date from St Mary's Church, Canterbury, showing (a) decorative openwork on the exterior, and (b) the separate internal receptacles for the three kinds of holy oil—chrism, oil of the sick, and oil of the catechumens

One of the more acceptable explanations for the rebuilding of chancels such as occurred both at Asheldham and at Sandon is the developing ritual of the thirteenth-century parish church and the increasing elaboration of its furnishings. We know from the inventory taken in 1297 that Sandon itself was very well equipped with service-books, vestments, and church plate. And we have, moreover, a list published in the synodal statutes of Bishop Quinel of Exeter, just a decade earlier, of what every parish church, in the view of the bishop, should indeed be expected to contain, these being the minimum requirements. Each church must have at least one chalice of silver or silver gilt; it must have a cup of silver or pewter (a *ciborium*) for use at the Eucharist to hold the sacramental bread and for the visitation of the sick; it must have a pyx (a little box frequently of silver or ivory) for the reserved sacrament, and another for unconsecrated bread. It should be equipped with a pewter chrismatory for the holy oils, with a censer and an incense boat, with a pax brede (for the Kiss of Peace), with three cruets and a holy-water vessel. There should be at least one altar of stone, fixed and immovable, with its cloths, canopy, and frontal; there was to be a font, also of stone and securely locked to prevent superstitious misuse of the baptismal water; and there were to be two images, one of the patron saint of the church, the other of the Virgin Mary. For special services and for processions, the candlesticks and crosses should include a multiple candleholder for the Holy Week services known as the *tenebrae*, with a paschal candlestick, again for Easter, two processional tapers, and two great crosses, one of which had to be portable. Marriage and death had each to be provided for, the former with a nuptial veil, the latter with a pall to be spread over the coffin, with bells, and with a lantern and hand-bell to be carried before the priest when visiting the sick and the dying. Vestments were to be comparatively simple, one better set to be kept for festivals and another for ordinary use, with a rochet (a white linen vestment) and two surplices. But the emphasis that the bishops were now commonly placing on the literacy of their clergy is established by a long list of required books. The priest was to have the guidance of a good manual, taking him through such occasional offices as baptism, marriage, and burial; another manual, the ordinal, gave him the offices to be recited through the ecclesiastical year, while the missal kept him instructed on the words and ceremonial order of the mass. For prayers, the priest must have a collect book, and for readings, a *legenda* with lessons from Scripture and with edifying passages from the lives of the better-known saints. The music of the church required a gradual (for the mass), a troper (for other special services), a venitary (for the invitatory psalms at matins), an antiphoner (for the canonical hours), a psalter, and a hymnal. Included with the books, and housed with them and the vestments in a great church chest, should be a copy of the statutes of the synod.[24]

23 An early-fourteenth-century parish chest, with decorative iron scrollwork, from Icklingham Church, Suffolk

Ten years later, in 1297, Sandon parish church lacked an ordinal and one of the two psalters was damaged, but it had a good missal, manual, and antiphoner, with other books required by the vicar. It was without a maniple (the silk strip worn over the vestments at mass) and was missing the ivory pyx that should have hung over the altar, yet it had three sets of vestments in place of the required two and two enamelled processional crosses where only one was necessary, while among the items of equipment considered to be good were two surplices and a censer with an incense boat.[25] In Bishop Quinel's own diocese, despite the terms of his statute, deficiencies might certainly be worse. It is true that in 1301, while Thomas Bitton, his successor, was in office, the chancel at Dawlish had been newly rebuilt by the dean and chapter of Exeter and the church there was very well equipped with, among other things, a 'noble' gradual and two 'very beautiful' processional crosses. But at Ashburton, in the same county and diocese and at the same date, the report of the commissioners fell very far short of enthusiasm:

> At the present visitation there were in the church: A fairly good antiphoner, and another old antiphoner not altogether of the use [of Exeter], with a collectare, capitulare, and hymnal. A legenda, according to the seasons, with a corresponding antiphoner, much worn and defective. A good legenda of the saints, by itself. A tolerably good ordinal. Item, a missal, with good musical notes, but with a corrupt lettering now and then. Another old missal not of the use [of Exeter]. Only one gradual, by itself, without a troper. A troper by itself, hardly good enough. A sufficiently good processional. A fairly good copy of the statutes of the Synod.
>
> Two fairly good sets of vestments complete. Three cruets in poor condition and worn out by age. Four sets of corporals. A wooden pyx for the Eucharist, without a lock, not hanging over the altar. A wooden chrismatory, with a lock. Two processional candlesticks of pewter. A small cross of metal, which is not good enough for processions. But there was another good processional cross. Two surplices, with one good rochet. Three paxes. A fairly good thurible. A new and decent banner. A good lantern. A chalice too small, scarcely weighing half a mark; and another smaller, hitherto belonging to the chapel of Saint Laurence. The nave of the church is too dark. The bell tower is not wholly roofed with lead now, but is being reroofed.[26]

The failure of two of the service books at Ashburton to correspond to the liturgical 'use' of Exeter recalls a complaint frequently heard before the enforcement of conformity in the sixteenth century. Many dioceses maintained their own customs of divine service, and the situation in individual parish churches was often further confused by the possession of books of 'monastic use', an occurrence which Bishop Quinel himself gravely deplored as bringing disrepute on the clergy. Not long afterwards, in 1342, another Exeter visitation, conducted in the archdeaconry of Totnes, found and condemned seventeen of these books—the casts-off of monastic appropriators with no further use for them in the abbey church, or the bargain purchases of an absentee rector anxious to fulfil the requirements of his office at the smallest possible expense.[27] Almost everything, indeed, in the furnishing of the chancel, depended on the willingness of the patron of the church to meet his traditional obligations. Bishop Quinel was reciting what was already by his time standard practice when he reminded his audience that the repair of the chancel was the responsibility of the rector, as that of the nave by convention was the charge of the parish.[28] And what he said of the fabric of the church was just as true of its equipment. It was the plain duty of both rectors and parishioners to make sure, as one diocesan statute put it, that their 'churches and chapels be decked according to ability with proper ornaments'.[29] Yet there were those, particularly among the absentee rectors, who attempted to get away with much less. At one of the Canterbury churches at Deal, in Kent, a visitation of 1327 catalogued the neglects of a rector who was away at his studies and who 'does no good in the parish':

> The paten belonging to the week-day chalice is broken, one phial is lacking, the troper requires binding, there is no martyrology nor ordinal, one antiphoner requires binding, one psalter requires binding, the ceiling in the chancel is cracked, one blessed cloth for the Sunday vestment is insufficient, the surplices are in bad condition and dirty, one choir-cope is in bad condition and torn, two glass windows in the chancel are broken, the chancel door is broken and without a fastening . . .

To all appearances, the rector's substitute (the parish chaplain) was little better than his absentee paymaster. If a parishioner came to ask the chaplain to visit the sick and the dying, he would be sent away unsatisfied, with 'bad words'.[30]

The rector of Deal's neglect of his charge at least met with correction in due course. And certainly more remarkable than the sins of the few was the progress that everywhere rewarded the bishops in the attaining of their declared ideal. The windows of the chancel at Deal were broken, but they had been glazed and could be repaired. Many churches, as Deal had been, were supplied with glazed windows at this time; they were painted internally with complete decorative schemes; they were beautified with sculptures in wood and in stone; and they were both re-roofed and re-floored with tiles.

Whereas stained glass, for example, had been known in England within a century of the Anglo-Saxon conversion, there is little evidence of its extensive use, even in cathedral churches, before the late twelfth century, and nothing to suggest that it came to the parishes before a generation or so after that. Interestingly, it arrived almost fully developed. Nevertheless it would be hard to find parish-church glass earlier than the fine decorative roundels of St Catherine and St Mary Magdalen in the east window of West Horsley Church (Surrey), and their dating at between 1210 and 1225 places them far in advance of the generality of such glass as it became common much later that century. Of some assistance to the spread of stained-glass windows through the lesser English churches was the introduction of new, more economical techniques. The so-called 'grisaille' windows of the thirteenth and fourteenth centuries made use of only small panels of the more expensive coloured glass to break the monotony of white-glass windows, otherwise just painted and leaded. Early in the fourteenth century, too, came the recognition of the properties of sulphide of silver in staining white glass yellow, enormously enlarging the range of the glass-painter, especially in the decoration of backgrounds and borders which could now be embellished with yellow-to-orange foliage and with architectural details hitherto obtainable only by laborious and expensive leading.

24 Donor figure of a lady, with coloured robe but grisaille head and surrounding panels, from a north window of the nave at Waterperry Church, Oxfordshire; early fourteenth century

With the fourteenth century, and partly as a consequence of the introduction of the new techniques, English stained glass, as much in the parish churches as in the great monasteries and cathedrals, entered its most glorious period. The characteristics of fourteenth-century glass-painting, which it shared equally with contemporary manuscript illumination and sculpture, were gaiety, naturalism, and invention. And all of these are to be found in what is surely one of the very finest products of the period—the matchless east window of the parish church at Eaton Bishop, in Herefordshire. Dated to between 1317 and 1321, the window is rich in decorative detail, much assisted by the extensive use of silver-staining in the mode only recently developed. Its figure-painting, too, has a vivacity and a confidence reminiscent, even in this remote parish, of the sophisticated 'court' style of the painters of Westminster and Paris. With other fine-quality windows like those at Madley, in the same county, and Stanford-on-Avon, in Northamptonshire, the glass at Eaton Bishop stands at the peak of a High Gothic tradition which began as far back as the mid-thirteenth century with the work of such sculptors of international significance as the so-called 'Joseph Master' of Rheims.

As with stained glass, we know that the practice of wall-painting in English churches goes back into the seventh and eight centuries. However, surviving decorative schemes are of course much later, beginning in the parish churches with the fragmentary Late Saxon Nativity series at East Shefford Church, in Berkshire.[31] There is no saying how many more pre-Conquest village churches may have been decorated in this way. Yet it is abundantly clear that the commissioning of ambitious wall-painting cycles was everywhere an element in the great parish-church rebuildings of the twelfth and thirteenth centuries, and that it took an important part in the programme of instruction in the faith with which the bishops were continually concerned. One of the earliest and the finest of these complete decorative schemes is the remarkable Last Judgement cycle at Clayton, in Sussex, displaying to the congregation, as the many late-medieval parish-church Dooms familiarly would do, its Latter Day prospects at 'hell door'. The church at Clayton itself is a pre-Conquest building, and the wall-paintings, which date to the late eleventh or early twelfth centuries, may almost certainly be associated with the granting of the patronage of Clayton to the Cluniac priory of near-by Lewes, as a part of William de Warenne's founding endowment of that house. With the other stylistically related paintings at Coombes, Hardham, Plumpton, and Westmeston, all of them Sussex parish churches, the murals at Clayton seem to have been the work of a single team of painters, strongly Anglo-Saxon in tradition yet responsive also to Romanesque influences from the Continent.[32] They provide us with one of our most human records of what it was like to live in such a period of cultural, as well as political and ecclesiastical, transition.

25 Head of the prophet Ezechiel from a former Tree of Jesse window at Madley Church, Herefordshire; in this portrait, sulphide of silver was used to stain the beard and hair of the prophet yellow; early fourteenth century

26 A Last Judgement scene of *c.* 1100, or a little later, painted over the chancel arch at Clayton Church, Sussex; Christ in glory is supported by angels, with apostles to left and right

27 Detail of heads, showing the considerable dramatic force of this early mural, from the south wall at Clayton

In the Sussex churches, the drive to instruct the folk in the great principles of their religion is already apparent in remote country parishes by the early twelfth century at latest. And even at that date it is perhaps less remarkable that the paintings should have occurred in such a context than that they should have been executed at such an extraordinarily high level of competence. In this, however, they are not unique. Before the end of the twelfth century, the diminutive Romanesque chancel of the church of St Mary at Kempley, in Gloucestershire, had been decorated in an expensive and a sophisticated style with a total scheme, covering side-walls, end-wall and vault, representing Christ in Majesty, with the Virgin, St Peter, and the Apostles in attendance.[33] The murals at Kempley belong to that period of Byzantinization in English art, visible especially at contemporary Winchester and Canterbury, brought about by the dynastic alliances and overseas possessions of the first Angevin kings. They are of high quality, and they demonstrate convincingly the incorporation of the English Church—even in the further tendrils of its remote country parishes—within the larger system of Rome.

28   The chancel arch, with painted chancel beyond, at Kempley Church, Gloucestershire; second half of the twelfth century

29 Frescoes on the tunnel vault of the chancel at Kempley; a seated Christ surrounded by symbols of the Evangelists, with the Virgin and St Peter, and with Seraphim; fine-quality work displaying strong Byzantine influence

Of less quality, but of parallel interest, are the paintings only recently fully uncovered and restored at another isolated Gloucestershire church, at Stoke Orchard, not very far from Tewkesbury. The church is of small size, being a simple two-cell building of which the nave alone survives from the late twelfth century, while the chancel is a fourteenth-century re-build. Nevertheless, despite its architectural insignificance, Stoke Orchard Church was to be decorated within a generation of its first construction with an elaborate cycle of frescoes commemorating the life and miracles of St James the Great, to whom the church is dedicated.[34] Other similar dedications to St James of Compostella were not uncommon in twelfth-century England, as the cult of the saint, with pilgrimages to his shrine in north-west Spain, built up. And what again they show (assisted by the clear Byzantine inspiration of the Stoke Orchard cycle) is the mounting sophistication of religious life in the localities under the influence of an international Church. Neither Kempley nor Stoke Orchard, whatever the experience and inclinations of their patrons might have been, could ever have counted as centres of population or of the intellect. Yet both were to be supplied, within a short space of their building, with refined and thoroughly up-to-the-minute decorative schemes that took them at once into clear association with the main contemporary current of religious experience in the West. No reforming bishop could surely have asked for more.

The unease later to be felt about the misuse of images was still some way distant in the thirteenth century, beginning only with the late-fourteenth-century Lollards. And few could have doubted the instructional value of a good set of moralizing paintings. Especially, of course, this would have been the case where many subjects were treated in one building. At Wissington (Suffolk), for example, the very wide range of the surviving imagery is undoubtedly more typical of the average parish church in this century than the merest fragments which have elsewhere come down to us would otherwise have tended to suggest. Thus, at Wissington, the mural scheme which two painters would seem to have executed between them during the third quarter of the thirteenth century, covered all four walls of the nave, to constitute an important visual aid for the preacher. In this small aisle-less country church, on the borders of Suffolk and Essex, he could draw the attention of his congregation to the heartening story of Christ's miraculous birth—to the Annunciation, the Flight into Egypt, the Massacre of the Innocents, the Magi warned in a Dream, the Nativity, the Angel appearing before the Shepherds, and the Adoration of both Magi and Shepherds. He could point to scenes of Christ's early life—to the Presentation in the Temple and Christ among the Doctors—and he could take his audience through the drama of the Passion (the Entry into Jerusalem, the Last Supper, Christ washing the feet of his Disciples, the Betrayal, Christ carrying the Cross, the Crucifixion, the Anointing of the Body, and the Resurrection). He could tell them about St Nicholas (the original Santa Claus): how he saved three boys from the

30 *Left* Detail from the extensive mural scheme at Wissington Church, Suffolk; second half of the thirteenth century

31 The centre panel of an early-fourteenth-century retable at Thornham Parva Church, Suffolk; high quality work in the contemporary 'Court' style, not original to this church

pickling-tub, and the legend of the Miracle of the Cup. He could instruct pregnant women in the life of their patron, St Margaret of Antioch, and in the torture and beheading that ended it. He could tell his flock about St Francis preaching to the birds, about the Decollation (beheading) of St John the Baptist, about the Twelve Apostles, and about the 'histories' of a number of now unrecognizable saints. Finally, he could ask them to look back at the west wall behind them, reminding them of the promise of a Second Coming, of a Last Judgement and Resurrection of the Dead.[35]

The paintings at Wissington are not of the highest quality. Nevertheless, they display the lively invention and easy naturalism of their period, and it was this deliberate reaching down into the affections of the folk that inspired the high level of contemporary patronage. In about 1250, when the chancel of Brook Church (Kent) was decorated with scenes from the Holy Infancy, from Christ's Public Ministry, and from the Passion, the financing of the work would have been the responsibility of the rector of Brook—the monks of Canterbury Cathedral Priory. However, a generation later, following alterations to the church which included some enlargement of the windows, a new decorative scheme took in the painting of the nave as well, which must have fallen to the charge of the parishioners. Hiring a painter at least as good as the one previously employed by the priory, they set him to work on a cycle commemorating the life of the Virgin. No doubt they chose the subject, which was a popular one in any event, because of the dedication of their church to St Mary.[36]

Certainly, the best work in the English parish churches, although likely to have

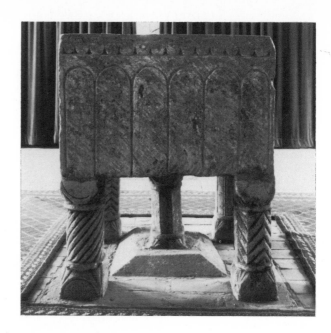

32 *Left* Wall-paintings of *c.* 1250, seen through the chancel arch at Brook Church, Kent, recording events in Christ's Infancy, Public Ministry, and Passion

33 A twelfth-century font, characteristically massive and low, at Burnham Norton Church, Norfolk.

occurred within the chancels and to be the choice of an individual discriminating rector, was by no means restricted to that area. Among the principal masterpieces of English mural-painting is the Life of Christ cycle, painted during the first decades of the fourteenth century at Croughton Church (Northamptonshire). It includes, on the north wall of the nave, a magnificent Last Supper scene of considerable sophistication and high quality, the whole being probably the work of London painters brought in for the purpose by the parishioners.[37]

What the men of Croughton were prepared to pay for the decoration of the nave of their church, others were to invest in similar projects, from major rebuildings to the replacement of inadequate or out-of-date church furnishings. Fonts, for example, which had already been handsome in many twelfth-century churches, were to reach new peaks of architectural exhibitionism in such thirteenth-century work as the font at Eaton Bray, in Bedfordshire, or the fourteenth-century fonts at Rattlesden and Hadleigh (Suffolk), at Patrington (Yorkshire), Brailes (Warwickshire), and St Mary Magdalene (Oxford). Carved chancel screens, unknown in Anglo-Norman England and still uncommon through most of the thirteenth century, had multiplied certainly before the end of that century, and would be found by early in the next century in such fine surviving examples as the graceful stone screen at Ilkeston (Derbyshire) and the timber screens at Edingthorpe and Watlington (Norfolk), or in their much simpler Suffolk equivalents at Fritton and Santon Downham.

34 An unusual early-fourteenth-century stone screen at Ilkeston Church, Derbyshire; the lower parts were restored in the nineteenth century

35 *Left* A thirteenth-century font, on foliated capitals of good-quality workmanship, at Eaton Bray Church, Bedfordshire

36 *Right* The font of St Mary Magdalene Church, Oxford, highly decorated with architectural ornament; second half of the fourteenth century

37 *Left* A good-quality mid-thirteenth-century piscina in the chancel at Skelton Church, Yorkshire

38 *Right* Piscina and sedilia together at Newton Church, Suffolk; early fourteenth century

39 *Below* A canopied set of piscina and sedilia at Swavesey Church, Cambridgeshire; fourteenth century

In the chancel itself, a new elaboration, implying considerable expense, was beginning to show during the thirteenth century in such equipment as the piscina (a basin, usually set in the wall, for washing the priest's hands and the chalice and paten at mass), the aumbry (a recess, or cupboard, for keeping books and sacred vessels), and the sedilia (a set of seats, usually three, for the priest, deacon, and subdeacon, built into the south wall of the chancel). There are fine thirteenth-century piscinas at Skelton (Yorkshire), Shepton Mallet (Somerset), and Ashby and Troston (Suffolk), with fourteenth-century examples, characteristically more elaborate, at Pettistree (Suffolk) and at North Marston (Buckinghamshire), where a canopied piscina is placed on either side of the great east window of the church. A combination quite

frequently seen is of piscina and sedilia together, the whole enclosed within a sculptured frame which might vary in decorative emphasis from the comparative simplicity of Newton (Suffolk) to those more ambitious canopied sets at Ilkeston and Sandiacre (Derbyshire), at Swavesey (Cambridgeshire), at Rushden (Northamptonshire), or at Hythe and Cliffe, in Kent.

Among the more spectacular of the surviving sedilia are the exceptionally ornate early-fourteenth-century sets at Hawton (Nottinghamshire) and Heckington (Lincolnshire), and it is of some interest that each of these is associated with an Easter Sepulchre of the same date and of probably identical workmanship. Before the late thirteenth century, as continued to be the practice in many parish churches thereafter, the Easter Sepulchre had been no more than a wooden chest intended to hold the consecrated wafer between Maundy Thursday and Easter Sunday, and placed during this time either in some convenient tomb recess or on a temporary wooden frame of its own. However, the Easter Sepulchre ceremonies were an important element in the rites of the pre-Reformation Church, and it was characteristic of church-building practice in the decades on either side of 1300 that a number of parish churches at just this time should have been equipped with permanent sculptured Easter Sepulchres, for which a place would be found on the north wall of the chancel, opposite the piscina and sedilia. Besides the Easter Sepulchres at Hawton and Heckington, there are other good examples of these at Navenby (Lincolnshire) and Patrington (Yorkshire). They would have shared the north chancel wall with an aumbry, or locker-like cupboard, which was usually plain but which could be elaborated, as in the contemporary aumbries with arched and pinnacled frames at Gazelely and Rattlesden, in Suffolk.

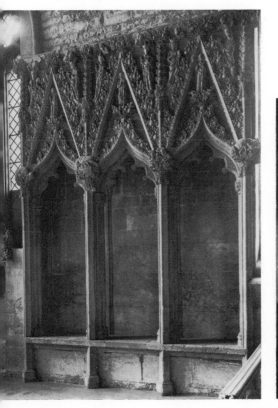

40 *Left* Canopied sedilia in the full richness of the Decorated style at Hawton Church, Nottinghamshire; first half of the fourteenth century

41 *Right* The north door, founder's tomb and Easter Sepulchre at Hawton, built (with the rest of the chancel) by Sir Robert de Compton (d. 1330)

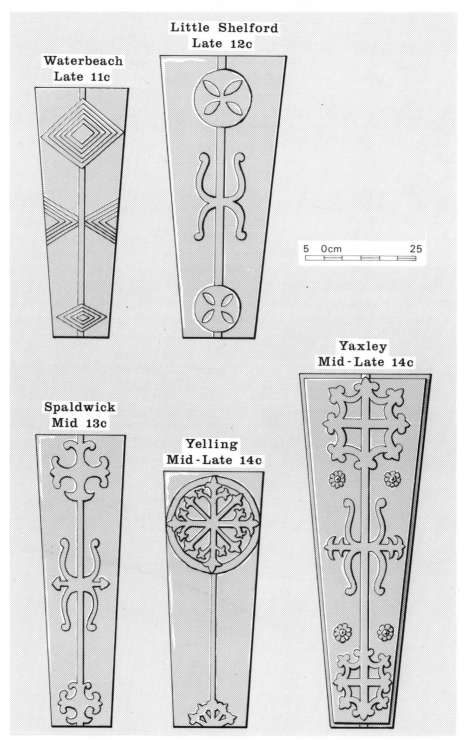

42 Growing sophistication in the grave-slab sculpture of the Barnack and Cambridgeshire regions from the eleventh to the fourteenth century (Lawrence Butler)

43 Life-size brass, one of the earliest to survive,
to Sir Robert de Septvans (d. 1306) at
Chartham Church, Kent; the brass is of the
highest quality, as well as being an
invaluable record of the armour and
costume of the period.

Good examples of the more handsome piscinas and sedilia are harder to find after the mid-fourteenth century, and although this in some degree may have followed from a change in architectural practice, it can also be taken as an indication of the extent to which the parish churches already found themselves adequately provided for. The same, of course, could not be said for tomb sculpture which continued throughout the later Middle Ages to provide an outlet for spectacular individual expression. Yet this too had begun to take its new form scarcely earlier than the thirteenth century. It was still uncommon even in the twelfth century for any but priests to be buried in the church itself. Moreover, although it was during that century that figure-carving on the grave slabs of prominent ecclesiastics became common for the first time in the cathedrals, sculptured effigies in full relief were not to be found even in the greater churches before the thirteenth century, nor was it much before the end of that century that they began to be met with quite frequently in the parishes. In the meantime, a general movement in taste towards greater elaboration can be charted in the work of the coffin-lid, or grave-slab, sculptors of a provincial industry like Barnack, meeting the demand in the twelfth and thirteenth centuries of a wide East Midlands market. For them, what began as a simple cross-slab would develop through the centuries into increasingly intricate cross and foliage designs, to end in the mid-fourteenth century with quite creditable imitations of the complex pierced patterns more economically achieved by the monumental brass-makers of that period (Fig. 42).[38] It was to these last, eventually, that the Barnack sculptors lost the richest part of their business, just as the monumental masons of Purbeck, in Dorset, found the hard black marble in which they worked displaced by the softer freestones, alabaster, and wood more suitable for the naturalistic effigy-carving becoming popular round about 1300.

What happened in monumental sculpture was less that the stone cross-slab was displaced altogether than that it descended in class to become the memorial of humbler and less wealthy men. Moreover this, to a large extent, was already the case before the opening of the fourteenth century. It is true that the alabaster monuments that would crowd the churches in both the late-medieval and early-modern periods were only just beginning at this time to flourish, most particularly from the 1350s. Yet knight images, first in Purbeck marble and then in the more easily worked freestones and wood, are known in the parish churches from a century earlier than this, while handsome monumental brasses were already beginning to compete with incised stone portraits in the last decades of the thirteenth century. The earliest of these, in Stoke D'Abernon Church (Surrey), is of Sir John D'Abernon (d. 1277), and it is a brass, even at that date, of such sophistication as to suggest a long history for the craft. Between them, monumental sculpture and fine incised and pierced brasses were to make many village churches the permanent memorial of a local dynastic line. Not uncharacteristically, Sir John's brass in Stoke D'Abernon Church is accompanied by that of another Sir John D'Abernon, probably his son, who died in 1327. In effect, Stoke D'Abernon was fast becoming, if it had not become so already, the tomb-church of the lords of the manor. And it was this function that guaranteed in the most obvious way the preservation and embellishment of its fabric.

The elaboration of tomb sculpture—both memorial in purpose and an object of beauty in its own right—was of course an essential part of the architectural taste of the period. Yet it lent itself more than anything else to competitive expenditure, with

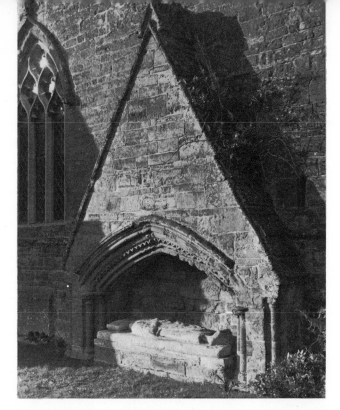

44 Gabled and canopied tomb of a priest on the outside wall of the parish church at Great Brington, Northamptonshire; late thirteenth century

the result that monuments and effigies in the latest manner very rapidly spread through the parishes. The tall gabled tomb of a priest, datable to 1275, on the outside wall of the parish church at Great Brington, in Northamptonshire, is already a handsome enough monument, even pointing the way, in the style of its canopy and gable, to the fashions of the following century. Yet it has nothing of the grandeur of a similar priest's tomb, only a generation later, at Welwick Church, in the East Riding of Yorkshire, as remarkable for the fine detail of the effigy it holds as for the complexity of its gabled and pinnacled canopy. One of the outstanding characteristics of the Welwick monument is the evident realism of its portrait of the priest in his final repose. And realism of quite a different, more dramatic kind was to characterize the exactly contemporary knight effigies of the early fourteenth century, where the knight is shown with his hand on his sword, as if ready to spring from the tomb. This particular form of vivid expressionism was to be relatively short-lived. By the middle of the fourteenth century, it had subsided into the alert repose— the 'martial recumbency'—of the knight effigy at Reepham Church, in Norfolk, while the principal emphasis in later sculptures would more usually be on rest.[39] Nevertheless, in the brief period that the style survived, it inspired what are certainly among the more memorable monuments known to military art. One of these knight effigies, at Hanbury (Staffordshire), has the added interest of being executed in that new material, alabaster, which would become so fashionable in memorial sculpture as its suitability for the medium was recognized. And there are some remarkable fragments of no fewer than seven realistic knight figures at the Berkshire village church at Aldworth. But the most striking of the effigies—and surely the best known—is the freestone figure in the former abbey church at Dorchester, in Oxfordshire. It has been a source of inspiration in naturalistic sculpture ever since.

The Dorchester knight effigy is on a plain free-standing tomb chest, and it owes at least some of its dramatic force to this austerity. Yet the more common instinct of the period was towards greater elaboration in the monument, and of this the Reepham knight memorial is one of the better examples. At Reepham, the effigy—probably of Sir Roger de Kerdiston (d. 1337)—is placed on a tomb chest decorated along its length with mourners, or 'weepers', in conventional poses of grief. The knight himself is shown austerely, on the pebble bed of a field of battle. Yet over him there rises a fine gabled and pinnacled architectural canopy, the precise equivalent in fourteenth-century monumental sculpture of the elaborately decorated sedilia, piscinas, fonts, screens, and Easter Sepulchres that still remain as the mark of the period.

Payment for a funereal monument was, of course, the charge of the family concerned. And no doubt (as we know to have been the case in the later Middle Ages) individual parishioners had come to compete with each other by the early fourteenth century not merely in the commissioning of suitable memorials but in the provision of new items of more splendid church equipment—chalices and altar-cloths, cruets and censers, chrismatories, candlesticks, and crosses. The rector too, whether seized by a

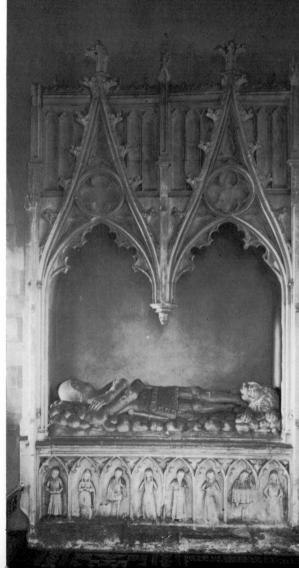

45 *Far left* Monument to Sir Oliver de Ingham (1344) at Ingham Church, Norfolk; here the vigorous sculptural style has survived unusually late

46 *Left* Monument to Sir Roger de Kerdiston (1337) at Reepham Church, Norfolk; Sir Roger lies on a bed of pebbles, perhaps of the battlefield, as does Sir Oliver de Ingham, but he has assumed a pose of 'martial recumbency' more in keeping with the usual late-medieval emphasis on rest

47 *Right* Freestone effigy of a knight, datable to *c.* 1280, in the former abbey church at Dorchester, Oxfordshire: an outstanding example of this comparatively short-lived tradition of vigorous naturalism

generous mood or anxious to placate his bishop, might put new investment into the chancel, modernizing its fixed furnishings (altar, piscina, aumbry, and sedilia), re-flooring it with glazed tiles in the up-to-date manner currently being adopted in the manor-houses,[40] or rebuilding its structure, as at Sandon (above, p. 26), on an altogether more magnificent scale. However, the church—as place of worship, assembly hall and council chamber, emergency storehouse, monument, and landmark all in one[41]—would also have been regarded as a public responsibility, being a charge on the parish as a whole.

Contributions to the church-fabric fund feature already in the earliest surviving wills, and they would remain a conventional gesture of piety, seldom neglected by testators, throughout the rest of the medieval period. Yet of particular interest, as it reaches down through the folk, is such a record as the bell-founding account of the church at Bridgwater, in Somerset, datable probably the the twelfth year (1318/9) of Edward II's reign. Parish collections at Bridgwater, and the sale of individual vessels of lead and brass, raised just under £11, or the bulk of the cash that was needed. But a substantial contribution had also been made by those who had no more than an old brass pot to offer to the Bridgwater collectors. About a tenth of the metal used in the casting of the new bell had come from the '180 lb. of brass received from gifts as in jars, plates, basins, ewers, chattels, mortars of brass and mill-pots.'[42] It was not just the wealthy who had been called on at Bridgwater, but the widow to contribute her mite.

Chapter 3

The Clergy

As the people, so the priest.

An enlarged and fully equipped parish church might assist the priest, but it made new demands on his capabilities as well. The liturgy of Holy Week, for example, with the complex ritual of the Easter Sepulchre, must frequently have been too much for the restricted learning of the average parish priest. Accordingly, it became a duty of the bishops, assisted by the authors of the more popular homiletic guides, to arm the priesthood with sufficient 'great answers' to meet the malicious questions of 'lewd men which be of many words and proud of their wit' concerning 'things that touch the service of Holy Church'.[1] On this particular occasion, it was questions about Holy Week itself that were anticipated. But to follow correctly the complex ceremonial round of the liturgical year, the parish priest would have to have, as we have seen above, a private library of service-books and manuals. Furthermore, to be kept abreast of the latest thinking of the remote theologians of Holy Church at Paris, Rome, or Avignon, he would require the regular instruction of his bishop.

It was John Pecham, archbishop of Canterbury (1279–92), who published the best-known of these instructions, later used everywhere in England as a model. Four times a year, Archbishop Pecham directed in 1281, the parish priest was to instruct his flock in Six Points—the fourteen Articles of Faith, the Ten Commandments of the Law and the two of the Gospel, the Seven Works of Mercy, the Seven Deadly Sins, the Seven Virtues, and the Seven Sacraments. The archbishop himself found it necessary to remind his clergy of the form of administration of the sacraments, placing special emphasis on the sacrament of Penance (contrition, confession, and satisfaction) which had taken on new importance in the parishes after the Fourth Lateran Council in 1215 had required annual confession to the parish priest and not just to any visiting confessor.[2] Six years after his first instructions, on 8 July 1287, the hearing of confessions was again given prominence among those qualities that Archbishop Pecham listed as essential in the parish clergy (the rectors and vicars) of his diocese. He drew up his list following a second visitation of the Canterbury churches, and it is plain that even at that date he found cause for concern both in the calibre of the clergy as spiritual directors of their flocks and in the very common neglect of church property. The eight articles he published on that occasion began with the injunctions to the clergy to recite their offices regularly and with proper reverence; they were to preach, to administer the sacraments, and 'especially' to hear confessions, allowing in friars to do these duties if incapable of performing them themselves; they were to direct surplus church revenues to the support of the poor and to the maintenance of hospitality at the vicarage; they were to keep church buildings (the vicarage and its barns) in good repair, avoid injurious contracts that might threaten their successors, recover all alienated property immediately, and sell tithes and other church revenues only with the consent of the archbishop.[3]

Pecham's injunctions of 1287 were intended to be copied into one of the service-books of every parish church in the diocese. However, they survive only in the archbishop's own register; and a better—and certainly much fuller—guide to the duties of the clergy may be obtained from a popular manual like William of Pagula's *Oculus Sacerdotis*, a work of the mid-1320s. William of Pagula, who was vicar of Winkfield (Berkshire) from 1314, was among those who used Pecham's constitution of 1281 as the basis for his own ideal programme of instruction in the parishes. Four times a year, that is, the parish priest must lead his congregation, in a language they understood, through the required Six Points. But he had other obligations in his teaching as well, based very probably on William's own pastoral experience at Winkfield, some of which seem as much like the duties of the modern social worker as of the solemnly ordained and instituted priest. In particular, William was concerned with child mortality, although he probably saw it less in terms of the welfare of the infant than of the sin of homicide as it might be committed by the responsible parent. Immediate baptism was usual in the Middle Ages, to secure the future of the baby who died shortly after delivery, and one of the obligations of the parish priest was to show the parents how to baptize, even as laymen, in an emergency. Smothering in the cradle was to be guarded against; babies were not to be tied into their cots, or left for too long unattended. Confirmation, too, was to be sought early, if possible before the child was five years old, although that might very well have to wait on the convenience of a migrant bishop. Other duties of the priest included the inculcation of a proper reverence in his flock for the church itself and for the churchyard, neither of which were to be put, even at festivals, to an improper or frivolous use. Similarly, sexual morality in the parish came under the priest's charge, and he was to be on the look-out for—and be ready with penalties if necessary to stop it—the persistence of heathen and magical practices in the village. Incantations alone, William of Pagula reminded his readers, could do nothing to drive away sickness. In the words of an earlier West Country penitential, which nevertheless had a wide circulation and may even have been known to William of Pagula over a century later:

> He who places his child upon a roof or in an oven to restore his health, or who for this purpose uses charms or characters or things fashioned for sorcery or any trick, and not godly prayers or the liberal art of medicine, shall do penance for forty days . . . He who practises divinations from the funeral of any dead person or from his body or from his clothing, lest the dead take vengeance, or in order that another not in the same house shall die, or to gain by this something to his advantage or health shall do penance for forty days. He who at the feast of St John Baptist does any work of sorcery to seek out the future shall do penance for fifteen days. He who believes that anything comes out favourably or unfavourably because of the croaking of a young crow, or a raven, or meeting a priest or any animal shall do penance for seven days . . . He who in visiting a sick man draws any inference of good or evil from the moving of a stone in going or returning shall do penance for ten days.[4]

William of Pagula chose to round off his manual with a discussion of the arguments for and against matrimony, which seem genuinely to have left him in some doubt. He would probably have agreed with St Paul that 'it is better to wed than to burn', and might also have gone along with the later proverb—'Wedding and hanging are destiny'. Nevertheless, it was clear to him that, for the scholar, a wife could hardly do less than bring serious interruptions to his studies, whereas for others, William's reflections on the likely miseries of the man who married too rich or too beautiful a wife echo the contemporary proverbial wisdom that—'Many a man sings that wife home brings; wist he what he brought he might weep.'[5]

William of Pagula lived in difficult times, of public as well as private distress, and it was the imperfect justice and extortionate taxation of Edward II's unhappy reign that no doubt lent particular eloquence to his denunciation of the sin of avarice. Yet he was not as specific about the true source of these oppressions as was the author of the almost contemporary *Memoriale Presbiterorum* (1344), a manual for the parish priest as confessor. Written for such a priest, the friend of the anonymous author, it sets out, among other things, the likely tyrannies of both manorial lord and over-wealthy villein, with the duty of the clergy in moderating them. The peasant proprietor and accumulator of lands had become by this date a well-known phenomenon in village society, especially evident in the decades before the Black Death when labour was cheap and land in short supply, even unfree tenure commanding a substantial premium. It would be for the priest to correct the abuses by which such men drove their way, often in association with men like themselves, up through the ranks and gradations of village society. As he was warned:

> In the first place they [the villeins] come together and make conventicles and illicit pacts, swearing and conspiring against their neighbours and especially against the poor, who have nothing to offer them, and disinherit them, and in many other ways cause them to be oppressed in the courts of their lords, against God and justice, and yet they get no profit out of this . . . Moreover a rich villein strives to sin in greater matters, and is less afraid to sin than a noble . . . Of such a rich man it is said: the rich criminal fears no penalty because he thinks he can buy himself off with money . . . Item, villeins often deceitfully accuse their neighbours to their lords and their bailiffs of fictitious crimes and shortcomings, and so they are unjustly harrassed and lose their goods.[6]

Yet bad though the villein might be, his lord could be very much worse, and here also the village priest had to face up to the duty of correction:

> It happens sometimes that temporal lords violently exact and extort both from their villeins and from their free tenants many goods beyond what the tenants ought and have been wont to pay, and they tallage them against their will and without cause, at their own will, sometimes once a year, sometimes more often, or whenever they like, now more, now less, extorting many goods by violence, whence it sometimes happens that such tenants being reduced to poverty have scarcely enough to provide themselves and their families with victuals; nor do

such lords think they sin in this, because by civil law . . . it is laid down that whatever the serf acquires, he acquires for his lord, and so temporal lords, relying on this law, seize at their will all the goods of their villeins as their own. But they are badly mistaken, for no temporal lord ought by natural or canon law to exact anything from his tenant beyond what is owed him by the same, by custom or by contract made between him and the tenant, or by imposition made from of old, and if he has exacted more, he ought to confess this . . . This ought to be enjoined upon him in confession and he should be effectively induced to it, namely that all that has been exacted beyond what is his due, should be restored to those from whom he extorted it or to their heirs, if he wishes to be saved . . . You ought therefore to say to such lords, if they confess this to you, that all who do such things are robbers and men of bad faith. And that no custom can excuse them in this case from sin.[7]

'Cart and plough,' it might be said with some bitterness, 'bear up clergy and chivalry.' Nevertheless, the role of the Church as mediator had obviously much to commend it where, even at the level of the parish priest, it could correct and chastise the oppressor. Certainly, this could never have been the case had the parish churches remained, as they were before the twelfth century, the private property of the local landowner. Nor could it have been so if the bishops had been unsuccessful in their long campaign to improve the learning, protect the income, and raise the social status of their clergy. Much depended, of course, on the elevation of the individual parish priest into the ranks of a professional caste distinct from lay society. And in no way could the differences be made more clear than through the enforcement of clerical celibacy.

A chaste priesthood had been the objective of reformers since the fifth-century reception of Christianity by Rome. But for many centuries the ideal of chastity had not been thought to apply to those below the rank of subdeacon, and when Archbishop Lanfranc, a decade after the Conquest, first came to grips with the problem of the married clergy and of the clerical families in England, he made it clear that although, in future, no priest was to marry, those parish clergy who already had wives must be allowed to continue to enjoy them. Lanfranc's humane legislation of 1076 suited a period in which the Norman clergy were no less uxorious than the English. Yet the position he took was, by his time, clearly a compromise, and if clerical marriage still had its skilled contemporary defenders in theologians like the so-called Anonymous of York, it was its opponents who, by the end of the day, clearly had command of the field.[8]

Growing sophistication in liturgy, both then and later, played its part in separating priest and congregation: the priest who, at the Eucharist, held Christ's Body and his Blood in his hands, must be the purest of conductors of God's word. Nevertheless, what was probably more important in driving forward the reformers was the recognition, not for the first time, of the danger of tolerating practices in the Church which might threaten, and even deprive it of, its property. If marriage had had no such consequence as children, it could very well have survived in the Church. It was the clerical family that presented the danger, far more than the parish priest's lust for his wife.

In the event, clerical dynasties were hard to eradicate, and hereditary succession in the parish priesthood survived, in many country areas, through into the thirteenth century—sometimes later. There is the case, for example, of Letheringsett Church, in Norfolk, which was kept in the hands of the founder and his kin from the early twelfth until the mid-thirteenth century, to be given over, whenever the benefice fell vacant, to the youngest son of the then patron.[9] Similarly, the chapel and later the church of Eye (Herefordshire) was to remain through that period the private property of the lords of the manor, while the cure of souls in the parish of Eye passed from father to son and brother to brother within the family.[10] Across the border in Wales, clerical marriage persisted so commonly throughout the Middle Ages that, by the sixteenth century, it had become established as immemorial custom.[11] Nevertheless, it would have been impossible for a married priest in twelfth-century England to have been unaware of the irregularity of his union, at least as hurtful in the descending status of his wife as it was damaging to his prospects for a career. With the growing confidence and assertiveness of the papacy itself, the campaign against marriage at almost all levels among the clergy gathered momentum during the late twelfth and early thirteenth centuries, to find a place among the statutes of the Fourth Lateran Council (1215) and to inspire the many mandates subsequently sent by the pope to the English bishops, requiring them forthwith to rid their dioceses of married priests as well as of those who had wrongfully succeeded to the cure.[12] Inevitably, and perhaps rightly, the parish priests were to take their time over purging their vicarages of their 'hearth-companions'. And still, in the 1260s, a bishop of Winchester would find himself compelled to warn his clergy of the penalties they risked by such indulgence:

> We direct also that clergy, rejecting all sinful lust, whereby ecclesiastical propriety is grievously blackened, live continently, and do not keep concubines either in their houses or in other places. We have determined to compel them to this by suspending them from office, withdrawing the fruits of their benefices, and finally by deprivation if they remain obstinate.[13]

A full generation later, in the diocese of Canterbury, a visitation of the Kentish churches conducted by Richard of Cliffe, a monk of the cathedral priory, during a vacancy in the archiepiscopal see, uncovered a number of illicit unions which were promptly and severely punished. Many of these concerned parish clerks, living openly with their wives, who were thenceforth prohibited from serving the priest at the altar.[14] But a more serious case was that of the vicar of West Hythe:

> Aylward vicar of West Hythe kept in his house long ago a certain woman by whom he had ever so many children and who died in his house as if she were his wife, and at length he took a certain Chima Tukkyld a woman whom he keeps openly and he enfeoffed her with a certain house and he often knows her in a hut and on banks to the scandal of the whole [priestly] order. The said vicar confesses in the visitation that he has indeed a bad reputation where Chima Tukkyld is concerned, though he is blameless concerning her as he says. He appears and sworn to speak the truth confesses that at some time or other he had two children by the one who is dead and eight years have elapsed since he last knew her, and a year since she died in his

house. He says also on oath that he has no connection with the surviving woman mentioned, and on this he submitted himself to an inquisition to be made on Friday, and the said survivor, Chima, appears, denies on oath the fact and says that the said chaplain never enfeoffed her with any house and submitted herself to inquisition . . . afterwards that Aylward was deprived and the woman renounced her sin and suspect places and whipped three times through Hythe market-place and three times round the church of West Hythe.[15]

God's vineyard, sad to say, had its weeds.

Aylward, of course, had committed a double crime. He was no Pierre Clergue, the now notorious priest-lover of Montaillou, but he was both morally at fault in taking his two women and criminally culpable of alienating the property of the Church. John Gervais, bishop of Winchester, had made the connection clearly enough in his diocesan statutes of 1262–5. 'We order further,' he had said, 'that no clergy, beneficed or in holy orders, build or buy houses or possessions for the use of their concubines or sons, nay more, that they do not presume to apply any money for them'.[16] Yet such abuses, under pressure like this, were already fairly obviously on the wane. The bishops were never fully successful—indeed, how could they have been so?—in enforcing strict celibacy upon their clergy. But where they triumphed more particularly was in the suppression, by the abolition in turn of all its rights in law, of the continuous clerical family. Hereditary succession in the parish church had become a rarity by the thirteenth century:[17] the priest's sons were unacknowledged and his wife had become his concubine. Nepotism would survive and might be especially rampant in the upper and career grades of the Church. But essentially Church property was secure.

Driven underground, clerical incontinence was no longer a scandal that could permanently damage the standing of the priesthood as a whole. However, the quality of the parish clergy hinged on more than its celibacy and good intentions. If the parish priest were to take his stand against the bullying of his wealthier parishioners, he must be well informed and literate as well.

It was to this purpose that the bishops published their 'instructions' (above, pp. 48–50), more numerous and comprehensive in the thirteenth century than at any other time. But they took precautions also of a more practical nature in the examination of candidates for ordination, as well as trying to maintain some continuous check on the literacy of the priests they had instituted. Just as clerical marriage had exercised the papal legislators of 1215, so the decrees of the Fourth Lateran Council included provisions both for the instruction of the clergy before ordination and for the punishment, by deprivation of the right to appoint to a cure, of the bishops who failed in this duty.[18] Not many years later, Robert Grosseteste of Lincoln, the most distinguished of all English bishops of the period, was to lay down, in the first of a set of statutes probably datable to 1239, what he took to be the basic syllabus of learning for the parish priest. So that he might expound them successfully to his parishioners, the priest must know the Ten Commandments; he must be able to discourse to them on the Seven Deadly Sins, to understand himself the Seven Sacraments (especially the sacrament of Penance), and to have a basic knowledge of the faith.[19] Bishop Grosseteste was a wise and a humane man, and what he required of the Lincolnshire clergy was no more than a 'simple' understanding of the more complex of the sacraments and the creeds. Yet to possess just this was already an advance on what had been expected of the parish priest before. It would equip him with at least some of the 'great answers' he would certainly need if the 'lewd men . . . proud of their wit' (above, p. 48) were to be kept successfully at bay.

Traditionally, the examination of candidates for ordination, usually conducted by the archdeacon, took place at the four Ember seasons, being groups of three days (Wednesday, Friday, and Saturday) following the first Sunday in Lent, Whit Sunday, Holy Cross Day (14 September), and St Lucy's Day (13 December). Successful candidates would be ordained by the bishop himself on the Saturday, and would say their first mass on the Sunday. But before ordination, they would have had to satisfy their examiners on a number of important points. In general terms, they had to establish their good character and suitability for holy orders. In addition, they had to offer proof of age, of legitimacy of birth, of title (source of income or private means), and of learning. It may very well be that the examiners were lenient over the last. They did not have a great deal of time to conduct their enquiries, and they would have been under pressure especially to establish beyond doubt the means of support of the candidate who, if he came through the ceremony lacking these, might become a personal charge on the ordaining bishop. Nevertheless, the essential elements of Bishop Grosseteste's syllabus provided a clear guide as to what the archdeacon might expect, and there are instances enough of candidates refused admission to a rank above subdeacon, the lowest of the major orders, or sent away for a year of further study.[20] Furthermore, the examination of the clergy did not necessarily end with such enquiries before ordination. Among the directives of John Gervais, bishop of Winchester in the 1260s, was a programme of continuing education, at least up to the mark of Grosseteste's syllabus:

> And since many ignorant and illiterate persons to the peril of their own souls usurp the pastoral office, we enjoin both our Official and the archdeacons, by the sprinkling of the Blood of Jesus Christ, that personally they make frequent and anxious inquiry whether any rectors or vicars are greatly deficient in learning; and concerning sacerdotal and parochial matters let frequent trial be made whether they know the decalogue and the ten precepts of the Mosaic law, the seven sacraments moreover, and the seven deadly sins, and whether they have at least a simple understanding of the faith; and whether they know how to explain all these to the laity in the vulgar tongue, and to instruct the people committed to them thereon.[21]

Bishops William de Blois and Walter Cantilupe, who between them ruled the diocese of Worcester from 1218 to 1266, were not above threatening their clergy with surprise tests of their learning. Every priest who came to a diocesan synod while William de Blois was bishop would have to bring with him a copy of the episcopal constitutions, which he might be required to read aloud or on which he could be tested. At each archidiaconal chapter, Walter Cantilupe provided, the bishop's constitutions and his tract on penance were to be read out and explained to the parish clergy, any one of whom might be called upon to read in turn without any previous warning.[22]

It was at the end of the century, in 1298, that Boniface VIII's constitution *Cum ex eo* gave powers to the bishops to dispense incumbents from the obligation of residence in their parishes for a period of up to seven years' study. And although these powers were used less and less from the mid-fourteenth century onwards, as the bishops attempted to control the abuse of non-residence without substitute provision for the cure, the fact that dispensations were granted quite freely during the first decades of the century underlines the rising status of the parish clergy as they were lifted into a graduate profession. Of course, with a body of clergy that was very locally recruited (as, for example, it has been shown to have been in late-thirteenth-century Lincolnshire) literary attainment remained low. However, even in Lincoln diocese before *Cum ex eo*, a 'substantial number' of the parochial clergy were already Masters of Arts.[23] And when the sums are done again, as they have been for the archdeaconry of Cleveland (diocese of York) in the third and fourth decades of the fourteenth century, some 11 per cent of the vicarages were held by graduates and twice as many (22 per cent) of the rectories. Interestingly, too, it was the graduate vicars—the rectors were usually non-resident—who took a particularly active part in the administration, at a local level, of the diocese.[24] Like the learned William of Pagula, vicar of Winkfield and penitentiary of the archdeaconry of Berkshire, who had become a Doctor of Canon Law at Oxford,[25] the Yorkshire graduate clergy provided a pool of locally resident talent which could be drawn on regularly for church business. It was among the graduates that the archdeacon of Cleveland found his officials and sequestrators, his penitentiaries and rural deans. These, among the parish clergy of their time, were the élite.

To maintain an élite, it is not enough merely to give it an educational advantage. 'The labourer is worthy of his hire' (St Luke x. 7), and if recruitment to the clergy were to be kept at any sort of standard, new resources would have to be found.

Traditionally, the parish clergy had a number of established rights. From his benefice, the priest had effective ownership of the lands of his church (the glebe), with the entitlement to tithes from the parish; from his cure of souls, or spiritual charge over his parishioners, he might expect to receive both voluntary offerings and fees. However, none of these, with the possible exception of the glebe, came to the clergy without dispute, and it became part of the organizational task of the Church in the central Middle Ages to re-define, and if possible to extend, its entitlements.

Particularly vexatious and especially important to the clergy, for it threatened a very large part of their income, was the problem of tithes—*praedial* (on crops growing in the ground), *mixed* (on animals and their products 'nourished by the ground'), and *personal* (on wages and on the profits of industry and trade). At first voluntary, the payment of tithes in England had become enforceable by the state as early as the mid-tenth century (above, pp. 3–4). But the limits of tithe obligation were obscure, and although the Church felt with some reason that such a tax, due to God, should be exacted 'to the uttermost farthing', its efforts to do so led it inevitably into a succession of the most painful confrontations, both locally with reluctant tithe-payers and nationally in the courts of the king.

Where the national conflict touched the Church most obviously was in the claims it began to make, seemingly at variance with established custom, to the new profits of an expanding economy—to tithes on minerals (slate and stone, lead and coal, lime and potters' clay etc.), on agistments (rights of pasturage and waste), on newly built mills, and on cut wood, whether 'great wood' (timber) or underbrush.[26] On a few of these, and especially on the last, the Church would suffer some major, and humiliating, defeats. But what is especially interesting about its actions at law to protect its rights, is that they take their part in a clear general pattern of encroachment and enlargement of Church receipts. Thus, while praedial tithes on wood had been claimed since as early as the eleventh century, the quarrels about their collection began only from the thirteenth century when the Church had started looking on every side for new means to protect and increase its revenues. In just the same way, tithes of hay, only occasionally exacted in the twelfth century, were secured generally by royal grant in 1226, to take their place among the other tithes listed and claimed in the episcopal statutes of the period.[27] Further claims to mortuaries (a fixed levy on the estate of a deceased parishioner) and to miscellaneous oblations (formerly voluntary gifts at the altar) were given new definition in the statutes, while fresh customs were allowed to establish themselves—the right of the clergy, for example, to assist in will-making, of course putting a price on their services, or the duty of the parishioners to maintain the church fabric (nave and tower) and to meet at least some of the expenses of church services.[28]

So common did disputes on tithe-paying latterly become that advice for healing them found its way into the contemporary manuals. One especially interesting example of this occurs in the *Regimen Animarum*, an anonymous treatise compiled in 1343, just when pressure on tithe-payers was at its strongest, for the instruction of parish priests:

> And what if it is not the practice to pay tithes on certain things, when by law they ought to pay tithe? Say that then one should proceed according to law, but on account of the discord which can arise between a curate and his parishioners, this ought to be done cautiously and discreetly, and this can be done in two ways:
>
> In the first way, thus: the curate ought to speak in a friendly way to his parishioners: 'My very dear sons, because this or that ought to pay tithes, and because this is not the practice among you, I counsel you that you choose two or three good and faithful men from among you, to come in my company before the ecclesiastical ordinaries [justices], to have a dicussion at my own expense, and I will be a faithful helper in your business and mine, because by no means do I desire your loss in temporal things, but I desire the salvation of your souls.' This first method works well in many dissensions which occur between very good curates and their parishioners who are also very good, or even middling good. But where there are middling good curates and middling bad parishioners, nay even very bad ones, then this first method is no good, but this following:
>
> The second method is thus: Let the curate go cautiously and silently to the official, or to the archdeacon if it is a great matter, none of his parishioners knowing for what cause, and let him say to him privately: 'My lord, such a thing in my parish ought to pay tithe, as it seems to me, but this is not the practice among my parishioners and so will you see whether they ought by law to pay tithe on the aforesaid things, and I pray you, that in your visitation at my church, you will

inquire of the men cited before you from my parish, among other inquiries to be made, whether they pay tithe on such things, as they are bound by law, or whether they do not pay tithe; and so it will be detected before you, in my absence, whether they say that they pay tithe, or that they do not pay; and let it be put into writing; and by your leave I will have a true copy by me, and will notify it to them.[29]

The advice is sound and is generally humane, but it does not admit of a compromise. If the parishioners indeed desired the salvation of their souls, they would have to meet their debts in this world to the full. It was the duty of the priest thus to help them.

He had other duties as well, many of which, similarly, could be expected to bring him some reward. The justification for the mortuary, or 'second legacy' due to the Church, was that it made up for tithes not paid in full during his lifetime by the deceased. In addition, the priest collected the customary offerings at Christmas, at Easter, and at other feast days, including the dedication day of his church; he might draw a small income from 'Sunday pennies' at mass every week, and would certainly get something from the 'mass pennies' offered at anniversaries, when a requiem mass might be said for the departed, and from 'confession pennies' collected usually at the annual Easter communion. Not all of these oblations came in their entirety to the parish priest, for an absentee rector was quite frequently entitled to his share. Nevertheless, the priest could anticipate gifts in kind—eggs, cheese, and chickens—at particular times of year, and although he was forbidden to exact fees for the church services considered to be routine, any additional effort beyond the call of duty almost certainly brought with it an offering. Thus visiting the sick would attract a gift, and the services at marriage and burial brought, as they still do today, a fee to the officiating priest.[30] It was these rewards, no doubt, which preoccupied the chaplain of Woodchurch (Kent) even on an occasion as important as a visitation. Required to appear before the prior of Canterbury's commissary on a Friday in January 1293, he failed to do so, but 'since there is good reason to believe that he hath a corpse awaiting burial, he is excused'. The next day, Roger the chaplain did indeed show his face at Ageney, one of the priory's manors, where the commissary, Brother Richard of Cliffe (above, p. 52), waited to see him. However, he 'asked to be allowed to make his obedience there and then because he certified that he had another corpse awaiting burial on that day, and in order that he might bury the aforesaid corpse, he was permitted to make his obedience in the accustomed manner'.[31]

48 Woodchurch, Kent: it was the chaplain of this church who, in January 1293, failed to attend a visitation enquiry on the grounds that 'he hath a corpse awaiting burial'

Obviously, it was in the interest of all concerned that Roger the chaplain should both do his duty by the parishioners of Woodchurch and be reasonably rewarded for his pains. And it was a like double preoccupation with the cure of souls and with the quality of the clergy who had charge of it, that engaged the bishops from an early date in the fixing of minimum stipends. There was to be, inevitably, some variation in the required minimum between dioceses, which might range from forty shillings a year at Worcester or Exeter to five marks (66s. 8d) in the dioceses of Winchester, Chichester, and York.[32] But this was not the only way in which the thirteenth-century English bishops sought to protect and improve their parish clergy, and one of the most important of the new measures they embarked on was the setting up and valuation of vicarages at appropriated parish churches, wherever the rector himself was non-resident. The bishops' concern in this matter was not unprecedented: they had done what they could to keep adequate priests in the villages from the moment, usually during the twelfth century, that the churches had ceased to be proprietary. Nevertheless, there is no doubt that Innocent III's Fourth Lateran Council (1215), and the great surge of episcopal legislation that followed it, stimulated new interest in the cure of souls in the parishes and in the plight of the clergy who ministered there. Accordingly, alongside concern with the morals, the learning and the income of the village priest, came a fresh anxiety: to see that a man of his standing in the community should be adequately—indeed, appropriately—housed.

Where the bishops showed themselves most active was in those parishes where the rector, being an appropriating monastic house, was permanently absent from the cure. From the beginning, the monks' concern with parochial service—the exercise of pastoral functions at their churches—had been limited.[33] They saw the parish as a financial asset, and may have kept a rectory with its tithe-barns as a base there, to be used occasionally as a holiday retreat. But they were content, for the most part, to entrust the ministry to a substitute chaplain, paid a fixed wage out of the receipts of the rectory and otherwise left much to himself. No doubt the system worked well enough in a good number of the parishes where it operated. But instances of abuse were sufficiently numerous to attract the attention of the more active of the reforming bishops. One of the conditions they now usually made before agreeing to a full-scale appropriation of a parish church, its tithes and other revenues, was an adequate provision for a vicarage. They saw to it that the vicar was equipped with some land, secured for him the guarantee of at least the 'small' tithes (on minor produce) from the parish, and not infrequently added some stipulations about his house.

It had probably been the practice in the majority of monastic parishes to find the chaplain quarters in the monastery itself, if that were near enough,[34] or in one of the buildings of the rectory. However, the need for separate accommodation for the village priest, where his parishioners might seek his help at all hours, had come to be recognized by the thirteenth century. In one of the earliest surviving agreements for such a house, to be built in 1268 by the Benedictine monks of Eynsham Abbey, in Oxfordshire, for the vicar of their Cambridgeshire church at Histon, the quarters were already quite lavish. The vicarage, which was to be built of good oak timbers, should contain a hall at least twenty-six feet by twenty, with a buttery at one end and, at the other, a 'competent' chamber with its garderobe; there was to be a kitchen, a bakehouse, and a brewhouse.[35]

It was exactly the problem of independent accommodation for the parish priest, 'fitting for the status of the vicar', that exercised Ralph of Shrewsbury, bishop of Bath and Wells (1329–63), when he gave directions to the Augustinian canons of Keynsham (Somerset) for a vicarage house at their near-by rectory at West Harptree. In 1336, the vicar had been assigned for his own use the existing rectory buildings with the exception of the barns into which the canons would have gathered their tithes. However, by 1344 the bishop had changed his mind:

> . . . we think that the vicar should have a house separate from the houses of the rectory and nearer to the church. We ordain that the vicar shall have the whole house of the tenant of the church opposite the gates of the rectory with the curtilage and close adjacent fitting for the status of the vicar, viz., with the hall and two solars and two cellars, one solar with the cellar at the front end of the hall, and another solar with the cellar at the back end of the hall. Also a kitchen, a grange, a stable for three horses, and a dovecote to be built within six months from the time they shall have possession of the church at their costs. The vicar shall maintain the house. The vicar shall have five acres of arable land, and two acres of meadow pertaining to the mansion and tenement of the tenant, with free common of pasture for his beasts at all times of the year in the fields and hills, and common feedings and pastures of the township of West Harptree and free faculty to mow heath in the hills of Mendip, as much as he wishes. . . . If the abbot and convent [of Keynsham] do not build the house within the time, or the vicar cannot have the house with the lands, etc., as above, we will that our first ordinance [of 1336] shall remain firm.[36]

One of the few such vicarages to have survived substantially intact is the priest's house at Muchelney, in Somerset, modified in various particulars in the fifteenth and sixteenth centuries, but retaining the basic plan and the three-part arrangement it must have had from its earliest beginnings. These, in all probability, date back to the agreement of 1308 between Bishop Walter Haselshaw, one of Ralph of Shrewsbury's predecessors in the see of Bath and Wells, and the Benedictine monks of Muchelney Abbey, appropriators of the church in their parish, by which the terms of the vicarage were laid down. The vicar was to draw a good part of his sustenance, including a dish of meat on Sundays and Tuesdays and of eggs or fish on the other days of the week, direct from the monastery kitchens. But he was to have a house of his own, rebuilt on its present scale presumably within a few years of the contract (Fig. 49). What that house is now is a handsome stone building, rectangular in plan, with a central hall, originally open to the roof, entered by way of a screens-passage, still having its early-fourteenth-century arched doors, at the western end. A parlour, with another chamber over it, adjoins the hall on the east, while beyond the screens-passage, on the west, the ground-floor service room (buttery or kitchen) again has a chamber above it. The square-headed eight-light windows at the upper end of the hall are improvements of the late fifteenth century, although they must have taken the place of a pair of somewhat smaller arched and hooded windows contemporary with the surviving fourteenth-century doors.[37] Such a well-planned and com-modious house as this, fully the equal of many of the smaller contemporary manor-houses, would not have been the lot of every vicar in the kingdom. Many, indeed, would have had to be content with a simple house in the churchyard like the one excavated in 1966 at Highlight (Glamorgan), divided into no more than two basic chambers and half the length of the vicarage at Muchelney.[38] Nevertheless, a hall with two chambers—Histon (1268), Muchelney (after 1308), and West Harptree (1344)—was far from exceptionally the standard of accommodation expected at the medieval vicarage. It had to be so not merely to accord with the status of the parish priest, but to find room for his chaplains, his deacons, and other helpers, including the *aquebajulus*, his holy-water clerk or boy.

49 Elevations and plan, at ground-floor level, of the Priest's House at Muchelney, Somerset; first half of the fourteenth century, with additions (W. A. Pantin)

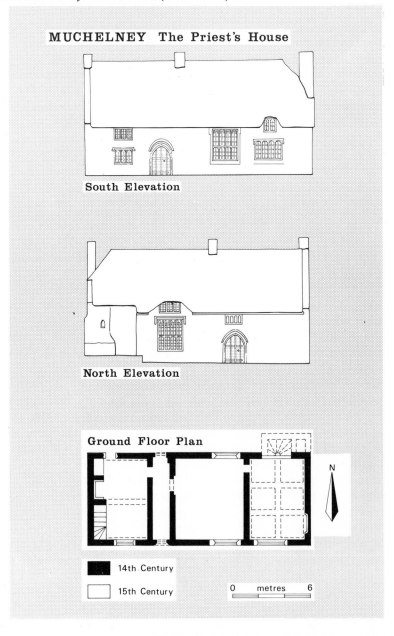

50 The Priest's House at Muchelney, as it is today

Bishop Robert Grosseteste of Lincoln had provided, in his diocesan statutes of 1239, that at every parish church that could afford it, there should be a deacon and a subdeacon, while at others there ought at least to be a clerk, capable of assisting the priest in divine service.[39] And there is no reason to believe that these minimum standards failed to be observed in the majority of parish churches, even where the stipend of the vicar was very small. At Donington (Lincolnshire), in 1285, the staff of the parish church included a chaplain, a clerk, and an *aquebajulus*, in addition to the vicar himself; the vicar of Whitchurch (Oxfordshire) had a chaplain and boy-servant, both of them living in his house; and the ill-endowed vicarage at Buckland Brewer (Devonshire) had even so to support a chaplain. With two dependent chapels to be served, the clerical community at Breedon-on-the-Hill (Leicestershire) consisted of the vicar, two chaplains, a deacon, and two clerks, although not all of them were expected to share the same vicarage.[40]

It is communities like these, in the wealthier parishes, that explain the scale of such considerable late-medieval rectorial complexes as Ashleworth, in Gloucestershire, and Brook, in Kent, the property of St Augustine's (Bristol) and Christ Church (Canterbury) respectively, where church, tithe-barn, and ecclesiastical manor-house survive in close association.[41] But at every parish church the priest-in-residence would have had to have a helper of some kind, commonly paid out of his stipend, for the proper conduct of the liturgical round would have been next to impossible without one.

What this assistant was expected to do obviously depended on the scale and resources of the parish, yet he is unlikely ever to have been idle. Basically, the duties of the parish clerk were to assist the priest in church by singing or reciting the

51 A surviving rectorial complex at Ashleworth, Gloucestershire, with a rectory (left) of *c*. 1460, a stone-built tithe-barn (right) of *c*. 1500, and a church dating originally from the twelfth century but extensively rebuilt in the fifteenth

breviary with him, by answering the responses, and by reading the epistle at mass; in addition, he would be expected to teach the children at the parish school, if any such existed in his day. But this was far from the limit of his obligations, and what may more usually have been extracted from the clerk is set down in a remarkable surviving 'job description' of 1481, detailing in no fewer than forty sections the duties of the parish clerk and assistant clerk (here referred to as the 'suffragan') of the church of St Nicholas, Bristol. The document is headed 'Howe the Clerke and the Suffrigan of Seynt Nicholas Churche Aught to do in the sayde Church After the use laudable of yeris paste & the Agrement nowe of all the worshypfull of the paryshe', and it includes, of course, the traditional duties, with very much else besides. Both clerks were to 'sing' with the priest daily and to be present at all services of the church unless by special dispensation of the vicar. In addition, the senior clerk was to read the epistle every day at mass, while his teaching responsibilities in the parish school are referred to obliquely in the clause that requires him to seek the authorization of the churchwardens of St Nicholas before removing books 'for childeryn to lerne in'. Inevitably, a large part of the time of both parish clerk and suffragan was taken up by the routine tasks of cleaning the church and preparing it for the daily round of church services. It was the suffragan who opened up the church in the morning, having locked it carefully the night before after his usual search for 'sleepers'. It was he again who cleaned the church steps and the stair down to the crypt as often as necessary, who swept out the church, after laying the dust with water, every Saturday, and who saw to the laundering of the church linen. Together with the clerk, the suffragan was to sweep all windows, walls, and pillars once a quarter, to clean the pews and choir-stalls whenever they needed it, and to dust the altars and images (ridding them of cobwebs) before every principal feast. It was the clerk's responsibility to order the 'springals'—the bunches of twigs used for the sprinkling of holy water—and to see to the church organs before they were likely to be played. Meanwhile, the suffragan tended the lamps before the Rood, fetched in oil for the lamps and 'fire' for the censers (using a firepan and not the censers themselves), and found at his own cost palm (in this case willow, *Salix caprea*) and flowers for the decoration of St Nicholas at Palm Sunday. It was his duty, too, to change the holy water in the stoup.

In general, the suffragan (assisted by his 'under-suffragan') had the charge of the lights of the church, while the clerk had the major responsibility for the bells. Thus it was the under-suffragan who saw to the sacring torches (burning at mass at the Elevation of the Host) and to the lights in the body of the church, although the suffragan himself took over the care of the torches at festivals and at the daily private masses financed by parishioners of St Nicholas. As for the bells, it was the clerk whose task it was to check the clappers and ropes, warning the churchwardens if either needed renewing; it was he who rang the bell for memorial services, taking his accustomed fee for doing so; and among his duties were the ringing of curfew on feast days at the earlier than usual time of 8 pm, the ringing of the compline bell in Lent, and the oversight of the tolling of the bell at the high mass sacring (the Elevation), ringing it himself at festivals. On ordinary days, the suffragan rang the curfew at the normal time of 9 pm, also taking charge of ringing the first peal to matins and then to evensong. The clerk rang the second peal and both then rang the last. With two bells again, clerk and suffragan rang to nones (the office said at the ninth hour, about 3 pm), as well as daily to high mass.

Perhaps the most essential duty of both clerk and suffragan was that of attendance on the priest. They laid out the books in the choir before matins and evensong, replacing them after each service; they dressed the altars with frontals and altar-cloths, and put out the priest's cope, it being the suffragan's duty to remind the churchwardens (as custodians of the church plate) to get out the censers, candlesticks, and incense-boat, which must be ready before the last peal. The suffragan then assisted the priest to put on his cope and to cense the altars and images. When matins were over, there was mass to be provided for. It was the suffragan's task to prepare the cruets of water and wine, and to put the mass-book and chalice on the high altar. With the clerk, he had to take the vicar's chasuble (worn when celebrating the Eucharist) and other 'ornaments' after mass, fold them and put them away. Miscellaneous duties included the dressing of the boy-bishop's throne for St Nicholas's Day (6 December), and the preparation of the Easter Sepulchre and tending of its light. It was the suffragan who accompanied the priest on his visits to the sick, carrying the surplice and stole, chrismatory (for the holy oil), and book, while the clerk looked after the church in his absence. Both were charged with the duty of carrying the cross at funerals from the house of the deceased to the church.[42]

The Bristol job description of 1481 ends with a list of the 'casual avails' (the perquisites) belonging to the offices of clerk and suffragan, and these would in part have supported them. Yet it is easy to see from the list of their duties both how necessary the priest would have found their assistance and how costly, in their wages and other expenses, the running of a church might have been. One of the earliest surviving churchwardens' accounts is that of the church of St Michael without the North Gate, Bath, dated 1349, and it ends up, after setting rents and miscellaneous receipts (including the Christmas and Easter collections) against rent-charges and the daily expenses of the church, with a clear deficit over the year.[43] Of course, such an account is only of limited value in recording the true worth of a church. Many monastic appropriators of parish churches expected, and received, a substantial income from them. Nevertheless, any impression we may obtain of the wealth of the clergy—and particularly of those in the parishes—needs to be set against a list of their accumulated and still growing obligations. Many of these charges, including the cost of repairs to the chancel and the provision of adequate church furnishings, would customarily have fallen on the rector, to be met out of the great tithes of the parish. Yet the vicar of Loddiswell, in Devon, as was not unusual in the diocese of Exeter, had to meet himself the expense of refurbishing his chancel; he had to find lights for the altars and books for church services; he had to carry the burden of royal taxes, increasing in frequency through the thirteenth and early fourteenth centuries, might be called upon to meet levies by the pope, and was always liable to such more local dues as the synodals and procurations of the bishop.[44]

Synodals, in point of fact, were a small charge of a shilling or two, levied on those who attended the episcopal synod. Ranking with other lesser payments like the 'quadragesimals', payable to the bishop on collection by the incumbent of his chrism, or holy oil, they would have compared hardly at all with more serious obligations like the finding of funds for the proper staffing of the church or the relief, wherever possible, of the poor. However, a formal annual payment like the procuration, to which the vicar commonly became liable in lieu of entertainment of the bishop or archdeacon on the visitation round, might conceal an obligation which, as the Church establishment expanded, had quite frequently become a major burden. Despite all attempts to control it, the cost of such hospitality had risen in the thirteenth century, to be the cause of grievous complaints. As the rectors, vicars, and parish priests of Holderness reminded their superiors before the end of the century, in 1281:

> If the beginnings of the early Church are called to mind it will be remembered that its members were one in faith, one in spirit, one in baptism, and that having pooled their resources they all promised to supply the wants of the poor and to regard the needs of all as their own. . . . But today the Church is not only without nourishment but is even abandoned and rejected, weighed down with new burdens and unwonted oppressions, and there is scarcely anyone to bring her solace in all her troubles.
>
> For when long since, beyond the memory of living men, the archdeacon's official with the rural dean and his clerk, or sometimes with only one of them, used to visit us and our churches to hold their chapters, they came with three or four mounted retainers at the most; but nowadays the official brings his companion and the rural dean his clerk, with your sequestrator in addition, and an apparitor— recently inflicted upon us by your official—and thus they descend upon us with a retinue of eight or nine for holding their chapter. In this way not only the rectors and vicars but also the parish priests are unduly burdened at a time when their livings have been greatly reduced by various disturbances in the realm in these latter days, while at the same time the number of poor people (to whom the goods of the Church belong) is daily increasing. Thus are the clergy grieved by reason of this oppression as were the Children of Israel under Pharaoh.[45]

Chapter 4

A Crisis of Faith

When the head is sick, the limbs ache.

When the clergy of Holderness spoke of the disturbances in the realm 'in these latter days' and of the daily increase in the numbers of the poor, they were not overstating their anxieties. The population growth that had served the economy so well in the twelfth and early thirteenth centuries had now dramatically overstepped itself. Land was expensive and in short supply; prices were rising as productivity failed to match up with demand; many, including the lesser clergy among them, lived perilously close to the margin.

The next generation of Holderness clergy would see things worsen rather than get better. The Church itself had its troubles. After a century of triumphs which had included a major victory over the German emperors, churchmen had witnessed in 1303 the humiliation, imprisonment, and death of Boniface VIII, one of their more assertive leaders, while just a few years later, in 1309, the long sad story of papal exile and 'captivity' under French tutelage at Avignon had begun. Nearer home, natural disaster and civil disturbance rocked the state. In a low-lying, waterlogged area like Holderness, the deterioration of the climate over the decades on either side of 1300, characterized by heavy rainfall and great storms, resulted in serious coastal inundations and river floods.[1] Nor were examples lacking, in conditions of mounting disorder, of explosive anti-clerical feeling. Just south of the Humber, in Lincoln diocese, there are a number of recorded cases of assaults on the clergy dating to the late thirteenth century. More serious, a wave of 'offerings strikes', which seems to have begun at Langtoft (Lincolnshire) in 1296 with a dispute over the scale of fees demanded at occasional offices (marriages, churchings, and funerals), continued thereafter for nearly two decades, featuring strikes and riots in many parts of the diocese and even, at Gedney in 1299, a 'sit-in'.[2]

The rage of the poor was not directed exclusively at the Church, and this was the time when men everywhere were building walls and digging moats round their manor-houses, in a fashion they had found quite unnecessary before.[3] But the collapse of public order, both politically and economically inspired, could not have failed to have its impact in the parishes. In 1304, one aggrieved evicted rector was attacking his substitute, with the assistance of a hired band of criminal thugs, at Weston Subedge, in Worcestershire.[4] And although incidents like this could of course have occurred at any time during the Middle Ages, they were very much more likely when the Scottish wars and baronial rebellions were preoccupying the king and his armies, when inflation everywhere was pushing up prices to the distress of the landless poor, and when harvest failures of such disastrous proportions as those of 1315, 1316, and 1321 brought many to the point of starvation. It had been a mistaken monetary policy, keeping over-large stocks of silver in the country and coinciding fatally with a contemporary boom in English wool exports, that had brought about the inflation of 1305–10.[5] Then, only a few years later, the agrarian crisis of 1315–22 had followed as a consequence of livestock murrains and of persistently unfavourable weather.[6] In such conditions, crime rates rose in direct proportion to the inflated price of cereals; the courts were choked with cases, criminal gangs roamed the countryside beyond the arm of the law, and property was everywhere at risk.

With the improved harvest yield of 1322, the worst of the agrarian troubles were over. Contemporaneously, a contraction in the money supply, reflecting an overall European shortage of silver, contributed to the bringing down of prices. But the great expense of the king's wars, at first in Wales and Scotland and then (from 1337) on a major scale in France as well, brought newly oppressive levels of taxation to all grades of society, laymen and clergy alike. And it was at an already diminished, unhappy, and impoverished population that the Black Death struck in 1348–9, bringing England its first traumatic experience of the bubonic plague that would remain endemic throughout Western Europe for the rest of the later Middle Ages.

This 'dreadful pestilence' and 'cruel death' spread everywhere, in the chronicler Henry Knighton's words, 'following the course of the sun'. It had come, he thought, from India, although we now know that it is more likely to have travelled the Mongol trade route from China, originating ultimately in the northern steppes of Asia. And it had spread quickly across the Middle East and Europe, from its occurrence in Georgia in 1346 and transmission to Constantinople across the Black Sea within a year of the first rumours of catastrophe. The stories grew in the telling, and there can have been few people in England in the summer of 1348 who were not aware of the plague and its approach. Still, in late July 1348, the principal purpose of the penitential processions required of his clergy by Bishop John Gynwell of Lincoln was to seek God's assistance for 'the more easy obtaining of peace [in Scotland and France] and mercy, and the enjoyment of tranquil weather'. But the anger of the Saviour, which needed assuaging in this way, 'brings vengeance upon sinners in divers ways . . . from pestilences, stormy weather, and the deaths of men in sundry parts of the earth', and this judgement of one high ecclesiastic was endorsed by another when William Zouche, archbishop of York, just a few days later urged similar measures on his clergy to hold off the 'mortality, pestilence, and infection of the air now threatening England, whereof the sins of men are the cause'.[7] Yet God, it appeared, would not listen.

52 The Black Death graffiti on the north wall of the tower at Ashwell Church, Hertfordshire; they record the onset of the plague in 1349, describe it as 'wretched, fierce, violent', and conclude, in the liberal Dickins translation, 'the dregs of the population live to tell the tale' (described and illustrated in Professor Dickins's appendix to V. Pritchard's *English Medieval Graffiti*, 1967)

Opinions have differed ever since on the degree of the mortalities and on the details of their local incidence. Nevertheless, the immediate havoc wrought by the plague on individual communities is indisputable, while its long-term effects, compounded by further major outbreaks of the sickness in 1361 and 1368–9, were (if possible) still more grave. As the plague reached their dioceses in the spring and summer of 1349, having penetrated first the southern counties in the late autumn of the previous year, both Archbishop Zouche and Bishop John Gynwell were called upon to license new churchyards. Before the end of April 1349, the churchyard at Melton Mowbray (Leicestershire) had had to be extended, and a few days later, on 4 May, Bishop Gynwell was at Great Easton, in the same county, dedicating a new graveyard at the chapel-of-ease there, formerly without any such provision. As he told the men of Great Easton and of the mother-church at Bringhurst: 'There increases among you, as in other places in our diocese, a mortality of men such as has not been seen or heard aforetime from the beginning of the world, so that the old graveyard of your church [at Bringhurst] is not sufficient to receive the bodies of the dead.' Archbishop Zouche's licensing of a new churchyard at Newark (Nottinghamshire), dated 15 May, was explained in very similar terms:

> The plague of mortality which had afflicted divers parts of the world for some long time past, has now begun to trouble the town of Newark, and has withdrawn from this light certain dwellers and inhabitants within the same, and, which is a grievous thing, waxes therein day by day more and more, insomuch that the churchyard, by reason of its straitness and narrow compass, will not suffice for the burial of the men that die in that place.[8]

It was of this same East Midlands region that Henry Knighton, himself a canon of Leicester Abbey, spoke with first-hand knowledge when he lamented the scything-down of the local priesthood and its inevitable consequences:

> At this time [1349] there was so great a scarcity of priests everywhere that many churches were left destitute, lacking divine offices, masses, matins, vespers, and sacraments. A chaplain could scarcely be obtained to serve any church for less than £10 or 10 marks, and whereas when there was an abundance of priests before the plague, a chaplain could be obtained for 5 or 4 marks, or even 2 marks with his board, at this time there was scarcely one who would accept a vicarage at £20 or 20 marks. Within a short while, however, a great multitude of men, whose wives had died in the plague, flocked to take orders, many of whom were illiterate, and almost laymen, except that they could read a little but without understanding.[9]

Leicester Abbey, which was one of the largest and wealthiest of the Augustinian houses, had many parish churches of its own, and Henry Knighton would certainly have known what he was talking about. Moreover, there is the directly contemporary evidence of episcopal institutions to the parishes to support what he had to say. In the diocese of Worcester, where the worthy Bishop Wolstan de Bransford was himself carried off by the plague on 6 August 1349, institutions to vacant vicarages and rectories rose to as many as 217 in the first seven months of the year, as compared with only fourteen over the comparable period in 1348. Of these, the great majority (78 per cent) followed on the death of the previous incumbent, while two of the new rectors were to be instituted by Wolstan even on the day that he died.[10] Similar calculations for the great diocese of Lincoln have shown a peaking of new institutions, as at Worcester, in the summer months of 1349, with Bishop Gynwell's 250 institutions in July alone considerably exceeding the total number of institutions he had made (212) over the first eighteen months of his episcopate. Again as at Worcester, while exchanges of benefices were one cause of these institutions, they were greatly outnumbered by the many new appointments to parish cures left vacant by death.[11]

Some idea of the likely quality of the new parish priesthood—just what Henry Knighton found most distasteful in it—may be obtained from the scale and rapidity of promotions to vacant cures, filling the gaps in the line. With the 76 deacons who Bishop Gynwell ordained at his Christmas ordination ceremony of 1349, there were 60 subdeacons (the lowest of the major orders) and 13 acolytes (in minor orders and

53 *Below left* A late-fourteenth-century travelling mitre case, thought to have belonged to William of Wykeham, bishop of Winchester (1367–1404), and now at New College, Oxford, one of his major foundations; the case is of iron, leather-covered, and bound with iron hoops; it testifies, as few documents can do, to the rigours of travel as the bishop made the rounds of his diocese

54 A shroud brass from Hildersham Church, Cambridgeshire: a not untypical product of the late-medieval obsession with death in some of its grislier aspects

dedicated to the service of the altar).[12] Before the plague, the deacons might certainly have hoped for promotion to vacant benefices, though many, even so, would not have got it. The subdeacons and acolytes would rarely, if ever, have been considered.

Inevitably, the shortage of clergy brought other pressures on the Church, among them an accelerating demand for better conditions and higher wages. Simon Islip, archbishop of Canterbury, whose own immediate predecessor, the canonist Thomas Bradwardine, had himself been a victim of the plague, led the way in the futile attempt to hold back wage demands in the priesthood. But the return of the plague in 1361 was too much for him. In an order of 1362 to Simon Sudbury, newly appointed bishop of London in place of another plague victim, the archbishop required strict enforcement of his earlier legislation of 1350. He had sought then to restrain the clergy from neglecting their cures in favour of more profitable offices and benefices, and had even agreed to some lifting of wages in the parishes. However, things had gone from bad to worse, and the second plague had done nothing, certainly, to help them. 'Nowadays' parish priests, even those of low quality, were barely content with double their former salaries. Moreover, they had taken to dissolute ways, frequenting taverns, dressing extravagantly, neglecting the tonsure (the shaving of the head), and resorting openly to brothels. To keep them in one place, Islip and his bishops agreed to fix wages—five marks for a priest without cure of souls, six for the priest with a cure of moderate size, and seven where the responsibilities were greater.[13]

Although reinforced by another similar order later in the year, such measures were unlikely to be successful. In the words of the contemporary acolyte-poet William Langland (c. 1330–c. 1400), who had himself taken the path he condemned:

> Parsons and parish priests complain to the bishop
> That their parishes are poor since the pestilence time
> Asking leave and licence to live in London
> And sing there for simony, for silver is sweet.[14]

There was nothing, perhaps, exceptional in the mobility of the clergy in a generation which, wherever it had an interest to advance, was on the move. Yet its consequences for the ministry were disastrous. Even during a period that included, in 1368–9, yet another return of the plague, it is a striking fact that exchanges of benefices while Simon Sudbury was bishop of London (1362–75) were a very much more common cause of the new institutions required of the bishop than were vacancies resulting from deaths.[15] 'A busy asker shall speed', it was said, and those who cared first for the welfare of their parishioners were not usually the most likely to obtain preferment. When Sudbury himself became archbishop of Canterbury, to which see he was translated from London in 1375, he was aware that the problems encountered by Archbishop Islip (1349–66) had certainly not gone away. As was his habit, he spoke out in his Lambeth constitutions of 1378 with a brutal disregard for the finer sensibilities of his audience, even while granting it a pay-rise:

> A common complaint is soundly made to us, and experience of things shows us, that priests of the present time, of our city, diocese, and province of Canterbury, are so tainted with the vice of cupidity that they are not content with reasonable

stipends but claim and receive excessive wages. These greedy and fastidious priests vomit from the burden of excessive salaries of this kind, they run wild and wallow, and some of them, after gluttony of the belly, break forth into a pit of evils, to the detestable scandal of all clergy and the pernicious example of clerics. And although the Lord Simon Islepe of good memory, lately Archbishop of Canterbury, our predecessor, while he was alive, established and ordained with the counsel and assent of his brethren, that chaplains celebrating anniversaries, and other clerics not having the cure of souls, ought to be content with an annual stipend of five marks and parish priests and chaplains and others having such a cure should be content with six marks annual wage . . . We, however, having considered the character of the times, with the counsel and advice of our brethren and suffragans . . . ordained and established on the salaries of the chantry and parish priests to be received henceforth . . . that whoever shall celebrate masses for the souls of the departed shall be content with seven marks a year, or food with three marks; but those who have a cure of souls shall be recompensed with eight marks a year, or food and four marks. No one is to charge more by any agreement, unless the diocesan of the place first orders it to be done otherwise with those who have the cure of souls. If any clerk shall presume to give or receive more against this our constitution, he shall incur the sentence of excommunication ipso facto.[16]

Almost exactly two years later, Archbishop Sudbury was to announce, in his capacity as chancellor of England, the poll tax of 1380–81 that would trigger off the Peasants' Revolt. He was rewarded for his insensitivity to the mood of his times with the brand 'spoiler of the commons', and would be executed by the rebels on 14 June 1381, driven on by the revolutionary preacher John Ball, one of his own excommunicate priests.

Plainly, what gave both peasants and priests their new power over their masters was the shortage of labour that had everywhere followed the plagues. Rich benefices were still in demand, nor was there likely to be any lack of applicants for the urban chaplaincies where a man might get his silver easily enough by singing requiems for the departed. But where parishes were 'poor since the pestilence time', no restrictive legislation on the part of the bishops could keep the clergy long at their posts. One Norwich diocese petition of the early fifteenth century speaks of the difficulty in finding priests willing to be instituted to the poorer churches of the region, with a consequential neglect of the cure of souls, of hospitality, and of the practice of divine worship in the parishes.[17] And a similarly acute shortage of priests in the rural areas has been noted, for example, in counties as different from each other as Rutland and Durham, persisting in some instances right through until the Dissolution and the Reformation together brought about a temporary flooding of the market.[18]

An obvious result of neglect in the parishes, although it followed too from the traumatic experience of the plague, was a return to primitive superstitions. Among countrymen, these had never lain far below the surface. In the early 1260s, Bishop John Gervais of Winchester was still finding it necessary to warn his priests—'Let no stones, logs, trees, or wells on account of some dream be venerated as holy, since we believe that from such things many perils have come to the souls of the faithful.'[19] Yet the attitude of the Church itself, to holy wells and wayside monuments as much as to any number of originally pagan beliefs, had always been ambiguous, and Bishop Gervais would certainly have been among those who encouraged the faithful to put their trust in the potent 'magic' of the Eucharist.[20] In point of fact, there was not much to choose between a prayer (encouraged by the priest) and a spell (condemned by him) in the healing of the sick and in the gathering of medicinal herbs to do this. The preventive medicine of the penitential procession, as urged on their priesthood in 1348 by Bishop Gynwell and Archbishop Zouche, was very close to the incantation of the magician.

Gynwell's successor in the see of Lincoln, Bishop John Buckingham (1363–98), found himself troubled by a number of incidents which, in more settled and less hysterical times, he might either have condoned or ignored. There was the case, for example, of the bacon and eggs ('a very foul abuse') blessed at the altar of Nettleham Church (Lincolnshire) during 'the most holy ceremonies of Easter' and subsequently distributed among the parishioners 'as a sort of holy offering, to the great scandal and dishonour of the Church of Christ and its sacraments, to the danger of the souls of these idolaters and, by example, to the souls of others.' And there was the wayside cross at Rippingale, in the same county, into the miraculous happenings at which the bishop ordered an enquiry in 1386:

> A serious complaint has reached us that many of our subjects have made for themselves a pretended statue vulgarly known as Jurdon Cros, in the fields of Rippingale, and have begun to adore it, and to report that many miracles are done there. They are preaching and ringing bells and holding processions, for the deception of the people and the increase of gain, and laymen are said to be converting the offerings to their own uses.[21]

Popular credulity, as the bishop well knew, left many wide open to the exploitation of the unscrupulous promoters of miracles. But what could he say when the pope himself, only six years later, overruled his ordinary, permitting a chapel of the Holy Cross to be built at Rippingale? And how could he deny the power of relics and images when an earlier holder of his own cure, the saintly Hugh of Avalon (d. 1200), had himself been such a fanatical collector of them? Among many similar stories, St Hugh's biographer tells us of an excursion to a shrine at Meulan, not very far from Paris, rewarded with a 'priceless' relic of the fifth-century martyred Bishop Nicasius of Rheims, which caused Bishop Hugh 'immense joy':

> Although his attempt to extract one of the teeth of St Nicasius whilst holding the holy head uncovered and keep it as a blessed relic was a failure, he did manage to put his fingers in the nostrils which had always breathed the good odour of Christ, and easily removed a delicate little bone which had separated the martyr's two eye-sockets. This he received with fitting devotion as a precious gift and pledge of God's favour, and with renewed hope that the Lord would lead him along the way of peace and salvation, with the assistance of this renowned bishop who had condescended to bestow on him a part of his very frame which had always until then remained between his most blessed eyes.[22]

Just this sort of enthusiasm would fuel such fifteenth-century cults, largely politically inspired, as that of Archbishop Scrope (executed 8 June 1405), in the Yorkist interest, or of Henry of Windsor (Henry VI: murdered 21 May 1471), in the Lancastrian.[23] It explains and gives force to the contemporary comment—'Flee reason and follow the wonder, for belief hath the mastery and reason is under.'

Superstition, obviously, was not created by the plague, being as old as man himself. Yet the plague, just as clearly, had some effect in promoting it, which was much the role the Black Death would play once again in such practical matters as appropriation. It is no longer thought that the plague alone was responsible for the many appropriations of parish churches which characterized late-medieval England. Indeed, the tide of appropriations had already reached full flood in the half-century before 1350. Nevertheless, the ravages of the pestilence rarely failed to be listed after this time among the reasons for a proposed appropriation. In the short term, the Black Death might force an appropriation, as it did on Worcester Cathedral Priory in 1350, troubled by the 'difficulty in getting in rents owing to the death of many tenants during the epidemic'.[24] In the long, it might so reduce the income from its parishes—the 'spiritualities'—of a monastic house, that no resort other than to further appropriations seemed available to the destitute monks. Such, certainly, was the experience of the little Cistercian community at Hulton Abbey, in Staffordshire, successfully arguing in 1354, on just these grounds, the appropriation of Audley Church, in the same county.[25] And so it would be again with the monks of Durham, permanently losing (by their own not inaccurate calculation) a third of their income from spiritualities after 1349, or with their brethren at Pershore who, in their petition for further appropriations in the 1390s, claimed to have lost fully a half of all receipts.[26]

It was the priory's conclusion at Durham in 1405 that 'the goods, rents and income of the said monastery have been so notoriously wasted and diminished that they no longer suffice to pay the usual debts and support the convent in all its necessities'.[27] And with no other resources to turn to, it was this poverty that justified a continuing programme of appropriation, exchange, and other manipulation of receipts at the churches of which the priory held the advowson. But there was, too, a strong element of habit in such transactions. Appropriations, bringing all the receipts of a parish church to the monastic rector, had usually proved to be profitable: so much so, indeed, that at every new reversal in the finances of the monks, they would turn once again to the same remedy. When Durham sought yet another appropriation in 1372, the resulting enquiry revealed that the priory had already absorbed in this way no fewer than thirteen parish churches, as well as six lesser monastic houses.[28] As one fifteenth-century observer shrewdly remarked of the practice of appropriation so widely deplored in his day:

> Such an appropriation of one church becomes the cause and occasion of appropriating another to the same monastery; because, as soon as one appropriated church begins to decrease from its former revenue, they labour forthwith to get another appropriation, on the plea of poverty, and thus 'deep calleth to deep', and one appropriation provoketh another.[29]

It was Thomas Gascoigne's belief that the parishes were drained of their income by appropriation, just as the non-residence of a monastic rector, of which again he was an eloquent critic, deprived them of the cure of souls. And he would, with good reason, have found much to deplore in the argument put forward, a generation or so after his death, by the monks of Peterborough, successfully appropriating in 1499 the church of North Collingham, near Newark. They wanted a fresh injection of revenues to their house—

> Because the rivers, streams and other watery places, and especially the great water of Nene, that lie near to and round about the said monastery, and wherein from of old time and for years together fish were wont to teem and be bred in great multitude, to the very great profit and nourishment of the said lords abbot and convent, who are notoriously bound by the appointment of law as well as by the rule of St Benet [Benedict] to a fish-diet in many of their repasts, on account of the exceeding and unusual dryness of the weather which has befallen of recent years, are become almost dry and waterless, or at any rate empty of fishes and unproductive, to the grievous damage of the said lords abbot and convent. Wherefore, for the purchase and buying of the fish, which they were in time past accustomed, to their abundant profit, to have and get in the aforesaid waters and waterish places at light expense to themselves and almost ready to hand, they are now compelled to send, to their very heavy expense and intolerable burthen, to other parts and other places and markets far removed and distant from them and their said monastery.[30]

55 North Collingham, Nottinghamshire: appropriated by the monks of Peterborough in 1499 on the grounds that drought had dried up their fishponds, causing them much unanticipated expense

All too obviously, 'some medicine is for Peter that is not good for Paul'. A century before, when Glastonbury Abbey had made out its case for the appropriation in 1391 of the church of Longbridge Deverill, in Wiltshire, it had urged the usual reasons for such action: the debts of the house and the poverty brought upon it by pestilence, livestock murrains, and flood. But the true motive of Abbot Chinnock was probably rather different. He needed the money to meet his promise to improve the annual cash dole of the Glastonbury monks, already among the highest such portions in the land.[31]

In point of fact, these mixed motives and dubious reasonings had long been familiar to the bishops, some of whom had set their faces very early in the day against the practice of wholesale appropriation. Robert Grosseteste of Lincoln (d. 1253) had been among the first to speak out openly in favour of restraint, and it was one of the more able of his successors, Bishop Oliver Sutton (1280–99), who said, while sanctioning yet another such transaction, that 'appropriations of parochial churches, by converting the fruits and profits of them to the use of religious persons, were absolutely odious to all the prelates of the church'.[32] Just a few years later, Richard Swinfield of Hereford (1283–1317) would conclude in 1305 that 'an experience of nearly twenty-three years [in the episcopacy] has taught me that these appropriations of parish churches are fraught with so many perils and losses both to the living and to the dead, especially in my diocese, wherein the greater number of the parish churches have already been appropriated . . . that I cannot now rehearse them to your Excellency [Edward I] in this present letter'.[33] Thomas Cobham of Worcester (1317–27) saw one of the chief of these perils in the under-endowment of vicarages—'We receive constant complaints that in appropriated churches, and in others which have perpetual vicars, the portion assigned to the vicars is so small and mean that they cannot pay the ordinary dues, exercise hospitality, or fulfil other obligations. What is worse, others resort to the tables of religious houses and of other rectors, losing altogether the vicar's office and retaining only the name; and they have no home in which to lay their head.'[34] But he was aware too of just that insidious habit of appropriation, noted much later by Thomas Gascoigne (above, p. 73), into which the religious houses of his own day were already all too liable to slip. In all probability, it was the rich Benedictine community at Tewkesbury, seeking to appropriate Fairford Church, in Gloucestershire, which provoked in 1323 one of Bishop Cobham's more eloquent protests:

> We hold your monastery in a close embrace of heartfelt affection, and our desire is to add as much as we may with God's help to your profit and honour; but we would rather, if we are driven to it, offend you by candour than please you by flattery. So imagine our surprise that so soon after the church of T. [probably Thornbury, appropriated in 1315] had been appropriated firmly to your monastery, you should importune us to appropriate the church of Fairford also. We beg you to desist for a time from the violence of these petitions; for you must have noticed that, when we have been incited by the requests of the king and other great folks to take similar action in behalf of other monasteries and churches, we have urged against it the plea that is accepted both by God and by men and have declined to proceed. We could not do what you ask with a quiet conscience.[35]

Yet whether Cobham and others like him approved of it or not, the plain fact was that

56 Fairford, Gloucestershire: almost entirely rebuilt in the late fifteenth and early sixteenth centuries by John and Edmund Tame, wool-merchants, and earlier (1323) the subject of an appropriation appeal resisted by Bishop Thomas Cobham of Worcester

the number of appropriations was rising decade by decade throughout the first half of the fourteenth century, even before the additional boost given to the practice by the Black Death. In Worcester diocese itself, there were only two appropriations in 1300–09, but six followed in 1310–19, seven in 1320–29, nine in 1330–39, and no fewer than twelve in the final decade before 1350.[36] By one calculation, almost 50 per cent of the parish churches in the county of Lincoln had been appropriated before the changes brought about by the Reformation. In Yorkshire, this figure had risen to as much as 63 per cent, although such a total was certainly exceptional.[37]

Appropriations had not continued during the second half of the fourteenth century at the same speed that they had reached in the first. Papal interference, with a new insistence on expensive licences, had slowed them down, and many monastic houses preferred to look for easier pickings in the lands of the suppressed and formerly French-held alien priories, victims of the jingoism building up in England as one consequence of the Hundred Years War.[38] But another reason for this moderation in the pace of appropriation was quite simply the fact that the richest benefices had, in many instances, been marked out and absorbed already, while the notorious cost and delays of appropriation proceedings made the profit on the others less obvious. Bishop Cobham of Worcester, whose natural inclinations in any case leant that way, had once warned an importuning fellow-bishop: 'Your paternity knows that the appropriation of churches is a slow business and cannot be hurried'.[39] And even a wealthy and influential house like Westminster Abbey had experienced considerable difficulties in appropriating the clutch of parish churches, out of the revenues of which it had hoped to make good the damage it had sustained in the great fire of 1298.[40] However, the truth was, as the monks of Westminster later recognized, that appropriations, once the high initial costs had been met, could in the long run prove very rewarding. Appropriations, when all is said and done, were intended to make a profit, and measures could be taken, if necessary at the expense of the parishioners, to ensure that this was so. We know, for example, of an agreed disappropriation in 1455 when the Cistercians of Haverholme Abbey, in Lincolnshire, seeing no profit in retaining the tithes of the depopulated village of Thorpe-by-Newark, restored them to the vicar there in return for a fixed annual pension.[41] Half a century before, their colleagues at Kirkstead, similarly equipped with a very poor church, had engaged in a most disreputable transaction. They had negotiated in 1392 the appropriation of Woodhall Church (Lincolnshire) on condition first that the vicar be 'sufficiently endowed' and second that 'a competent sum of money' be set aside from their revenues for the poor. The following year, having done their sums again, they discovered that because of the small value of Woodhall, 'nothing would be left for themselves' if they kept to the terms of their agreement. They secured a re-grant of their licence to appropriate 'without paying aught to a vicar or the poor parishioners there', as required by the earlier concession.[42]

57 Woodhall, Lincolnshire: an isolated country church appropriated by the monks of Kirkstead in 1392 but found by them to be of only small value; now disused

The appropriation of parish churches, it has sometimes been said, could work out to the advantage of the parishioners. And it is certainly true that a perpetual vicar, properly endowed by the appropriator, would be in a better position to look after the cure than the temporary chaplain he would quite often have replaced. Nevertheless, there can have been few villagers who would have watched without apprehension such a ceremony as we know to have taken place at Pucklechurch (Gloucestershire) in 1396 when, in the presence of Nicholas More, clerk of the diocese and notary public, Master Richard Harewell and Master Richard Bruton, canons of Wells, formally appropriated the parish church on behalf of the dean and chapter. By the authority of a bull of Pope Boniface IX (1389–1404) and of a licence of Richard II, Master Richard Bruton—

> . . . opened the door of the said church, and entered therein, with Richard Harewell the said notary and the witnesses, and advancing to the high altar took possession of the church in the name of the dean and chapter, and in sign thereof took in their hands the books, missals, chalices and ornaments of the church, rang or caused to be rung the church bells, and remaining in the chancel while high mass was celebrated caused the said papal and royal letters to be published, and their effect to be declared before a great concourse of people in the vulgar tongue, and on the same day entered and took possession of the rectory manse : and after on the 13 November [the next day] held a court of the church tenants in the hall of the said rectory, who appeared before the said proctors and acknowledging the said dean and chapter for their lords, gave their oaths of fealty.[43]

One of the more frequent complaints about appropriation was that it might result, as at Woodhall, in the failure to appoint a parish priest. The religious houses, in the words of a Commons petition of 1391, 'do mischievously appropriate the said benefices throughout the kingdom, and beat dolorously to the ground the houses and buildings thereof, and carry all away, cruelly destroying and subtracting from the poor and needy those divine services, hospitality and other works of charity which were wont to be done in the said benefices.'[44] However, the removal of priests altogether from the cure, 'whereby, in many parishes of this kingdom, old men and women have died unconfessed or without other sacraments of Holy Church, and children have died unbaptized',[45] was certainly less common than the appointment of men of low quality, itself an abuse that was almost as serious. 'My youth is past,' wrote Archbishop John Pecham (d. 1292), 'and I have now reached old age ; yet, when I search my memory carefully, I can scarce recollect one occasion, even to the present day, when the Prior of Lewes and his monastery have presented any man to the cure of souls with the sincerity which it requires'.[46] Two centuries later, and despite all the labours of the bishops to the contrary, properly established vicarages were lacking at almost a third of the appropriated churches in Norwich diocese, visited during the five-month vacancy that followed the death on 15 February 1499 of Bishop James Goldwell. Particularly neglectful of their responsibilities had been the Augustinians of Butley, in Suffolk, one of the richer houses of that order. Five alone of their fourteen appropriated churches, as visited in 1499, had vicars serving the cure. At the remaining nine, unbeneficed priests had been left in charge of the parishes, and even this may have been largely a fiction, for three of these priests failed to show their faces at the visitation proceedings and another two were unable to produce any letter of ordination by the bishop.[47]

An abiding cause of the clergy's failure in the parishes was the difficulty of reconciling the duty of the cure of souls in the poorer livings with the needs and ambitions of a careerist priesthood in the Church. Among the earliest of the objections to appropriation itself had been that, by its means, 'the encouragement of young clerks and students was defeated, by cutting off their hopes of a future provision'.[48] And whether or not this proved to be the case, the viewing of a good benefice, both before and after appropriation, as the source of support for some cause (or person) outside the parish, continued to determine the choice and restrict the opportunities of the mass of the local clergy. To many well-to-do families, both country gentry and burgesses in the towns, the advowson (right of appointment) of the parish church remained a part of their anticipated inheritance long after the church itself had ceased to be private property. In late-medieval Warwickshire, for example, the Montforts of Ilmington presented no fewer than six of the rectors of that parish, while among other fourteenth-century family livings in the county were Frankton (the Palmers) and Newton Regis (the Sekindons).[49] In Lancashire, Wigan, Standish, and Halsall were each of them covetable family livings, while the same was true of Alderley and Grappenhall, in Cheshire.[50] The results of such patronage were not always disastrous, nor has the abuse, as is well known, been restricted to the pre-Reformation church. Yet it could lead to arrogance and to irresponsibility, with a control by the gentry of the parish churches quite as suffocating as their grip on the magistracy. George Brudenell, rector of Quinton (Northamptonshire) in the early sixteenth century, was one of the Brudenells of Buckinghamshire, the neighbouring county. By 1519, when his misdeeds were listed, he had fathered a daughter in Quinton rectory, he owed money to the church, had neglected its buildings, and had bullied his parishioners on the matter of rights of common. In short, he had behaved according to the very worst standards of his class.[51]

Gentlemen-clergy had their faults, and none more so than Master Brudenell. Nevertheless, they shared one virtue with the humbler priesthood in their primary interest in the locality. Very little is known of the social origins of that priesthood, for it belonged, for the most part, to the level of society that left little behind it in records. Unquestionably, though, it was essentially local in character, recruiting its members from the county or the city and from the class most appropriate to the office. Thus in the archdeaconry of Chester in the late fourteenth century, those who held the richer benefices were frequently of the gentry class, while the poorer livings, as was only to be expected, went to men of more obscure origins and of few hopes or pretensions for advancement. Lacking this, they made no mark, and we can do no more than guess at their character. However, their names alone are proof enough that they came from within the archdeaconry. With local family names like Poghden and Totygreve, Steresacre, Shalcross, and Shagh, or bearing place-names like Altcar and Coppenhall, Sandbach, Bromburgh, and Salghton, there is no doubt whatever that the clergy of the Chester archdeaconry were recruited from Lancashire or Cheshire. And what was true of the beneficed parsons can scarcely have been less so of that great sub-population of stipendiary clergy—the chaplains and deacons, the subdeacons, servers, and parish clerks.[52] A record survives of the manumission (the freeing) in

58 George Brudenell's church at Quinton, Northamptonshire, neglected in the early sixteenth century while Brudenell, a miscreant member of the local country gentry, was rector

1456 of John Pyndere, formerly a villein of Terrington, in Norfolk, to enable him to take holy orders.[53] Plainly, he was not the only man to have made such a journey, bringing to the Church a precious understanding of what it had been like to have been raised among the under-privileged and the poor.

Others—and their case was more common—came there by a different route. 'He sits high,' it was said, 'that deals out acres', and every man of property in late-medieval England had his clients among the lesser clergy. One indication of the evident and increasing worth of parochial patronage was the way it was accumulating, already in the thirteenth century, in the hands of the magnates and other greater landowners, at the expense of the smaller and less powerful. And it is significant, too, that the other class, both then and later, in the market for churches was that of the officials—careerist administrators building their fortunes by manipulating assets and by the calculated exchange of favours.[54] Among the more notorious products of this class, his greedy collection of benefices being at least one cause of the brutal execution by rebels that he suffered with his great patron Suffolk, was Adam Moleyns, bishop of Chichester (1446–50), keeper of the privy seal for the Lancastrian Henry VI. In addition to two London livings, Moleyns held rectories in nine different counties, his eventual total rising to fourteen livings. It is not much of a defence of the system that permitted this that he never held all fourteen rectories together.[55]

Patronage, certainly, was as important in the late-medieval Church as it was in contemporary government, and there are many known cases of individual churchmen whose rise through the ranks was entirely dependent upon it. Nicholas Crosseby, for example, a Warwickshire priest, owed his first step on the ladder (the gift in 1411 of Copston's chantry in Coventry) to Richard Crosseby, prior of Coventry and almost certainly a relative. It was Prior Richard again who found him a rectory, in the priory's gift, at Ufton, which he kept from 1417 until his presentation, in 1421, to the wealthy Coventry vicarage of Holy Trinity. The very next year, Nicholas Crosseby was granted study leave, with permission to absent himself from the cure at Holy Trinity on exceptionally favourable terms.[56] Not one of these stages would surely have been possible without the indulgence and support of his patron.

The Crossebys remained Warwickshire men whose fortunes were bound up with Coventry, of which Richard was prior for a term of fifty-four years. But if a man chose to hitch his waggon to the star of a rising magnate bishop, he might find himself almost anywhere at the end of it. Thomas Arundel, third son of Richard Fitzalan, earl of Arundel, was successively archdeacon of Taunton, bishop of Ely (from 1374), archbishop of York (from 1388), and archbishop of Canterbury (from 1396). And as he rose, he took the men of his household along with him. Thomas Barnard Castle, who ended his life as master of Peterhouse (Cambridge) in one of the offices linked with the bishopric of Ely, served for many years as Bishop Arundel's registrar, during which time he held successively the livings of Lolworth and Haddenham, Monks Risborough, Little Gransden, Barking, and Bluntisham, his last holding being Harrimere free chapel. In 1388, following his patron, he exchanged Harrimere for a prebend at Auckland (Co. Durham) and later held a canonry at York before returning to East Anglia in 1400 to the headship of a Cambridge college.[57] Within the bishop's circle, exchanges of livings to suit the convenience of individual clerks were common. Thomas Barnard Castle's admission to Cottenham (Cambridgeshire) in September 1388 followed only two years after Thomas Dalby, another of Arundel's clerks, had acquired it himself by an exchange with John Newton, the bishop's official at Ely. In the meantime, Dalby had become archdeacon of Ely in 1387 by exchange with Thomas Pattesley, and would abandon that office in 1388 in favour of the great Yorkshire archdeaconry of Richmond, where he could be of more direct assistance to his master. Thomas Dalby, along with others in Arundel's train, would have endured some black times during his patron's temporary loss of office and disgrace (1397–9). However, he died a rich man in 1400, once again in possession of his archdeaconry. The inventory of his effects has survived in full, and it shows him to have become, after a lifetime of service and loyalty to Arundel, a veritable prince of the Church. In cash alone, Dalby's executors accounted for just over £800. But they listed also considerable sums received for the sale of the archdeacon's plate, much of it evidently of the highest quality; and his clothes, books, linen, and other household furnishings were clearly just as fine. In Dalby's wardrobe, significantly enough, one of the two best cloaks was 'of the livery of the Archbishop of Canterbury', and Arundel certainly was among those listed in the terms of the foundation of Dalby's chantry at York, to be prayed for after his death. As for the archdeacon's own funeral expenses, recorded with meticulous care, they included £17 3s 9½d paid to Richard Blakburn 'for the purchase of victuals for a great funeral feast on the day of the burial', with similar sums spent on the purchase of black cloth for the funeral liveries and on marble and various works on the tomb. Among other charges were the hoods for mourners, torches for the procession, tapers for the hearse, candles for the choir, fees for the bell-ringers, and 'rewards to various cooks and other servants and labourers involved in the preparation of the funeral feast'. A notable preacher, Brother William Helmesday, was paid the then substantial fee of 13s 4d for 'preaching on the day of the funeral'.[58]

Thomas Arundel then, both as bishop and archbishop, looked after his household well. And the possessor of patronage on this sort of scale undoubtedly enjoyed great power. But the gift of advowsons could also bring with it some very considerable burdens. The prior and chapter of Durham, for example, with over fifty livings in

59 *Right* The livings in the gift of the early-fifteenth-century priors of Durham, with their other ecclesiastical dependencies (Barrie Dobson)

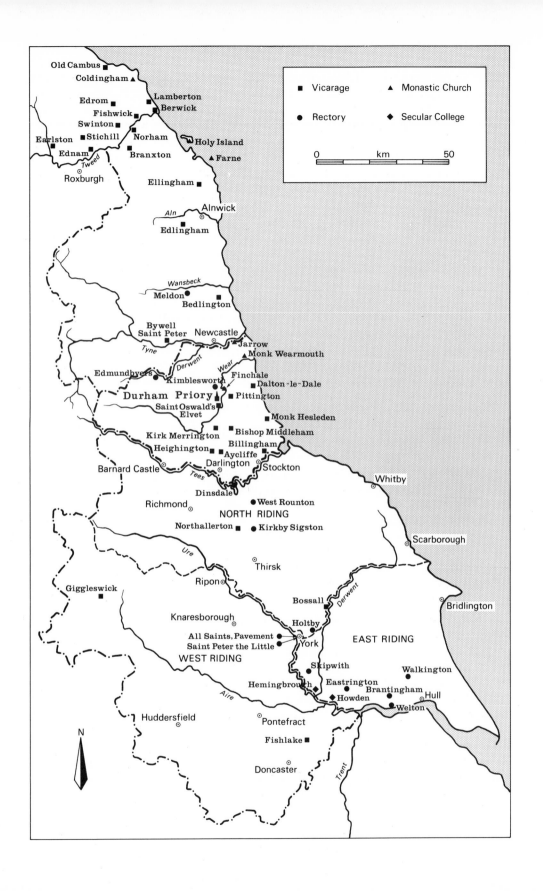

■ Vicarage	▲ Monastic Church
● Rectory	◆ Secular College

0   km   50

Old Cambus
Coldingham ▲
Edrom ■
Fishwick ■
Swinton ■
Earlston ■ Stichill
Ednam ■
Tweed
Roxburgh ⊙
Lamberton ■
Berwick ■
Norham ■
Branxton
Holy Island
Farne ▲
Ellingham ■
Alnwick ⊙
Aln
Edlingham ■
Wansbeck
Meldon ■
Bedlington ●
Bywell
Saint Peter ■
Newcastle ⊙
Tyne
Derwent
Jarrow ▲
Monk Wearmouth ▲
Edmundbyers ●
Kimblesworth ●
Finchale
Dalton-le-Dale ■
Wear
Durham Priory ▲
Saint Oswald's ■
Elvet
Pittington ■
Monk Hesleden ■
Kirk Merrington ■
Bishop Middleham ■
Heighington ■
Billingham ■
Aycliffe ■
Barnard Castle ⊙
Darlington ⊙
Tees
Stockton
Whitby ●
Dinsdale ■
West Rounton ●
Richmond ⊙
NORTH RIDING
Northallerton ■
Kirkby Sigston ●
Scarborough ⊙
Ure
Thirsk ⊙
Ripon ⊙
Bossall ■
Bridlington ⊙
Gigglewick ■
Knaresborough ⊙
Holtby ●
Derwent
All Saints, Pavement ●
Saint Peter the Little ●
York ⊙
EAST RIDING
WEST RIDING
Skipwith ●
Walkington ●
Hemingbrough ◆
Eastrington ●
Brantingham ●
Hull
Howden ◆
Welton ●
Aire
Huddersfield ⊙
Pontefract ⊙
N
Fishlake ■
Doncaster ⊙
Trent

their gift (Fig. 59), had continually to meet the requests of suitors for vacant benefices, some of them so powerful that they could not very readily be refused. For Prior Wessington and his successors, the writing of letters of explanation and excuse, putting off a petitioner without offending him too greatly in the process, became a necessary art; nor were they without their triumphs in balancing the claims of one importunate magnate against another. However, one obvious difficulty remained always that whereas everybody wanted the richer benefices south of the Tees, nobody was much interested in the poorer livings in the diocese of Durham itself, many of which were thin in tithe-payers and had continually been laid waste by the Scots. In the Durham archives, a collection of these requests for the preferment of protégés has survived from the fifteenth century, each of them making a powerful case and almost all of them ending with the somewhat threatening formula: 'as I may do things als mych to your pleisance in tyme to come'. One of these, dating to the early years of the century, originated from the prior and chapter's own steward at Hemingborough (Yorkshire), a rich benefice, worth over £100 a year, which they were shortly to convert into a college. Sir Robert Babthorp was not in pursuit of Hemingborough itself, which was certainly more fitting material for the candidate of a magnate or the king. But he wanted the vicarage of Eastrington, not very far away, in reward for good service already done for the priory and 'as I may do you service in time to come'. He wrote, expecting an answer by the hand of his own messenger—

> Right worshipful sir and father, I recommend me to you as heartily as I can, praying you that you will vouchsafe to remember how I stand your officer and steward of Hemingborough and Hunsley, and how I have laboured for you in saving of your right and St Cuthbert's franchise. And how I have put you in possession of felon's goods where you had none before, and with great labour and cost put away the king's officers from them that they might have no interest there, which will be a great furthering to you and your house and to St Cuthbert's franchise in time to come, with all other profits and service that I have done for you at Hunsley and in other places also, and yet will to the best of my power. That you will vouchsafe for my prayer at this time to grant me the next avoidance of the church of Eastrington for a priest of my choosing. I will undertake that he is an honest priest and an able one.[59]

Sir Robert Babthorp's assurances about the quality of his protégé, whoever that might be, were no doubt sincerely made. However, the power of clientage in fifteenth-century England was such as to make sure that it was the young man with 'cosynage' who made good progress, where others more able might have faltered. This was no part, of course, of the deliberate intention or declared policy of the bishops. Yet even the ablest of them, like the beleaguered prior of Durham himself, would have had to agree to some compromises, and most, by the end of the fifteenth century, had learnt to live with at least some abuses for which there appeared to be no obvious cure.

Where the parishes were concerned, the chief among these abuses (and quite the hardest to tackle) were the practices of holding in plurality and of non-residence, the one usually following from the other. Nobody could doubt the Church's attitude in general to pluralism (the holding of two or more churches by one priest), and one of the more forceful declarations against it had been Alexander III's canon of 1179, urging his bishops already into action—'Seeing that some men's covetousness has now gone so far, that they are reported to have not two or three churches, but six or more, although they cannot make due provision even for two, we give charge that this be amended by our beloved brethren and fellow bishops.' Yet even at that time Alexander's concern had not been just with the cure of souls in the parishes, important though he would have held that to be, but with the promotion opportunities of well-qualified clergy, excluded from vacant benefices by the scandalous greed of the pluralists. Inevitably, administrative considerations of exactly this kind continued to preoccupy the leaders of the Church, hampering any truly out-and-out attack on what all freely admitted to be wrong. When Innocent III in 1215 repeated the main terms of Alexander's canon of which, as he admitted, 'no fruit or scanty fruit has come', he found himself compelled to admit an exception, later much exploited by the unscrupulous. He had stood out firmly against pluralism of any kind. 'Nevertheless,' he said, 'as regards noble and lettered persons, who ought to be honoured with larger benefices, there shall be power of dispensation by the apostolic see, whenever reason shall require'.[60] It was this exception that the 'noble' Bogo de Clare (d. 1294), younger son of the earl of Gloucester and 'invader of many churches', exploited to build up what was certainly one of the most notorious collections of benefices ever made. And it was the actions of pluralists like Bogo that both drew down the anger of the popes on the abuse and demonstrated equally how little they could do to prevent it.

Of particular interest in the long series of such assaults is the constitution *Consueta* (1366) of the Avignon pope Urban V, with the special rider it contains for England. Urban started his constitution by castigating in the usual way the 'blind avarice of certain churchmen' who, whether with or without dispensations from his predecessors, were holding 'more than one priory, dignity, parsonage, administration, office, church, canonry and prebend, pension and other ecclesiastical benefice with cure or without cure'. These practices had led, he pointed out, to a 'lessening of divine worship, want of hospitality, destruction to the liberty of the church and its laws, and decay of goods, dilapidation of estates, ruin of buildings and of the churches themselves, abundant growth of vices, peril of souls, and cause of complaint and offence to certain bodies of men that are without the governance of their own rectors'. In general synods everywhere, archbishops and bishops, or their vicars general, were to warn all pluralists to make a return of what they held, which would ultimately be considered by the pope. But special regulations applied to England 'since it has come to our ears, on the report of many trustworthy persons, that in the realm of England certain clerks have the presumption to hold several dignities, prebends and other benefices and ecclesiastical offices in a number excessive and forbidden by the sacred canons; wherefrom the above-said and many other evils and grievous scandals are known to have proceeded hitherto and continually to proceed, and others that are greater are feared in all likelihood for the future'. Although bound to return details of their holdings as before, the English pluralists were to be deprived automatically after six months of all but two of their benefices, to be chosen not by themselves but by the bishop.[61]

The English returns were undoubtedly made, and were followed by their quota of deprivations. But there were always good reasons for not being resident in a parish, and the richer benefices, throughout the later Middle Ages, continued to provide incomes for absentees. Non-residence and pluralism, as watched out for and controlled by the bishops, were perhaps not the abuses in the fifteenth century that they had been under Bogo and his associates in the thirteenth. Moreover, other evils like multiple or over-rapid exchanges had been brought under some kind of check, having reached their maximum in the late fourteenth century while the papacy endured the Great Schism. Nevertheless, non-residence—usually temporary in the poorer parishes but frequently semi-permanent in many of the richer—continued to be experienced and complained of. In Norwich diocese in 1499, the forty absentees denounced or merely noted in a visitation of 478 churches do not in themselves seem excessive.[62] However, in the diocese of Lincoln at approximately that time, as many as a quarter of the parishes are thought to have been subject to non-residence in one form or another, while at perhaps half of these the priest is likely to have been absent more or less continuously.[63] By far the largest number of those whose reasons for absence are known—over three times as many as the incumbents in the next largest category—were what have been described as 'pure pluralists', with one other benefice or several more. After these in order of frequency were the university men (teachers and administrators as well as students), private chaplains and royal servants, regular canons residing at their priories, diocesan officials, and priests away on some such spiritual exercise as a pilgrimage.[64] In general, the better qualified a man might be, the less likely he was to be resident.

John Colet, dean of St Paul's and friend of Erasmus, had himself been a non-resident pluralist on a very considerable scale. Yet he spoke out for what was best in the Church in a celebrated sermon delivered to convocation in 1511, castigating the greed of the clergy. 'Let the laws be rehearsed,' he urged, 'that command personal residence of curates [those holding the cure of souls] in their churches. For of this many evils grow, because all things nowadays are done by vicars and parish priests; yea, and those foolish also and unmeet, and often times wicked; that seek none other thing in the people than foul lucre, whereof cometh occasion of evil heresies and ill christendom in the people.' Convocation had been summoned to consider new measures to suppress the Lollard heresy, just then experiencing a revival. But it was not of this that Colet preached, seeing the need of reform from within. Covetousness and pride were two of the great evils he saw around him:

> . . . how much greediness and appetite of honour and dignity is nowadays in men of the Church? How run they, yea, almost out of breath, from one benefice to another; from the less to the more, from the lower to the higher? Who seeth not this? Who seeing this sorroweth not? . . . O covetousness! St Paul justly called thee the root of all evil. Of thee cometh this heaping of benefices upon benefices.[65]

Pluralism and non-residence, it is now sometimes argued, were less the cause of contemporary troubles in the rural parishes than Dean Colet and others might have judged them. On the evidence of visitations and of ecclesiastical court proceedings, the quality of the pre-Reformation parish clergy has been shown to have been comparatively high, while the incidence of offences, of whatever kind and seriousness, was scarcely higher, it appears, among the lightly supervised clergy of the appropriated parish than among those where the rector was resident in person.[66] Yet, as a proverb of the times put it, 'all are not holy that heave their hands to heaven', and it was becoming increasingly difficult, as the clergy themselves experienced mounting oppressions, to pretend that reform within the old framework was still possible.

Chief among the clergy's troubles—and the explanation of almost everything else—was a very noticeable deterioration in their incomes. This might, of course, have had special causes, as at Hornsea in East Yorkshire where a descent in the vicar's revenues of 28 per cent between 1423 and 1483 seems to have followed from a local decline in the number of livestock kept by tithe-payers in the parish.[67] But it was aggravated, too, by three other more general conditions, the first of these being the widening net of royal and ecclesiastical taxation, the second the growing difficulty experienced by many clergy in collecting the tithes and other dues owing to them, and the third the onset of inflation. It was not as if clerical incomes, at parochial level, had started particularly high. By the sixteenth century, an income of at least £15 a year would have been necessary to meet comfortably the parish priest's customary expenses, yet less than a quarter of the parishes of England could find that amount for their priests. Taking vicarages alone, as distinct from rectories, almost 90 per cent were worth less than the desirable figure of £15, with some 70 per cent of the vicarages in total bringing in between £5 and £10 only.[68] The accounts of the clerical subsidy of 1526, recording the incomes of the parish clergy well after inflation had had plenty of time to erode their worth, establish that the average income of, for example, the Buckinghamshire village priest was no greater than £5 per annum.[69] In the same year, the net average stipend of the Lincolnshire vicar has been calculated at £6 13s 1½d.[70] Sir Richard Brone, rector of Harston (Leicestershire), close to the Lincolnshire border, died in 1519 worth only £8 10s 8d, of which household goods and clothing together accounted for not much more than £1. His income, even as rector, had been just over £8 per annum during the years that he held the living, and he had clearly had little to put aside from it for luxuries. He lived in a two-roomed cottage, of which the 'hall' doubled as kitchen and the 'parlour' as sleeping-chamber. Neither was furnished in any better style than that to be found in the houses of many of his parishioners.[71]

If—which is unlikely on figures like these—Parson Brone had indeed enjoyed a surplus, he would have lost it soon enough to the tax collector. With other incumbents, he would always have been liable to occasional taxation, whether originating in the king or in the pope. But both the incidence and the weight of taxation were rising in the late fifteenth and early sixteenth centuries, and what was equally destructive to the clergy as a whole was that it touched them at an ever lower level. While the archbishop's charitable subsidy, or 'gift of grace', was always designed to be a 'moderate' tax from which generous exemptions should be allowed, it was nevertheless levied on no fewer than seven occasions between 1463 and 1489, after a lapse of eighty-six years. Moreover, in its application now to the relatively new class of stipendiary chaplains, ignored in the earlier subsidies, it caught up the poorer fixed-income parish priests along with the better-off private chaplains and with the already tax-liable beneficed clergy. Annual stipends of between £5 and £6 13s 4d (10 marks) attracted a tax in the first of these subsidies of 6s 8d (half a mark), the tax levels rising as the stipends themselves improved. Before the end of the century, an annual stipend of only £2 was being taxed at the rate of 3s 4d.[72]

Perfectly justifiably, the archbishops Bourgchier (1454–86) and then Morton (1486–1500) had sought to include in the tax-paying categories the multiplying class of unbeneficed clergy who were often very well off. At the same time, they had hoped to protect the poorest chaplains by granting exemptions to those with surviving parents still to support, to others who were studying at the universities, and, of course, to the aged and infirm. However, one of the consequences of establishing these new lists of clerical tax-payers was that the king could adopt them as well. John Morton was chancellor of England as well as archbishop of Canterbury. Like Thomas Wolsey, in the same position a generation later, he opened the pockets of the clergy to the king. Still, until Wolsey's measure of 1523, benefices worth less than £8 (12 marks) continued to be exempt from the long series of clerical subsidies granted, for one reason or another, to the king. After 1523, the £8 limit made only the difference between the levy of a fifteenth and a tenth.[73]

There are obvious difficulties in establishing the real value of the parish priest's stipend. He had his house and the entitlement to occasional offerings, and might have access to glebe land and common grazing as well. However, there is no doubt that the fixed and larger portion of the stipendiary chaplain's income was taking a severe beating from inflation from quite early in the sixteenth century. Prices were rising markedly in the second decade of the century, to enter an especially steep ascent in the 1520s and to more than double by the 1550s.[74] And while it is true that those in possession of land did outstandingly well from the inflation—and that among these were included many of the more comfortably-off beneficed clergy—for others the consequences were less happy. In the circumstances, it is hardly surprising that the clergy everywhere found themselves obliged to collect in full measure every conceivable due that was owing to them. And of course the public outcry was immediate.

Indeed, it is hard to resist the conclusion that the real forcing-bed of the Reformation in England was less a theological than an economic revolution. Even before inflation could bite really severely and before the highest levels of clerical taxation had been reached, Dean Colet had complained in 1511 of the covetousness (perhaps better read as desperation) in the Church from which had proceeded 'all the sueing for tithes, for offering, for mortuaries, for dilapidations, by the right and title of the church . . . these chargeful visitations of bishops . . . the corruptness of courts, and these daily new inventions wherewith the silly people are so sore vexed'.[75] Predictably, the first decades of the sixteenth century were characterized by tithe-strikes and by sometimes violent disputes on mortuaries and fees of all kinds, exactly as had occurred in similar conditions of uncontrollable price movements just over two centuries before. In such a situation, the Church's administrative efficiency, perfected over the years, worked against it. Able ecclesiastics like Archbishop Morton, under pressure themselves from the king, increased their efforts to protect the rights of the Church.[76] Yet, as they did so, they met opposition in the royal courts, sometimes amounting to deliberate harassment, and would find themselves, to their genuine bewilderment, under open attack from the Commons. By 1532, when the Commons submitted their 'Supplication against the Ordinaries', the real issue was probably the heresy proceedings of the previous three years which, for the first time, were touching gentry and professional men like the members themselves and which were filling the episcopal prisons. Nevertheless, the grievances listed in the 1532 document were the familiar complaints, for which indeed there had come to be good reason, against excessive activity in the ecclesiastical courts and unwarranted increases in customary dues—in probate fees, mortuaries, and tithes.[77] It was just these discontents again which gave the necessary fire to that scabrous document of the English Reformation, Simon Fish's *A Supplication for the Beggars* (1528). More anti-clerical than Protestant in sentiment, this popular satire took the form of a petition to the king from his 'poor daily bedemen . . . that live only by alms', recently much multiplied and dying for hunger because 'all the alms of all the well-disposed people of this your realm is not half enough for to sustain them'—

> And this most pestilent mischief is come upon your said poor bedemen by the reason that there is, in the times of your noble predecessors passed, craftily crept into this your realm another sort (not of impotent, but) of strong, puissant, and counterfeit holy, and idle beggars and vagabonds, which, since the time of their first entry, by all the craft and wiliness of Satan, are now increased under your sight, not only into a great number, but also into a Kingdom. These are (not the herds, but the ravenous wolves going in herds clothing, devouring the flock) the bishops, abbots, priors, deacons, archdeacons, suffragans, priests, monks, canons, friars, pardoners and summoners. And who is able to number this idle, ravenous sort, which (setting all labour aside) have begged so importunately that they have gotten into their hands more than a third part of all your realm. The goodliest lordships, manors, lands, and territories are theirs. Besides this, they have the tenth part of all the corn, meadow, pasture, grass, wool, colts, calves, lambs, pigs, geese, and chickens. Over and besides, the tenth part of every servant's wages, the tenth part of the wool [sic], milk, honey, wax, cheese and butter. Yea, and they look so narrowly upon their profits that the poor wives must be accountable to them of every tenth egg, or else she getteth not her rights at Easter, shall be taken as a heretic. Hereto have they their four offering days. What money pull they in by probates of testaments, privy tithes, and by men's offerings to their pilgrimages, and at their first masses? Every man and child that is buried, must pay somewhat for masses and dirges to be sung for him, or else they will accuse the dead's friends and executors of heresy. What money get they by mortuaries, by hearing of confessions (and yet they will keep thereof no counsel), by hallowing of churches, altars, superaltars, chapels, and bells, by cursing of men, and absolving them again for money? What a multitude of money gather the pardoners in a year? How much money get the summoners by extortion in a year, by asciting the people to the commissaries court, and afterwards releasing the appearance for money? Finally, the infinite number of begging friars: what get they in a year?[78]

Simon Fish's statistics were far from accurate, and his exegesis was bawdy and libellous in the extreme. But his shafts struck home. Even the king is reported to have embraced him.

Chapter 5

The Community of the Parish

Help yourself and God will help.

Those discontents with the clergy that Simon Fish voiced in 1528 had long before resulted in almost every parish in the development of an alternative organization. Inevitably, there were responsibilities for the spiritual life of the parish which the priest alone could carry. But care for the church fabric, the supervision and replacement of its furnishings and ornaments, custody of the plate, and management of Church properties and rebuilding funds—in all of these, the parishioners themselves found a voice.

We know rather little of the origins of the office of churchwarden and still less of the vestry meeting in its earliest form. Nevertheless, it is plain that one of the consequences of the administrative tidying-up of the Church in the thirteenth century had been the deliberate unloading on the parishioners everywhere of the principal charges for repair and new building at their churches. With this had come the need for a new kind of machinery for interpreting and then implementing the common voice, not dissimilar to the existing machinery already perfected within the community of the vill. There would have to be a meeting of interested parties, which would certainly include all those in the parish becoming liable to what we have since come to call the Church rate. If the decisions of the meeting were to be translated into action, officers would have to be appointed. Although the first surviving churchwardens' accounts are not much earlier than the mid-fourteenth century, both churchwardens and parish rates are identifiable in the records from the late thirteenth century, if not before. Usually they occur there because of a dispute that had arisen with the rector.[1]

Tithe and offerings strikes, we know, were a characteristic of just this period (above, p. 65). And it is hardly surprising that the men of the parishes should have preferred, wherever an opportunity presented itself, to divert their charity and that of their friends to a purpose more directly their own. Thus at Reculver (Kent) in 1296 and at Newark (Nottinghamshire) in 1310, the incumbents were to complain that their parishioners, in setting up fabric-fund boxes within these churches, had deprived them of the alms that would otherwise have been given at their altars. Furthermore, it was reported, this shift in allegiance had been deliberately fomented in each parish.[2] The competition in loyalties that had probably always been felt between the church as a building belonging to the village and the pastor as its spiritual director, had at last begun to surface.

It was a competition that the pastor could never hope to win. Not only was he the collector of tithes and other dues in the parish—the tenth part and more of every income—but it had become his duty over the years to enquire into the morals of

60 A fifteenth-century wrought-iron alms-box, with the arms of England on the front panel (Museum of London)

individual parishioners and to denounce them, if necessary, at the rural chapter, the inquisitorial court of the archdeacon.[3] These unpopular tasks of the parish priest, from which the zeal of the rector, the rural dean, and the archdeacon's apparitor (summoner to court) gave him no rest, contrasted sharply with the intercessory role of the patron saint and with the functions, clearly beneficial to all, of those 'proctors' and 'kirkmasters', 'church greeves' and 'keepers of the fabric' who came commonly to be known as the churchwardens.[4] Our first surviving set of churchwardens' accounts—those of the church and parish of St Michael without the North Gate, Bath, dating to 1349—shows them already to have had a wide range of responsibilities, not restricted to the care and supervision of the church fabric. They administered rents and took charge of the moneys left to the church for memorial masses and obits (anniversary masses on the mind-day of the deceased); they bought wax, candles, and oil for the church, and paid the wages of minor church servants; they saw to the repair of damaged service books, sold surplus church furnishings, and bought, in what was undoubtedly the most important transaction of the year, an expensive new missal, or mass-book.[5] The churchwardens were not as yet handling poor relief in the parishes, exercising those functions that would make them such powerful men in the sixteenth century and after. But even here, in a characteristic example of an absentee rector shelving his responsibilities, the Dominican friars of Kings Langley in 1400 were to transfer to the churchwardens of their appropriated church of Great

Gaddesden (Hertfordshire) the annual duty of distributing alms to the poor.[6] Almost certainly, the churchwardens would have done this a good deal more efficiently than the friars.

In point of fact, the range of duties of the late-medieval churchwarden was always liable to be enlarged. The churchwardens of St Michael's, Bath, in compiling their account for 1349, made no reference there to the plague which must recently have visited their parish. But the Black Death, for all that, was an important factor in the promotion of new devotional movements among the laity. And these, with their emphasis on memorial masses and on the sad celebration of the dead, brought a flood of fresh properties to the parish church. Already before this, in the late thirteenth century, the richer parishioners had begun to remember the church fabric and its furnishings in their wills.[7] At the same time, occasional moneys, however received, had been diverted by custom to the parish church, and would be held and accounted for by the churchwardens. By the fifteenth century, with programmes of church rebuilding and repair active on all sides, the churchwardens were busy with every fund-raising device to keep their own churches at least as well equipped as their neighbours'. One well-recognized method was to organize a charitable performance of a play in the parish, from which the proceeds would then go to the fabric fund or to the purchase of new church ornaments. But the churchwardens of Pulloxhill (Bedfordshire), in doing just this, found themselves embroiled in a Chancery case in an effort to recover the proceeds. William Lucas and Richard Taylor, 'wardens and keepers of the goods and ornaments of the church of Saint James at Pulloxhill', explained before the chancellor—

> that whereas one John Russell of Pulloxhill aforesaid with divers other persons, took upon them to make a play and so did within the same Town, and the profits thereof coming they promised should be to the use and behalf of the said Church of Pulloxhill. The said John receiving of divers persons at the same play of their good devotions which they had to the said Church £4 of lawful money of England. Which £4 the said Churchwardens often times hath required of the said John to the use of the said Church according to his promise, and that to do the said John at all times hath denied and yet denieth, to the great hindering of reparation of the said Church and of other ornaments of the same. And for as much as your said Orators be without remedy for any recovery of the said £4 to be had by the course of the Common Law, pleaseth it your grace the premises tenderly considered to grant a writ of *sub pena* to be directed to the said John, commanding him by the same to appear before your lordship in the King's Chancery there to answer to the premises at a certain day and under a certain pain etc.[8]

We have no record of how the case then advanced.

Another of the fund-raising methods quite commonly resorted to was the division of fines, levied in the manorial court for infringements of village by-laws, half to the lord and half to the fabric and other purposes of the parish church. At Elton, for example, in Huntingdonshire, it was agreed in 1446 that 'no one shall play tennis or penny prick nor other illicit games henceforth day or night under pain of 3s 4d to the lord and 3s 4d to the fabric of the church', while one of the contemporary by-laws of

Broughton, in Northamptonshire, ran—'It is ordered by the common consent of the lord and his tenants that no inhabitant shall call any of his neighbours who dwell there whoreson . . . or cuckold on pain of 40d of which one half to the fabric of the church and the other to the lord of the fee.'[9] Moreover, the peculiar interest of this group of shared fines is that they cluster quite noticeably within the fifteenth century, during which they might be associated with an individual building programme at a parish church. From late in the fourteenth century, for example, divided fines (half to the lord and half to the church) coincided with the beginning of extensive building programmes, stretching through several decades, at the churches of Leighton Buzzard (Bedfordshire) and Broughton (Northamptonshire). In both cases, the nave was substantially rebuilt: lighting was improved by the addition of a clerestory and a new roof had then to be provided. At Leighton Buzzard, the same treatment was given to the chancel, while Broughton at this period acquired a new west tower. Warboys Church (Huntingdonshire), on one of the principal manors of the great Benedictine house at Ramsey Abbey, was likewise rebuilt in the fifteenth century, soon after the villagers had successfully achieved a new degree of independence from their lord. It too was re-roofed and a clerestory inserted, and there, so long as the building works continued, at least part of the expenses was met out of the proceeds of the court.[10]

61 The late-fifteenth-century west tower at Helmingham Church, Suffolk, built to rival and overtop the towers at neighbouring churches at Framsden and Brandeston, from which many of the details of its design were borrowed

62 Northleach, Gloucestershire: it was John Fortey (d. 1459), a rich wool-merchant whose memorial brass is preserved in the church, who financed the building of the great clerestory at Northleach, with its unusual nine-light east window over the chancel arch; the Lady Chapel, south of the chancel, was another pious addition to the church, datable to 1489

Significantly, the building programmes at each of these churches were not restricted to the repair of existing structures, but included very important and expensive improvements. Among the most frequent complaints heard at episcopal visitations of the late fourteenth century had been that the chancels of the churches were 'dark and gloomy'; so much so that even at midday, mass had to be celebrated by candlelight.[11] And it is plain that the churchwardens and other leading parishioners who made these complaints would not long rest content with the standards of church provision which had perfectly satisfied their forefathers. Naturally enough, they all wanted a parish church that was light and dry, one of their principal anxieties (often expressed) being the defective roofs that let rain through onto the altar. However, they were to show themselves, too, ready to find the money for luxuries—for towers and porches, pinnacles and decorative buttresses, clerestories and battlemented roofs. And they would mind the cost less if they thereby improved upon and substantially up-staged their neighbours. Church-building contracts of the later Middle Ages, of which a fair number survive, not infrequently cite near-by buildings as the model for proposed additions or improvements. When the men of Walberswick (Suffolk) in 1425 engaged masons to build them a church tower, they stipulated that the tower should follow the general design of the 'steeple' at Tunstall, with a west door and with windows 'as good as' those of the tower at Halesworth, both of these being churches in the same county.[12] Later in the century, again in Suffolk, the church tower at Helmingham in 1487 was the last of a trio to be built in the adjoining parishes of Helmingham, Framsden, and Brandeston. Characteristically, it borrowed features from both of the others and was given just enough extra height to overtop them.[13]

Some of these works were the result of individual benefactions—the product of the generosity of a wealthy parishioner whom they afterwards served to commemorate. But many also were communally undertaken in a popular effort which brought in

63 The spire at Bridgwater Church, Somerset, the construction of which, in 1366–7, was financed by parish collections

every manner of contribution. It was parish collections, benefactions, and individual small gifts which financed the construction of the spire at Bridgwater (Somerset) in 1366–7.[14] Similarly, the rebuilding of Bodmin Church (Cornwall) in 1469–72 was made possible by the contributions in cash and kind of the trade gilds and the many parish fraternities of the town, while something like 460 of Bodmin's inhabitants are recorded as subscribers to the work.[15] Among the many handsome rebuildings of the fifteenth century, an outstanding example is the parish church at Swaffham (Norfolk) where the rector himself, from the mid-fifteenth century, played an important role in the initiation and direction of what was to be an almost complete reconstruction. It is his name, John Botright (rector 1435–74), that heads the Bede Roll (list of benefactors) of Swaffham, and it was probably his reorganization of the resources of the church that made it possible for the work to begin. After this, individual townsmen and their wives gave generously to the furthering of the programme. It was William Coo and Anne, his wife, who paid for the roof of the porch, while Walter and Isabel Taylor were among the contributors to the exceptionally handsome timber roof at Swaffham, its finely carved hammer-beams terminating richly in angels. It was John Walsingham who found the money for the glazing of the great window in the Lady Chapel, Ralph Hammond who paid for the pews in the Trinity Chapel, John and Agnes Langman who provided the bulk of the seating in the main body of the church, and Thomas Cocke who did the same for the south aisle. Especially prominent among the subscribers to the works at Swaffham Church were Simon Blake, 'gentleman', and Jane, his wife, contributing, with other things, the sum of £40 to the noble tower, completed there in 1510. But important practical aid was also given by such as Robert Payne, who gave twenty tons of good quality building stone towards the construction of the tower, and Nicholas Wright, whose contribution was a lime-kiln and five roods of land. Of all the subscribers, none were more generous than John Chapman and Catherine, his wife, who 'made the north yle, with glasyng, stolying [seating] and pathyng [paving] of the same wyth Marbyll, and gave £120 in money to the makying of the New Stepyll'. Appropriately enough, they were portrayed as carved figures on the Pedlar's Seat at Swaffham, a prayer desk so-named after the spirited carving of a pedlar (chapman) and his dog which still recalls the source of the benefactor's fortune.[16]

64 Bodmin, Cornwall; rebuilt in 1469–72 on the proceeds of collections taken from the gilds, fraternities, and townspeople of Bodmin; the contemporary spire was demolished in the late seventeenth century

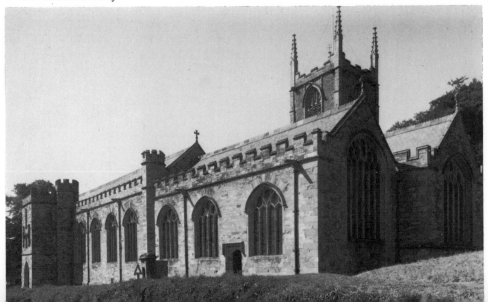

65 *Above* The fine double hammer-beam roof of Swaffham Church, Norfolk, towards the cost of which Walter and Isabel Taylor, among others in the parish, contributed; second half of the fifteenth century

66 The Swaffham Pedlar: carved figures of a pedlar and his dog, commemorating the substantial contribution of John Chapman to the rebuilding of Swaffham Church

67 The south porch at Walpole St Peter, Norfolk: an outstanding example, among
many, of the porches built during the fifteenth century at the expense of pious
parishioners

68 Castle Ashby, Northamptonshire: one of the cases where the chancel, in the fifteenth century, was
rebuilt at the same time (and to the same scale) as the nave

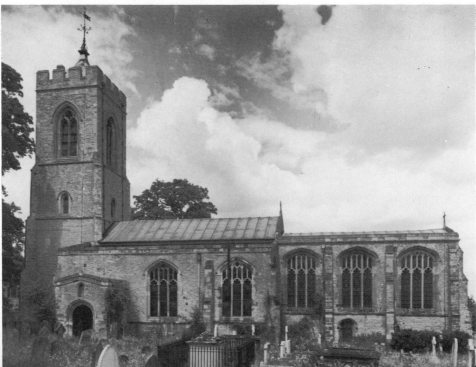

Swaffham was exceptionally lucky in its rector. Himself a native of the town, Dr John Botright was a man of learning and of considerable personal wealth, simultaneously rector of Swaffham, master of Corpus Christi College (Cambridge), and chaplain to Henry VI. During his time, the chancel at Swaffham would receive from him as much care and attention as his parishioners contemporaneously lavished on the nave, the porch, and the tower. Such cooperative action was not, however, very common, and it was more usually the case that the standard of maintenance on the chancel and its furnishings fell behind that of the rest of the church. Chancels certainly were rebuilt in the fifteenth century, whether as part of a total programme like that at Swaffham or as an individual project such as we know, from the record of a dispute, to have occurred at Surfleet Church (Lincolnshire) in 1418–20.[17] But wherever church-building was especially active, as it was, for example, in cloth-rich Somerset during much of the later Middle Ages, the difference between a reconstructed nave and tower (the responsibility of the parishioners) and an old-fashioned and unaltered chancel (the rector's charge) is often very obvious. At such great Perpendicular churches as Yatton and Weston Zoyland, both in that county, or Methwold in equally prospering Norfolk, the chancels, excluded by the parishioners from their major building programme, were left absurdly out of scale.

69 Methwold, Norfolk: an example of the dwarfing of a fourteenth-century chancel by a rebuilt fifteenth-century nave and spire

⌈Too frequently, the problem was not just the rector's failure to rebuild the chancel but his chronically persisting neglect.⌋ Early in the sixteenth century, the defects in the chancels of a group of Lincoln diocese churches outnumbered by three to one similarly recorded deficiencies in those same churches' naves and towers.[18] It was the monastic appropriators who were the most to blame for this neglect, and it was they also who appear to have paid least attention to the repeated instructions of the bishop to make the damage good. But circumstances, in any event, were against them. The contemporary downward drift of the real value of rectorial incomes left little in the purse for improvements. The ruin and decay of the chancel at Wisbech (Cambridgeshire), left unremedied from 1462 till 1479 or later, may just as likely have followed from the poverty of the living as from the neglect of a non-resident rector.[19]

⌈Inevitably, the temptation felt by most incumbents was to patch and mend, leaving major works to their successors.⌋ And with little machinery to pass on funds between one serving priest and another, the next incumbent could often find that he had taken on more than he could afford. Such certainly was the experience of John Mayhewe, the new parson of Saxlingham (Norfolk), who took a case to Chancery in 1476–7 to obtain compensation out of the estate of his predecessor, John Grey, for dilapidations in the chancel ('choir') and the parsonage. He had found the benefice 'in great dilapidation and needing great repairs, both in the choir of the said church and also in the house of his parsonage'. But Parson Grey had died intestate, giving what money he had to a friend, Thomas Gardener, from whom his successor now sought some remedy. The late parson, as the court proceedings made clear, had had little thought at the last of the problems he was leaving behind him. Having discharged a small private debt to Thomas Gardener, he had commissioned his friend to lay out a further sum to the benefit of his immortal soul. It was Gardener's case that—

> . . . the said John Grey upon his death bed delivered to the said Thomas 40s in money, praying the same Thomas that he would therewith cause him to be buried appropriately, and for the welfare of his soul to have Placebo and Dirige and a mass of Requiem with such other funeral service done and said for his soul at the day and time of his burial, with the same money; and if anything remained of the said 40s to distribute it forthwith in alms the same day of his burial, which the same Thomas Gardener so did and observed in every point well and truly according to the desire of the said John.

What was left unsaid was that there had been other assets, including a house and garden in Norwich, which had come to Gardener by the same deed of gift, side-stepping the rightful claims of the Church. On the consideration of this new evidence, judgement at last was given against Gardener to the tune of 26 marks.[20]

Parson Mayhewe, in the final event, did reasonably well from the settlement. However, he had not got to that point without hardship, nor was the lot of village clergy like himself to improve within his or the next generations. In contrast, the laity grew steadily more powerful, taking an ever greater interest in the management of their churches as the value of their investment in them increased. Parson Grey's relatively heavy outlay on a good and fitting funeral, with its crucially important memorial mass or requiem, was typical of a period to which the belief in Purgatory

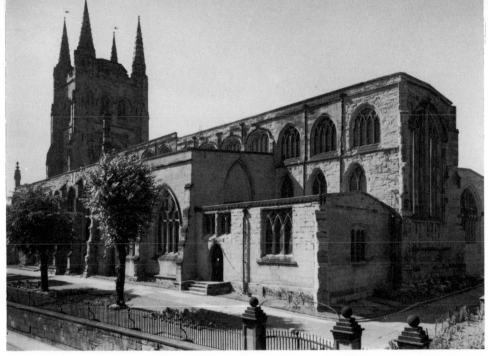

70 Tamworth, Staffordshire: a large collegiate church where the furnishings were so rich that the deacons were required to sleep in the church 'for the care and safe-custody of its books and ornaments'

was central, nothing being of more power to 'draw down the mercy of God' and to restore 'fallen humanity' than the 'solemn celebration of Masses'.[21] Of course, the parish church was always more than the memorial chapel or tomb-house of its parishioners; it had many other functions as essential to the daily routine of the community. Nevertheless, well before the Reformation swept much of this away, obit (or 'mind-day') had been piled on obit, one subsidized requiem mass followed quickly on another, there were memorial candles burning 'for evermore' at every altar, while among the heavier responsibilities of already over-burdened churchwardens was the care of many valuables, including church plate, donated in 'remembrance' of the pious. Not surprisingly, with all this to protect, the breaking into and robbing of parish churches was not uncommon in the later Middle Ages, several incidents of this kind being reported, for example, in a 1458 visitation of the churches belonging to St Paul's (London).[22] No chances were to be taken at Tamworth Church (Staffordshire) where, from the promulgation of new statutes in 1442, the 'deacons shall in future sleep and take their repose in the church itself for the care and safe-custody of its books and ornaments'.[23]

Tamworth was a rich collegiate church, certainly better furnished than most. Nevertheless, all parish churches had at least a minimum of equipment (above, pp. 27–8), and many, in the late fifteenth and early sixteenth centuries, were rapidly increasing their stock. The further endowment of the English parish churches took many forms, but one of its most appealing manifestations in the rural areas was the very obvious participation of the husbandmen. Among the church goods of Little Waltham, in Essex, as listed in a fifteenth-century inventory, were valuables which included a 'cross of silver', no fewer than three chalices, and a 'vestyment of gyfte of a cyteseyn of London'. However, the humbler sort had also made their contribution to the church by the gift of cattle and sheep, the leasing of which would yield an income usually devoted to the maintenance of lights. In the long list of 'all the ken [cattle] & shep longynge to the cherch of lytyl Waltham', among recorded donors were William Parnell who 'gaf ij ken for ij lampes to the rode [rood] lygt', Margaret Lurkes who 'gaf half a cow to seynt Margarete lygt' and a 'schep to seyny Anne lygt', and Thomas Cogeshale who, with other gifts to the lamps, gave 'a cow for the parson to synge with every day'.[24] Similar donations, including some as delightfully expressed, feature among the wills of the West Kent yeomen of an only slightly later generation. Thus John Sherman, of Fawkham (Kent), bequeathed to his parish church in 1502 for 'the maintaining of a perpetual light before the image of Saint Catherine in the church, a mother sheep and a lamb', while thirteen years later, by the gift of William Wadham, the church at Halling acquired a 'cow to maintain and find a lamp to burn before the rood in the church from the second peal to matins till high mass be done and from the second peal to evensong till evensong be done, for evermore'. To the church of All Hallows at Hoo, in the same county, William Forest in 1524 made the gift of a cow in terms that are authentically rustic: 'To Saint Christopher light one cow, and she to remain for evermore and to be registered in the mass book that she never decay.'[25]

William Forest's small bid for immortality was only one of many, up and down the country, as men of every walk and condition in life sought to ensure a swift passage through Purgatory both for themselves and for those whom they loved. It was Thomas Cumbe's wish, recorded in his will dated 15 October 1494, only a few days before he died, that his body should be buried 'in the church of Pulborough in the place there I have made for myself to lie in if I die within the shire of Sussex'. To recommend his soul, he gave twenty shillings to Pulborough Church towards the buying of a new 'portuous' (breviary), and added to this the further legacy of 'one of my mass books, two altar cloths of cloth-of-gold for the high altar, two cruets of silver, a pax of silver and gilt, a vestment of white damask, and a chalice, to pray for my soul and the souls of my both late wives'. In the same document, the church at Udimore, also in Sussex, was to have a vestment and a chalice 'to pray for the souls of my most Dearest Heart and Lady and for mine'.[26]

71 The large and expensively ornate tower of St Stephen's Church, Bristol, built at the expense of John Shipward and his son, merchants of Bristol and, in their turn, mayors of the city; fifteenth century

[Remembrance, and the obligations thus imposed on posterity, became a factor of overwhelming importance in the extension and the fitting out of churches. The church of St Stephen, Bristol, owed its tower to John Shipward and his son, both of them mayors of the city. But that was not the only contribution of John Shipward to his parish, for he set up a personal chantry at St Stephen's Church to pray in perpetuity for his family and himself, and gave the church two missals, a silver-gilt chalice, and six suits of vestments, on condition only that his chantry priests might use them when they needed. John Shipward's will was dated 1473. By 1494, when Richard Vaghan (churchwarden and himself one of a family of benefactors of St Stephen's) made his inventory of church goods, the plate at St Stephen's already totalled nearly a thousand ounces in weight, while in the next eight years the four chalices of Vaghan's counting were to rise in number to twelve. Of these, there was some uncertainty in 1502 who one of the donors had been—'as yet can no man tell who gave it'. But most benefactors (including, it was found, the donor of this chalice) were careful to record the fact of their generosity by an inscription, a coat of arms, or an initial. The problem chalice had 'writen yn the fote' *orate pro animabus Iohannis bayly & Elysabeth vxoris eius* (pray for the souls of John Bailey and Elizabeth his wife); others had similar inscriptions for John Collins and Catherine his wife, for Margaret Holbrook and Christine Fouke together, and for the soul (*pro anima*) of Hugo Hunt.[27]

72   The Peacock Chalice, Museum of London; the foot of a pre-Reformation pyx, carrying the date letter for 1507, to which was added in 1559 a bell-shaped cup, thus converting it for use in the reformed Elizabethan church. The pyx, which is mentioned in Sir Stephen Peacock's will, carries the inscription round the foot: 'Praye for the solle of Stewyn Pekoc and Marget hys wyff, which gave this in the worshippe of the Sacrement'; silver gilt

Competitive gift-giving in the richer city parishes had become a reality long before the St Stephen's inventories were compiled. St Peter Cheap in the City of London, one of the many parish churches destroyed in the great fire of 1666 and never subsequently rebuilt, was situated in the goldsmiths' quarter, its rich treasury of church plate and relics including a 'pece of the cross of Cryste'. In 1431, when an inventory of the vestments, plate, and service-books at St Peter Cheap was taken, this precious fragment was kept in a reliquary (a gold cross garnished with jewels, on a silver-gilt base) which was by far the most valuable single item listed among the *jocalia* (jewels) of the church. But it was accompanied too by a great range of plate, ornaments, and books, and by vestments, frontals, and painted banners and cloths far in excess of any reasonable requirements of the clergy. One of these last was a 'cloth of gold, the colour red and white with trees and birds and the arms of Robert Walter goldsmith', valued at twenty shillings. Another, perhaps from the same source and still more costly, was a set of cloth-of-gold altar hangings clearly commemorative in purpose. They were painted with angels and with birds, and were decorated further with the arms of Robert Walton (*sic*), 'and he, his ij wyves and his sonnes beynge therin'.[28] Before the end of the century, it would be the London goldsmiths who would find themselves most seriously embarrassed by the large number of memorial services and solemn processions they were required to attend to mark the well-endowed mind-days of other goldsmiths once of their fellowship. A conscientious attender of these obits, they discovered, could lose one working day in every twelve.[29]

73 A fifteenth-century embroidered altar frontal, carrying an Annunciation scene, from the Church of St Thomas, Salisbury

Not very far from St Peter Cheap was another parish church, St Margaret Pattens, again the proud possessor of a fragment of the True Cross in its reliquary of silver gilt and jewels. Like other London churches of its kind, it was richly equipped and its treasures were carefully recorded. However, for our purposes the chief interest of its surviving inventories lies in the list they include of the church goods acquired during the seven-year wardenship of Robert Bangyll and John Thrilkyld, both of the Company of Grocers—the 'Ornamentes and gyftys that was Gotten and gyvene to the use propyrlye of Seynt Margarete Patten Church' between 1 March 1479 and 7 March 1486 'att their gevyng upp off their Accowmpt'. The two churchwardens had been generous donors themselves. Robert Bangyll had given a mass-book bound in white leather, and John Thrilkyld and his wife an embroidered vestment. In addition, they had 'labered to be had in the same tyme' a whole suit of new vestments for priest, deacon, and subdeacon, with eight embroidered corporals, complete with cases, being the squares of cloth on which the bread and wine were placed for consecration during the celebration of the Eucharist. Especially generous, too, had been the parson, Master Thomas Houghton, whose gifts included a vestment of white buckram (fine linen), a reliquary cross, a carved and gilded cross-staff 'like goldsmyth werke with the crown of Seint Margarett', a long curtain 'steyned with Seynt Margarett' to hang before her image, several altar-cloths, cushions, and tapestries, some books (among them a hymnary, a manual, and two burial books), and a frontal for the high altar of white double damask 'with rosis of gold and ymages of Seint Margarett made in nedill werke'. Parson Houghton had paid also for the new making, painting and gilding of the cross on the rood-loft, he had seen to the repair and gilding of the font, and had made a contribution out of his own purse towards the building works, otherwise largely financed by a bequest of Richard Bowell and Elizabeth his wife, in the south aisle of the church, 'with many other necessaries done, and Ocupied to the behoofe of the forsaid Chirch Seynt Margarett Patten the which he will natt have rehersid nor knowen'.

Richard and Elizabeth Bowell had been patrons of St Margaret Pattens in other ways beside their contribution to its repair. They had given it its most important piece of church plate—a large silver-gilt cross with images of Mary and John on it—which had featured already in an inventory dated 1470. And eight pounds of their money was laid out during the wardenships of Robert Bangyll and John Thrilkyld towards the cost (£9 in all) of a white damask cope 'powdered with Archangelles', of which the orphrey (an ornamental strip or band) was embroidered with needlework scenes from the life of St Margaret—'and we paid the overplus'. Two other valuable copes had come to St Margaret's during the same period 'ffor the sowle off Sir John Thoode preest', being of white damask again 'powdered with fflowres of silke and gold', while 'for the same sowle' had come a red silk vestment, the great cross on the back being embroidered with Sir John Thoode's name. In just the same way, the vestment bequeathed by Master John Darbye, alderman of London, had had a cross on the back 'and his name in the myddes therof'. The four silk Easter banners 'had off my lady Edward', presumably in memory of her late husband, bore the coats-of-arms, in beaten silver and gold, of Master Edwardes and of the city of London.[30]

Many smaller gifts accompanied these greater ones during the Bangyll and Thrilkyld wardenship. However, although the church of St Margaret Pattens by

74 A fifteenth-century velvet cope, embroidered with saints under canopies, at Chipping Campden Church, Gloucestershire

1486, when they gave up office, was already quite certainly over-furnished, the flow of pious benefactions continued. Before 1500, St Margaret's had acquired a valuable damask cope embroidered with gold fleurs-de-lis, by gift of Master Harry Wayte, mercer and merchant of the Staple. During 1494/5 (the 'xth yere off the regne off Kynge harry the viith') it got forty shillings in cash by bequest of William Johnson, basketmaker; in 1498/9, an altar-cloth by gift of the wife of Richard Pound 'to the honor of god & Seynt margitt', and that same year a latten (brass) candlestick by gift of Margaret Harpham; in 1499/1500, another altar-cloth from Mistress Staunton, as well as four torches given by Mistress Bretten for the soul of her daughter Maud, 'the whiche maude decesid the laste day of App'ile A° h. vij° xv° [1500] on whos sowle Jesus have mercy'.

75 A late-fifteenth-century brass lectern, probably of East Anglian workmanship, at Chipping Campden Church, Gloucestershire; not original to the church

In the last decades before the Reformation, there is little to establish that the parishioners of St Margaret's felt any differently towards the church they had long since equipped so well. One of its most valuable acquisitions in the early sixteenth century was a suit of black velvet vestments for priest, deacon and subdeacon, with a cope of the same and orphrey worked with figures of the apostles and prophets, the whole valued at £22. And the donors of this suit—John Wilson, Robert May, and Joanna (wife in succession to them both)—were also to give St Margaret's, in 1504/5, an incense boat of silver gilt, complete with spoon, recorded thereafter among the more important of the church's many pieces of plate. It was probably in this period that St Margaret's collected its 'ij lytyll botels of Glasse wt Jesus Christ wryton on them', as well as the two costly mazers (wooden cups bound with silver), one of which carried the attractive inscriptions—'Of goddes hande blissed be he that taketh this Cuppe and drynketh to me', with (on the inside) 'God that siteth in Trynyte send us peax'e and unyte'. In 1536, as rumours gathered concerning the confiscation of Church treasures, these two 'grete masers' were delivered to William Gibson, then churchwarden, to be sold for the benefit of St Margaret Pattens. With them went the buckle of silver gilt which had perhaps been the one holding the 'coat' about the image of St Margaret herself, and the splendid reliquary, also silver gilt, that had housed the precious fragment of the Cross of Christ, now an object of contempt to the reformers.[31]

76 Roughton, Norfolk: a parish fraternity, founded here, declared its object to be the collection of ornaments for the church, at that time only scantily supplied with them

This great accumulation of church goods at St Margaret Pattens (London) resulted in part from nothing more sophisticated than civic pride. One of the finest of St Margaret's several coats—of black damask bordered with cloth of gold and fringed beneath with silk—carried a shield with the arms of the Company of Salters, and the church itself was hung with streamers of silk, embroidered or painted with a variety of arms and heraldic devices, including those of the Grocers, of the City of London, and of the Company of Merchant Staplers of Calais.[32] But important though the motive of civic pride must have been in the competitive furnishing of such richer city churches as those of London, of Bristol, or of Norwich, it was never as powerful as that other great promoter of lay generosity—the desire, felt everywhere equally, for a fitting commemoration of the dead. A parish fraternity at Roughton Church, in Norfolk, taking every possible precaution by naming as its patrons the Holy Trinity, St Mary, and All Saints, declared as its object the collection of the ornaments with which the church was but scantily supplied.[33] However, its founders did this, as they stated, for their souls' health, and this would have been as much the motive of the Brethren of St Margaret Pattens, whose gift to their parish church of a valuable silver-gilt chalice was carefully recorded on its base.[34]

For the very rich, commemoration might take the form of the foundation and endowment of a perpetual chantry, according to the terms of which one or more chantry priests would be hired to sing mass for the souls of the departed. 'It is befitting,' said the preamble of one such Yorkshire chantry ordination, 'to encourage with affectionate sympathy the sincere devotion of those who desire to give of their worldly goods to the increase of divine worship, the multiplication of the number of them that minister in God's Holy Church, and the establishment of celebrations of masses which are the more profitable to Christ's faithful people unto salvation, inasmuch as in the same the King of Heaven is placated by mystic gifts, and remedies for sins are more easily obtained by asking'.[35] And there were some parish churches, like Tormarton in Gloucestershire, that became almost exclusively the personal chantries of their appropriators. But Tormarton was expensive. Founded in 1344 by

John de la Riviere, lord of the manor and patron of Tormarton Church, the chantry was united almost immediately with the neighbouring Acton Turville, of which its founder again held the advowson, and was worth in 1348 the large annual sum of 100 marks (£66 13s 4d). As a collegiate institution, it was run by a warden (the rector of Tormarton), with a staff of four chaplains, two clerks (deacon and subdeacon), and three choristers. Between them, according to the very precisely expressed wishes of their founder, who still lies in the chancel at Tormarton, they were to maintain an elaborate liturgical round. John de la Riviere had an obvious enthusiasm for the proper use of liturgical colours. His priests, celebrating mass at the high altar at Tormarton, were to wear black vestments at the burial of the founder and his kin and at all subsequent anniversaries; at the five feasts of Our Lady 'and other solemn feasts of virgins', they must wear white; at Christmas and feasts of confessors, green; at Easter and feasts of the apostles and martyrs, red; at vigils, violet.[36] A similar colour-rule, still more elaborately expressed, has been found among the statutes of Pleshey College (Essex), founded in 1395 by a great magnate, Thomas of Woodstock, duke of Gloucester (d. 1397), at the rebuilt parish church of St Mary. At this chantry college, black was to be the colour for All Souls Day, vigils, funerals, and masses for the dead; yellow for feasts of confessors; green for all Sundays 'from the feast of the Trinity until Advent'; violet or blue 'within the octave of the Epiphany, of the Trinity, and of the Nativity of St John Baptist'; red for the feasts of Pentecost, the Invention and the Exaltation of the Holy Cross, the apostles, the evangelists, the martyrs, St Thomas of Hereford, and Ash Wednesday; and white for many of the remaining more solemn feasts, including Corpus Christi, the Circumcision and Ascension of the Lord, and the five feasts of the Virgin. On the feast of the Epiphany, Thomas of Woodstock's chaplains were to wear 'vestments with stars, if they have them, of whatever colour they may be'. On Christmas Day, on Easter Day, on Trinity Sunday, All Saints' Day, and the dedication day of the church, with the special addition of the feast of the Translation of St Thomas 'the martyr' (Thomas Becket of Canterbury, the duke's 'special patron and advocate'), the priests and clerks of Pleshey College were to select for themselves 'the best and most solemn vestments of whatsoever colour they please'.[37]

77 The handsome Perpendicular church at Lowick, Northamptonshire, which remains a memorial to the Greene family—Sir Henry (d. 1399), Ralph (d. 1415), and Henry (d. 1468)—by whom the rebuilding was chiefly financed

Pleshey College survived until the Reformation, and its colour-rule was still being observed, as the 1527 inventory of its church goods and other furnishings makes plain, well into the sixteenth century.[38] But the lavish endowments that such foundations as Tormarton and Pleshey required, very obviously put them beyond the reach of all but the very wealthiest patrons, while it is clear that even the individual personal chantry was becoming too expensive in the later Middle Ages for those who, in earlier generations, would not have thought twice about establishing one. The foundation of perpetual chantries had peaked in England during the first half of the fourteenth century, reaching its climax before the Black Death at just about the time that Tormarton itself was founded.[39] After the mid-century, a decline set in, and although chantries everywhere continued to be established for almost another two hundred years until the Protestant reformers put paid to them, the failure of some of the earlier foundations—their endowments swallowed by inflation—promoted a new circumspection among patrons. When Thomas Dursle, fishmonger and citizen of London, made his first will on 10 March 1428, he provided for an annual obit at St Margaret's, Bridge Street, by bequeathing his shop in that street to the rector and churchwardens of the parish, 'to be held in perpetuity on condition that they keep his anniversary and that of his wife Joan with tolling of bells and requiem mass'. Ten years later, drafting another will on 27 September 1438, he had evidently increased his fortune to such a degree as to be able to consider a chantry, for he left the reversion of all his property in the parish of St Edmund, Lombard Street, to St Margaret's Church to support a chaplain in perpetuity, praying daily for the souls of his parents, himself, and his successive wives. Yet he added a significant rider. If the rents and profits from his assigned properties proved insufficient to pay the upkeep of a full-time chaplain, then the rector and churchwardens 'at their discretion' were to use some of the money to pay the fees of a part-timer, employing what was left for the 'renewal, repair and alteration' of the church and for 'ornaments and other necessities'.[40]

Inadequate chantry endowments had already led to mergers and reorganizations well before Thomas Dursle made his own arrangements for the health of his soul. Robert Braybrooke, bishop of London (1382–1404), had encouraged other similar action elsewhere by agreeing to a rationalization of the chantries at St Paul's Cathedral by which, in a number of instances, the incomes of two or more foundations had been united to support a single priest.[41] And measures of this kind would always be necessary where founders continued, as they did, for example, at York, to assign incomes to their chaplains which, at only five or six marks per annum, were right down at the bottom of the scale.[42] A few, of course, were prepared to pay more, among them Joan Holmhegge, widow of a former mayor of Southampton, whose mid-fifteenth-century chantry foundation at the church of St Mary provided for a chaplain's stipend of £6 13s 4d. But Mistress Holmhegge expected her appointee to work hard. He was to celebrate mass daily at St Mary's, the mother-church of Southampton, and 'likewise he ought to be present on every Sunday and feast day at prime, vespers, matins, high mass and second vespers, and other canonical hours of the day from the beginning to the end. . . . Provided always that the said chaplain shall once in a week say services and commemorations for my soul, etc., and in like manner a requiem mass on the day following with a special collect, mentioning my name, to wit, Joan, in the same collect.' As one of the better endowed of such foundations in the town, the Holmhegge chantry survived until the Reformation, still supporting a full-time cantarist at the wage that Mistress Holmhegge originally had set for him.[43]

Yet it was, inevitably, just this inflexibility of income that had brought many similar projects to nothing, and they were wiser men in the later Middle Ages who

78 Brass to William Ermyn (d. 1401), rector of Castle Ashby, Northamptonshire, his handsome cope embroidered with saints under canopies

relied less on a stable economy. Rather as Thomas Dursle had done in London, John Shipward of Bristol, making his will on 14 December 1473, anticipated a future when his endowment might be worth less by providing that the two chaplains of his original chantry at the parish church of St Stephen's (Bristol) should be reduced in number, after twenty-five years, to only one.[44] At York, where a pronounced economic decline had set in during the fifteenth century bringing a descent in land values and in rents, the practice of perpetual chantry foundation, very popular in the city in better days, fell away almost to nothing. In its place, even the wealthier of York's late-medieval citizens preferred to put their money into short-term arrangements—twenty years, seven years, or just two. Robert Johnson's will, made during his mayoralty of York in 1497, set aside £35 for the hire of a priest 'to synge at the alter of our said Lady, daily, by the space of vii yeres . . . And I will that what prest that shall serve it every day, whan that he hath saide *Messe*, that he stand affore my grave in his albe, and ther to say the psalme of *De Profundis* with the Colettes; and then caste holy water upon my grave'.[45] Earlier in the same century, John Northby, also of York, had arranged that £100 of his fortune should be employed, after his death, in the commissioning of memorial masses. He believed, evidently, in a concentration of effort, for no fewer than ten priests were to work together to this purpose over a period of only two years.[46]

79 The Beauchamp Chapel, Devizes, Wiltshire: one of the more magnificent of the many chantry chapels added to parish churches in the late Middle Ages; late fifteenth century

Whatever the fate of the chantry, at York or elsewhere, there is nothing to suggest, before the second quarter of the sixteenth century, any appreciable falling-off in popular belief in the efficacy of the memorial mass. All chantry founders had specified the celebration of requiem masses, many of them one every day, and it was this duty that was always of overriding importance, exceeding that even of the chaplain's parallel obligation—the recitation of the office of the dead (*Placebo*, *Dirige*, and *Commendation*).[47] If a man was not able to pay for such masses on his own account—as most, indeed, were not—one course he could take was to unite in association with others in his position (his 'brothers' and 'sisters' in the parish) in the foundation of a fraternity, or church gild. It was precisely because 'they two alone were insufficient to do this' that William Everswell and Nicholas Clerk, soon after the Black Death, founded their Gild of St Mary at Tydd St Giles, on the Lincolnshire and Cambridgeshire border, having as their avowed purpose the hiring of a stipendiary chaplain to improve divine service in the village and 'for the benefit of the souls of the dead'. Like other associations of its kind, the gild kept a candle alight before the image of the Virgin, and paid for two torches to burn at the Elevation of the Host during the celebration of the Eucharist. Its members joined in prayer on the death of a gildsman, attended each other's funeral masses, and came together once a year on the feast of the Assumption of the Virgin (15 August) for the celebration of a solemn collective requiem.[48]

Liturgical sophistication and the terror of an unsecured death united in late-medieval England to promote such associations as the Corpus Christi gilds, especially prominent in the fifteenth century. It had been Pope Urban IV, in the early 1260s, who had founded the Feast of Corpus Christi, the central feature of which was to be a

80   An interior view of Tavistock Church, Devonshire, showing the clothworkers' second south aisle to the right; fifteenth century

solemn procession of the Blessed Sacrament. And at first the idea had been slow in catching on. Endemic plague then gave it a new setting. At Lynn (later King's Lynn), in Norfolk, the foundation narrative of the Corpus Christi gild makes the connection especially explicit:

> During the great pestilence which was at Lynn in 1349, in which the greater part of the people of that town died, three men seeing that the venerated Sacrament of the Body of Christ was being carried through the town with only a single candle of poor wax burning in front of It, whereas two torches of the best wax are hardly sufficient, thought it so improper that they ordained certain lights for It when carried by night or by day in the visitation of the sick ... and designed this devotion to last for the period of their lives. Others seeing their devotion offered to join them and thirteen of them drew up their ordinances.[49]

Less a parish association than an interest common to the whole town, the Corpus Christi gild in many of the larger centres soon accumulated great influence and wealth. Although of relatively late foundation, the Corpus Christi gild at York, originating only in 1408, had won a prominent place for itself in the feast-day procession within not more than a decade, its members subscribing 2d a year towards the cost of the ten great torches carried by the gild before the Blessed Sacrament. In

81 Ludlow, Shropshire: a great parish church which owed its fifteenth-century rebuilding almost entirely to the munificence of the wealthy Palmers' Gild

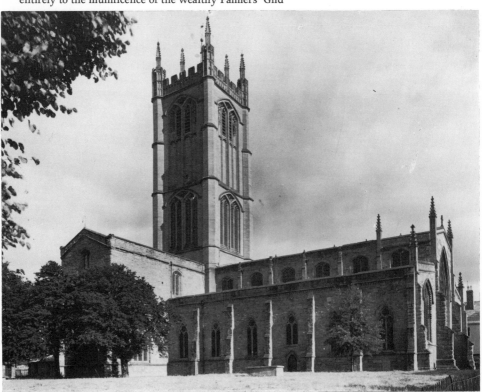

1432, the gild's privilege was extended to the carrying of the shrine itself, and in 1449 one of its wealthy members, Thomas Spofford, bishop of Hereford, bequeathed to the gild a fine new silver shrine, decorated with jewels and fashioned in the form of a church, which it now preserved as the centrepiece of its rapidly expanding treasury. Well before the end of the century, the processional order was fixed, giving the positions of greatest prominence to the gild. A priest, paid by the gild, carried the cross at the front, while the master of the gild, with former masters to his right and left, brought up the rear. Behind the cross, in the order of the torch list of 1501, the Corpus Christi gildsmen were preceded by the cobblers and porters, the ropers, glovers, butchers, bakers, fullers, carpenters, smiths, coverlet-weavers, the 'ffysshmongers fysshers and maryners goyng to gedir by tham self', the weavers, the cordwainers (shoemakers), the tailors and mercers, with the ruling twenty-four and the aldermen of York being the last in the procession before the gild.[50]

The York Corpus Christi gild, with its many important members both in the city government and among men of influence outside, was exceptionally wealthy; it was also unusually specialized, showing less concern than most gilds would have done for the health of its individual gildsmen's souls. More representative of the class of late-medieval parish fraternities as a whole was such an association as the Gild of St George at the church of St Peter, Nottingham, of which the account books survive, with the annual reckonings of the chamberlains of the gild from 1459 until its suppression in 1545–6. Typical of these reckonings is the account of John Cost and Richard Esott, chamberlains 'from the Feast of Saint George A.D. 1484 until the same feast then next A.D. 1485, to wit for one whole year'. They started the year with £28 3s 5d in hand, to which they were able to add 15s 6d received in rents during their term of office from gild properties, among them a house in Hundgate and another in Wheelwrightgate 'given and assigned for the support of the same Gild by John Thrompton for the welfare of the souls of his parents'. Other receipts, totalling £9 14s 1d, included £6 2s 6d 'for the money collected among the brothers and sisters of the aforesaid Gild for their payments in this year', with various small charges made for hiring out the gild pall at funerals, 18d 'for the moiety of the offerings found in the casket of St George' (the other moiety going to the church), and 41s 'collected by them in malt towards the breakfast (*jantaculum*) of the brothers and sisters'. To set against this income, the principal expenses met by the chamberlains had been those associated with the maintenance of the round of memorial masses and the repair of the various gild properties. During the year, the gild had lost one chaplain and had had to hire another, 14d being charged for the 'expense and labour for the men who rode to engage a Chaplain'. The priest chosen was John Blomeley who himself 'went away' the following year. In addition, two other chaplains had been hired for occasional services—20d to Roger Grene 'for celebrating the common Mass of the aforesaid Gild by the order of the Alderman', and 6s 8d to Thomas Williamson 'for the keeping of the Mass of Saint George'. Among the repairs, the largest item was 22s 11d paid for work on the chamber at the Franciscan friary where the gild had held its breakfast, with something too for the tenement owned by the gild in Hundgate. Miscellaneous expenses had included 12d for the washing of the gild's vestments and albs, and the same sum 'for wine and wax for the Masses celebrated for a moiety of the same year'. The chamberlains had spent 1d 'paid to Thomas Hall for making the tapers of the aforesaid Gild', with 8d 'paid for the carrying of eight tapers of the aforesaid Gild about the Body of the Lord on the day of Corpus Christi' and 3d 'paid for the carrying of three banners on the same day'. Henry Hobbes had charged a 4s fee 'for keeping the harness of Saint George clean in this year', while the gild had had to find another 1d 'for the protection of the armour of Saint George' from those who carried its torches in the Corpus Christi day procession. Painting the gild chest green had cost 6d; two new keys, priced at 3d, had been bought for the aumbry in the gild chapel at St Peter's; and 3s 4d had been paid to John Clyderowe, beadle, for his fee.[51]

It seems not to have been among the duties of the chamberlains of St George to keep the reckoning of their gild's annual 'breakfast'. But this common meal—a survival from the traditional drinking-bouts and feasts of the gilds merchant and other remote ancestors of the fraternities—remained the most important social event in any such fellowship's calendar, providing a very welcome relaxation after the solemnities of the annual gild procession and requiem. The Gild of St John the Baptist was only one of seven parish fraternities in the Norfolk church of St Peter and St Paul, Swaffham, the others being dedicated to St Peter himself, to the Holy Trinity, the Ascension, St Nicholas, St Helen, and St Thomas Becket. Yet, for the purpose of the feast, it kept a stock of its own of tableware which, as listed in 1496, consisted of five large pottery plates, five smaller pewter plates, three flat pewter dishes, and six saucers, all marked with the initial letter of the gild; in treen (wooden vessels), it had 18 dishes, 28 'great trenchers' and 3 other trenchers, and 17 wooden spoons. In other nearly contemporary inventories, the gild is shown owning three or four long tablecloths and a large brass pot; and all this equipment would certainly have been needed for the yearly dinner which every member attended, paying each one his share. In 1508, as we know from the accounts, the brothers and sisters of the Gild of St John the Baptist (Swaffham) sat down to a meal of beef and mutton, lamb, pork, and goose, with sauce and spices, bread, cheese, and ale. There were probably between forty and fifty gild members present for the occasion. Including the cost of minstrels (16d), torch-bearers, and cooks, the charge per head would have worked out at between five and six pence, or about as much as the individual member was expected to contribute yearly to the common fund and pious purposes of the gild.[52]

Of course, the Gild of St John the Baptist was a very small affair, representative enough of many such rural gilds, but concerned with little more than the maintenance of a candle (or 'light') burning before the image of John the Baptist at Swaffham and with the provision of torches at gildsmen's burials. Nevertheless, its members had clearly learnt the habit of regular contributions to the worship of their church, and wealthier fraternities in similar circumstances came frequently to be responsible for major improvements to the fabric of a church and to its stock of plate and other furnishings. There was no obvious need, for example, for the second south aisle at Tavistock Church (Devonshire), yet before 1450 the clothworkers of the parish had provided it.[53] Nor is there any more striking material evidence of the financial muscle of a single powerful gild than the Palmers' great collegiate parish church at Ludlow (Shropshire), which they were largely responsible for rebuilding. Both, in their way, are exceptional. But it was common in all parts of late-medieval England—not merely in the richer cloth-working regions—for the better-off fraternities to maintain chapels of their own and to keep them adequately furnished. Sharing the responsibility with the local trades with which many of them, in any event, were identified, they converted the greater parish churches, up and down the country, into memorial chapels for those who had been once of their fellowship.

An important urban church, like the Holy and Undivided Trinity at Hull, was especially liable to be used by the gilds in this way. Altars there, each maintained by its fraternity, were dedicated to Corpus Christi, to St John the Baptist, St Katherine, St Anne, and St Eloi (the seventh-century bishop who had himself been a goldsmith and whose cult afterwards thrived among the metal-workers).[54] At Coventry, prospering likewise in the later Middle Ages when other towns were not doing too well, the great churches of Holy Trinity and St Michael's were filled out in plan as one gild after another extended them (Fig. 83). One of the earliest of these extensions at Holy Trinity, Coventry, was a chapel dedicated to St Thomas, joining the north porch and transept of the originally cruciform church, while another chapel of St Thomas, extending eastwards from the south porch at St Michael's, was maintained by the Coventry cappers and cardmakers. In St Michael's, too, space was found west of the same porch for a chapel to be kept by the dyers; opposite it, in the north-west corner of

82 Holy Trinity, Hull: the largest parish church in England and the spiritual home of many late-medieval fraternities, each of which made its contribution to the fabric; fourteenth century with fifteenth-century improvements and additions, including the crossing tower

COVENTRY St. Michael

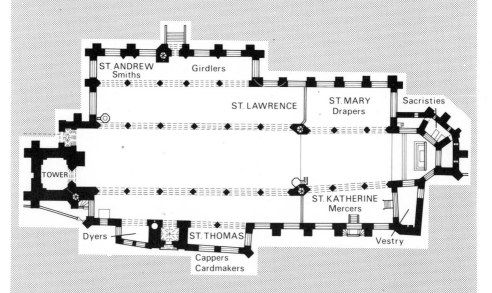

ST. ANDREW
Smiths

Girdlers

ST. LAWRENCE

ST. MARY
Drapers

Sacristies

TOWER

ST. KATHERINE
Mercers

Dyers

ST. THOMAS

Vestry

Cappers
Cardmakers

Holy Trinity

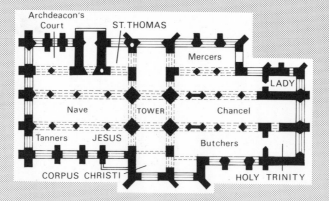

Archdeacon's
Court

ST. THOMAS

Mercers

LADY

Nave

TOWER

Chancel

Tanners   JESUS

Butchers

CORPUS CHRISTI

HOLY TRINITY

0   metres   20

the church, the smiths' chapel was dedicated to St Andrew (apostle and fisherman); the eastern end of the same north aisle became known as the Girdlers' Chapel; there was a chantry chapel of St Lawrence to the south-east of this, with St Mary (the chapel of the drapers) to the east again; in the equivalent position to the south of the chancel, the mercers had their chapel of St Katherine. When just such a chapel was projected at the church of St Mary-on-the-Hill, Chester, in 1433, the contract specified an extension of the type becoming common all over England at that time. Like so many other exactly contemporary chantry chapels, it was to be built to the south of the existing chancel with which it shared one wall. Eighteen feet in width and the same length as the adjoining chancel, it had to be 'as high as it needs reasonably to be'. It should be corbelled, battlemented, and supplied with three decorative ('honest') finials in the latest fashion, and must be equipped, 'in the best wise to be devised', with five 'fair and cleanly-wrought windows full of light'. The south wall was to be supported by four buttresses.[55]

83 *Left* Late-medieval gild and fraternity chapels at Coventry's great parish churches (*after* A. Hamilton Thompson)

84 The pulpit, crossing, and nave of Holy Trinity Church, Coventry; fifteenth century

85 *Above* Interior view of St Mary-on-the-Hill Church, Chester, showing (through the arch on the right) the chantry chapel for which a building contract of 1433 survives

86 *Right* Church of St Thomas, Salisbury: an interior view showing the Doom over the chancel arch, which would have been such a powerful visual aid for the preacher

Every chapel of this kind would have had, moreover, to be furnished to a good standard by its patron. The Fraternity of Merchant Taylors of Bristol, incorporated in 1392, was to acquire its own chapel not more than seven years later, dedicated to St John the Baptist and situated on the south side of the parish church of St Ewen's, from which it was separated by an enterclose, or partition. Within another three years, an inventory of the contents of the chapel, taken in 1401/2, shows it already to have been richly equipped by the gild. The fellowship of Merchant Taylors, also known as the Fraternity of St John Baptist, owned five cloth hangings painted with scenes from the life of the saint; they had five linen cloths for the altar and two rich altar frontals, both of cloth of gold—one with red trimmings, the other with green and blue. Of their vestments, one was a full suit in cloth of gold, three were rich 'pairs' for the priest alone, and another (of lesser quality) was for the chaplain's daily use. The 'great' chalice of silver gilt, weighing 33 ounces, was no doubt kept for the more important feasts, as there was another smaller chalice also of the same precious metal. Of the three corporals, similarly, the least fine was kept for everyday masses, while other gild equipment included two processional banners (one painted with the Lamb of God), two pewter candlesticks, various items of church linen, a large chest for storing the more valuable furnishings, and a smaller chest for the fraternity's records, including the book in which the inventory was written.[56]

The Merchant Taylors' fraternity, at Bristol as elsewhere, was one of the richest in the city. Nevertheless, all fraternities hiring chaplains of their own undertook some responsibility to equip them. The furnishings of the 'chantries, free chapels, gilds and fraternities' of Wiltshire, as listed at their sale for the Crown on 15 June 1548,

were not exceptionally lavish and may indeed already have experienced some plundering by those who could see appropriation on the way. Yet the Fraternity of St Catherine, Chippenham, even if it had no individual item of any real value apart from its silver-gilt chalice, still possessed two sets of vestments, complete with their albs and stoles, two corporals in their cases, three altar-cloths, a cruet, bell, chest, and 'seven pieces of evidence' (charters, account books, or other records). In the same county and at the same date, the Brotherhood of Trowbridge had two 'pairs' of vestments, an old silk cope, two corporals in their cases, a cloth of dowlas (coarse linen) and another of silk 'to hang before the altar', two red silk curtains, a 'little' pair of pewter candlesticks, and two mass-books, 'the one in print the other written'. Among the better-off of the Wiltshire trade gilds was the Fraternity of Tailors at the church of St Thomas, Salisbury, and there certainly the approaching confiscation of chantry goods had been anticipated. At the 'Feast of All Saints last past' (1 November 1547), the fraternity's chalice had been sold to Robert Gryffythe (later the purchaser of the rest of the gild equipment) for 40s, to be 'bestowed upon reparations of the lands pertaining to the said chantry as he saith'.[57]

St Thomas's, Salisbury, was a much cherished city church, extensively rebuilt and enlarged during the fifteenth century, and the home of at least three other important chantries besides that of the tailors' gild. The works, which had included the insertion of a clerestory and re-roofing throughout, had necessitated a new scheme of internal decoration and had resulted in the painting at St Thomas's, over the chancel arch, of one of the most remarkable 'Dooms', or Last Judgement scenes, to have survived at any English parish church. Seated before such a scene in the fixed pews that, only in the fifteenth century, had become a usual part of church furnishings, the tailors of Salisbury and their fellow parishioners were exposed to just that kind of apocalyptic preaching for which their own deliberate cult of the dead best prepared them. They would have been warned 'when men are merriest, death says checkmate'; they would have been asked 'where see you any rich dead man?'; they would have been told—and would have caught the blushes of their neighbours at the time—'if death would take bribes, many would overbid others'; and they would have been reminded, as the westering sun lit their expensive new Doom, 'be the day never so long, ever comes evensong'. It was just what they came to church to hear.

Last Judgement scenes were not, of course, exclusive to the fifteenth century. However, the favour they found then, as well as some of the characteristics they acquired, can tell us much about the abiding preoccupations of that society. The mysterious Christ of the Romanesque painting, calm amidst his symbols of majesty, had yielded before the fifteenth century to a much more human figure, wounded and life-like but none the less terrible for being so. In the Salisbury Doom, as was not uncommonly the case in these later paintings, Christ is shown flanked by the kneeling figures of the Virgin Mary and of John the Baptist, interceding for the souls of true believers, while much more play is made than in the past with representations of the blessed and the damned. The yawning Hell Mouth (shown as Jonah's whale) of the Salisbury painting is one of a great class of similarly horrifying moralities, pointing the path which even kings and bishops must tread. All the chaplains at St Thomas's would probably have read John Mirk's *Instructions for Parish Priests*, one

87 *Right* Hell Mouth detail, with devils and the damned, from the Doom formerly over the chancel arch at Wenhaston, Suffolk; early sixteenth century

of the more popular manuals of their day, and some of them may even have repeated his sermon on the familiar theme depicted so vividly in their Doom:

> Then woe shall be to him that shall hear this rebuke in that day; there shall no pleader help, nor gold nor silver, nor other gifts; but as a man hath done, he shall have. He shall have accusers above him, within him, on either side of him, and under him, that he shall no way escape. Above him shall be Christ his doomsman so wroth that no tongue can tell . . . under him hell yawning and gulping, and spitting fire and stench ready for to swallow him into the pain that never shall have end.[58]

Death, judgement, heaven, and hell—the 'four last things'—rarely failed to stir the preacher or to engage the interest of his audience.

Certainly, it was to meet a demand clearly intensifying from the mid-fourteenth century that painters, glaziers, and wood-carvers everywhere turned their attention in the later Middle Ages to the depiction of popular moralities. The great Life of Christ and Virgin cycles of the earlier taste were not abandoned altogether, but the fifteenth-century patron quite frequently had other (and grislier) preoccupations. The gildsmen of Stratford-upon-Avon, for example, chose to decorate their chapel with a painting of the Dance of Death, the first known version of which, at least in that form, was the great mural in the Cemetery of the Holy Innocents in Paris, painted in 1424–5.[59] Copying the French model, Londoners had their own version of the

88   The Descent into Hell, from the mid-fifteenth-century Passion cycle at Pickering Church, Yorkshire

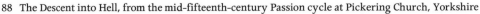

Dance, in which Death leads off men of all estates and conditions to the grave, at one of the chantry chapels of St Paul's, and although nothing of the St Paul's painting now survives, there are fragments of such dances still to be seen at Hexham (Northumberland) and Newark (Nottinghamshire), the latter designed to be the principal decoration of the early-sixteenth-century Markham chantry.[60]

A related but much earlier theme was the encounter of the Three Living and the Three Dead, usually at a cross-roads where three richly dressed huntsmen are brought up short before a vision of their immediate future—'As you are,' say the Dead, 'so we have been, and as we are, so you shall shortly be'. Known in English wall-paintings from the early fourteenth century, the legend became a favourite subject for church murals in all parts of the country, its simple message of vanity defeated being understandable to every audience. Perhaps the best preserved of these scenes, at the little country church of Widford, in Oxfordshire, is also among the earliest, having the delicacy—almost the gaiety—of much of the better-quality early-fourteenth-century work. By the mid-century, the emphasis had changed. The Three Dead of the immediate post-plague years during which the Peakirk (Northamptonshire) version of the legend was painted are corrupt and particularly terrible; they drip with slugs, beetles and worms as they confront the three richly dressed kings whom they threaten.[61]

89 *Left* The two surviving Dance of Death figures from panels in the Markham chantry chapel at Newark Church, Nottinghamshire; early sixteenth century

90 *Right* The Three Living and one of the Three Dead, from a fourteenth-century representation of the legend at Seething Church, Norfolk

John Mirk's *Instructions* had opened with the lines—

> God seyth hym-self, as wryten we fynde,
> That whenne the blynde ledeth the blynde,
> In-to the dyche they fallen boo [both],
> For they ne sen whare-by to go.[62]

And it is plain that one of the means employed by many parish priests to open the eyes of their audience was direct reference to the painted moralities by which, as a congregation, they were surrounded (above, pp. 36–7). With the Doom (behind the preacher and over the chancel arch), other common late-medieval instructional paintings included representations of the Seven Deadly Sins—pride, gluttony, anger, sloth, envy, lechery, and avarice—each conventionally shown with whatever symbols had become attached to these failings. Frequently opposing these were the Seven Virtues, or the Works of Mercy. There was often room too for a painted version of the Seven Sacraments, assisting the priest, as John Mirk urged, to—

> Teche hem thenne wyth gode entent,
> To be-leve on that sacrament;
> That they receyve in forme of bred
> Ys goddes body that soffered ded
> Up-on the holy rode tre,
> To bye owre synnes and make us fre.[63]

Similarly, Wheels of Fortune were very popular, as was a characteristically late-medieval version of the Weighing of Souls in which the Virgin, laying her hand on

91 *Left* The pre-Reformation pulpit at Burnham Norton Church, Norfolk, bearing an inscription which reads (in translation): 'Pray for John Goldale and Katherine his wife. They had it made.'

92 A Last Judgement painting on the west wall of Trotton Church, Sussex, with the Seven Works of Mercy on the right of the mural and the Seven Deadly Sins on the left, much worn; late fourteenth century

93 *Above left* St Michael presiding over a Weighing of Souls, from the Wenhaston Doom, Suffolk; early sixteenth century

94 A late-medieval mural of Christ and the Implements (also known as 'Christ of the Trades') in a window splay at West Chiltington Church, Sussex

the balance or her rosary in the scales, intercedes on behalf of the sinners.[64] Less common but certainly of the greatest social interest was the representation of Christ and the Implements, once mistakenly thought to have been a protest painting and consequently labelled as 'Christ as Piers Plowman'. The most remarkable of these paintings is the great crowned but otherwise nearly naked and wounded figure of Christ at Breage Church (Cornwall), surrounded by implements of husbandry and fishing, and of the cloth and metal-working trades. Perhaps a reference, in its many wounds, to the continuing Passion of Christ before Man's never-ending sins, it is likely also to have been used by the preacher as a warning to those who persisted in injuring Christ by breaking the sabbath that he had ordained.[65] Parish priests had always had the task of reminding their congregations of the duties to attend mass and to keep the fasts that Sundays and other feast days (the so-called *festa ferianda*) imposed upon them. Over the years, such festivals had multiplied with the result that considerable confusion had arisen as to when work should be allowed and when forbidden. For John Mirk and for others of his kind, publishers of lists and advisers on acceptable degrees of idleness, the best way of making sense of the system was to instruct the pastors who, alone in their parishes, were left with the task of urging the love of the saint and respect for his name-day against the routines of the farming year.[66]

95 *Above* The Earthquakes panel from the Pricke of Conscience window at All Saints Church, York; the legend reads—'Ye sevent day howses mon fall / castels & towres & ilk a wall'; early fifteenth century

96 The Hell Mouth group from the Last Judgement window at Fairford Church, Gloucestershire; late fifteenth or early sixteenth centuries

This task would certainly have been more difficult had the intercessory role of the saints in general not been so well understood. There are didactic subjects treated in English fifteenth-century stained glass—a Last Judgement, for example, at Fairford Church (Gloucestershire), a Ten Commandments window at Ludlow (Shropshire), and the 'Pricke of Conscience' window at All Saints, York, also known as 'The Pains and Terrors of the Last Fifteen Days of the World'.[67] However, far more common than these and than the narrative windows of the older tradition were the windows now dedicated to individual saints, the particular patrons of wealthy donors. In late-medieval England, the stained glass window, like the chantry chapel and the gift of inscribed plate, took on a commemorative purpose. It was there to remind the faithful of the virtues of the departed and to call upon each of them for prayers.

Much of this glass was destroyed in the sixteenth and seventeenth centuries by the reformers. Yet inaccessibility and the expense of replacement combined to save a number of fine specimens, among them the commemorative glass at Long Melford Church (Suffolk) which, in common with much of the rest of the late-fifteenth-century rebuilding, was financed by the Cloptons and their relatives. John Clopton it was who, as builder of the great Lady Chapel at Long Melford, had it inscribed—'Let Christ be my witness that I have not exhibited these things in order that I may win praise, but in order that the Spirit may be remembered.' And whatever the motives of John and his family, they made the parish church itself their memorial. In the east window at Long Melford, members of the family kneel on either side of the Virgin and Child, with St Dominic, St Edmund, and St Peter the Martyr below them. Their portraits, with others in the church, are enriched with the heraldry which is so characteristic of the glass of the period and which again drew attention to its essentially commemorative purpose.

97 John Clopton's Lady Chapel at Long Melford Church, Suffolk: a striking example of individual generosity with a commemorative purpose, dated by inscription to 1496

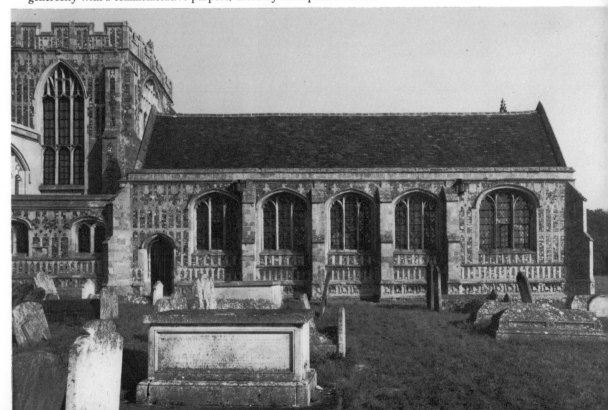

Fifteenth-century glass, if its message was not always as direct as in the Long Melford windows, usually exhibits some such purpose and meaning. Thus at Fotheringhay, the richly endowed Yorkist collegiate chantry in Northamptonshire, the representation of Archbishop Scrope in the windows of the nave, depicted there as the saint he never became, reflects the deliberate fostering of an anti-Lancastrian cult, while the choice of the other saints whose company he keeps seems to have been determined by the personal devotions of the Duchess Cecily, resident at Fotheringhay between 1461 and 1469 and the mother of the Yorkist Edward IV.[68] We may suppose that the Dance of Death scene surviving in a window at the church of St Andrew, Norwich, was ordered and paid for by the founder of a chantry, perhaps one of the city gilds. And it is certainly the case that the Corpus Christi subjects in four York windows (three in parish churches and the fourth in the south aisle of the Lady Chapel at York Minster) reflect the influence in that city of the powerful Corpus Christi gild (above, pp. 112–13).[69] On a very much more personal level, Henry Williams, vicar of Stanford-on-Avon (Northamptonshire), made provision in his will for two roundels of painted glass—'as gude glasse as can be goten'—to be found a place in one of the chancel windows of the church he had served while he lived. One of these roundels still survives. It shows, exactly as Parson Williams provided almost five centuries ago, 'my ymage knelyng in ytt and the ymage of deth shotyng at me'.[70]

98 *Left* The figure of Sir Robert Wingfield (d. 1480), donor, in the east window of East Harling Church, Norfolk

99 *Right* The great west tower and nave—the chancel was demolished in 1573—of the Yorkist collegiate chantry at Fotheringhay, Northamptonshire; fifteenth and early sixteenth centuries

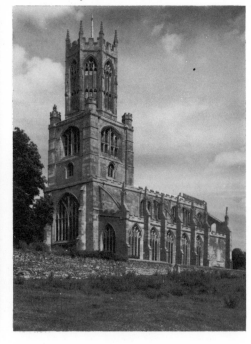

100 Panels from an alabaster altar or reredos at Drayton Church, Berkshire; fifteenth century

101 *Right* Panel from a fifteenth-century alabaster reredos, showing Christ bearing the Cross; Nottingham work of good quality, now at Yarnton, Oxfordshire, but not original to the church

102 *Left* A late-fifteenth-century oak lectern from Leverington Church, Cambridgeshire

103 *Above* A carved wooden pulpit, with angels supporting gabled canopies over saints, at Trull Church, Somerset; *c.* 1500

The subjects chosen for representation by a craftsman will obviously depend on the context for which they are intended. The glaziers at Fotheringhay, for example, with great windows to fill and all the wealth of the dowager duchess of York to support them, were well placed to get the best out of their medium. And similarly the carver of a church screen or of an altar retable usually had room to display his invention. On the alabaster tablets listed during a visitation of the St Paul's churches in 1458, many of the great themes of Christianity were represented—the Holy Trinity at Pelham Arsa (Brent Pelham), where there were also two tablets of the Five Joys of the Blessed Virgin Mary; a Last Judgement at Chiswick; a Resurrection at Tillingham; a Passion of Christ at Chiswick again and at no fewer than six other churches.[71] Yet when it came to the more mundane church furnishings, and in particular to the pews, lecterns, and pulpits with which so many parish churches from the second half of the fifteenth century were beginning to be provided, the emphasis had necessarily to change. Passion and Resurrection scenes were clearly better suited to a sculptured

104 The double hammer-beam roof, with angel supporters, at March Church, Cambridgeshire; *c.* 1500.

reredos, a great east or west window, or a wall-painting, than they were to the ordinary bench-end. Similarly, the angels with outspread wings which were frequently such a feature of the East Anglian hammer-beam roofs of the fifteenth century, were totally unsuited to the end of a pew on which even the unicorn, with his single vulnerable horn, had to be contorted to get him in position. In the circumstances, both for reasons of space and of suitability, the Virgin and Child subject was rare on bench-ends, while individual patron saints were quite common; the Seven Vices (as in the fine Norfolk set at Wiggenhall St German) appealed to the carvers, the Seven Virtues less so; there was heraldry (as at Wensley in North Yorkshire), and elaborate architectural ornament (as in the Suffolk churches of Woolpit, Fressingfield, and Dennington). Symbols of the Passion (the crown of thorns, the robe, the pillar, the sponge, the ladder—for the descent from the cross) are quite often seen, as are subjects from everyday life, among them tumblers and musicians, windmills, castles, and ships. Most common of all is that great menagerie of monsters and other fabulous or fantastic creatures which fifteenth-century wood-carvers were able to copy from the popular Bestiaries ('Books of Beasts') of their period. What these allowed them was a language of symbols that both pleased and taxed the ingenuity of their patrons. Thus the pelican, drawing blood from her own breast to nourish her young, signified Christ; the peacock, thought to have incorruptible flesh, stood for immortality; the ape and the dragon were the symbols of the devil; the owl, preferring darkness to light, symbolized the Jews, while the unconquerable unicorn, if seen (as in the legend) with a pure virgin in the forest, could be read as Our Lord's Incarnation and his Passion.[72] A parishioner seated among imagery like this, whether in wood-carvings or alabasters, glazed windows, sculptured roof-bosses, or murals, would have found himself in tune with the vision of his preacher and with both the magic and the mystery of the Church.

105 Fifteenth-century architectural bench-ends of high quality at Fressingfield Church, Suffolk

106 A fox and goose, carved on a brace of the roof
at Necton Church, Norfolk

107 *Right* A fifteenth-century ship under sail on a
bench-end at Thornham Church, Norfolk

108 *Left* The screen and pulpit, richly carved and painted, at Bovey Tracey Church, Devonshire; second quarter of the fifteenth century

109 *Below* The graceful fifteenth-century chancel screen at Scarning Church, Norfolk

110 *Right* Painted panels from the rood-screen at Ludham Church, Norfolk, erected in 1493 at the expense of John Salmon and his wife, Cecily; the figures (from left to right) are Mary Magdalene, St Stephen, St Edmund, King Henry VI, St Augustine, and St Ambrose. Henry VI's appearance in this company, although perhaps no more than a gesture of Lancastrian piety, could also reflect the growth of a contemporary cult

Few opportunities were neglected in art to increase this sense of awe. At the east end of the nave, between nave and chancel, was the Great Rood, a representation of Christ in majesty on the cross that was intended to bring out not the humanity of Our Lord but, as in the Doom, his supremacy. Sometimes set on a rood-beam of its own or suspended on chains from the crown of the chancel arch, the Great Rood often stood in its 'rood-loft' on the top of the chancel screen (or 'rood-screen') which was again one of the features of the late-medieval church that, by emphasizing the distinction between nave and chancel, increased the mystery of the priesthood. Such screens had been known since the thirteenth century (above, p. 38), but their ultimate flowering in the magnificent screens of East Anglia and the West Country during the later Middle Ages was to be one of the products of the substantial rebuildings that so often took place in that period. There is a difference in quality between these screens, the light and grace of such typical Norfolk screens as Litcham, Scarning, and Thurlton contrasting with the insistent over-ornamentation of Minehead (Somerset) or Marwood and Bovey Tracey, both in Devon. Yet the purpose of all of them was the same, being to enhance the sacred quality of the chancel area when every other tendency in the church architecture of the time was towards the introduction of more light and space. Certainly, whatever later reformers may have thought of such distinctions within the parish church—and every inclination among the first Protestants was to be rid of them—they were not considered invidious by contemporaries. The fine chancel screen at Worstead, in Norfolk, carries an inscription to the effect that it was put up in 1511 at the expense of John Arblaster and Agnes, his wife, parishioners of Worstead. In the same county, the rood-screen at Ludham is inscribed—'Pray for the sowle of John (Salmon) and Cycyly his wyf that gave forten pounde and for alle other benefactors made in the year of ower Lord god MCCCCLXXXXIII.'[73]

111 *Below* The unusual pre-Reformation font
   canopy at Trunch Church, Norfolk, formerly
   richly painted

112 *Left* Telescopic font-cover at Ufford Church, Suffolk, richly buttressed and pinnacled, and surmounted by a Pelican in her Piety: a Suffolk wood-carver's masterpiece unexcelled in England; fifteenth century

113 *Right* The Seven Sacraments font at Weston Church, Suffolk, with representations on the side panels of mass, ordination, penance, extreme unction, marriage, the baptism of Christ, baptism, and confirmation; fifteenth century

Surely the most extravagant of all expressions of late-medieval devotion are the remarkable fonts, and especially the font-covers, that celebrate the sacrament of baptism. Long before this, infant baptism at the font had taken the place of the earlier practice of adult baptism by total immersion, and this, of course, had had the effect of making the font both smaller and more elevated. Yet so crucial was the ceremony of baptism to Christian theology that it was natural enough for the pious benefactors of the later Middle Ages to seek to make the most of it architecturally. The richly carved hexagonal font canopy at Trunch (Norfolk), dominating the nave of this fine church, has a monumentality unequalled anywhere else. Nevertheless, scarcely less remarkable are the many fifteenth-century Seven Sacrament fonts, most of them again in East Anglia, so often distinguished by the quality of their stone-carving. Among the finest of these are the Suffolk fonts at Cratfield and Badingham, Laxfield and Weston, with similarly magnificent Norfolk specimens at Little Walsingham and Salle, the latter inscribed—'Pray for the souls of Thomas Line and . . . his wife and Robert their son chaplain and for those whom they are bound to pray who caused this font to be made'.[74] Like others of its kind, the Salle font is raised on a series of ornamented plinths; on the sides of the bowl, each panel carries a scene of one of the sacraments, while over the whole there rises a pinnacled and spired font-cover, twelve feet high, supported by a traceried bracket. Half as high again, the Suffolk font-cover at St Mary, Ufford, is the most theatrically spectacular of them all. Canopied and pinnacled, it ascends to the roof-beams in receding tiers, even incorporating (as further proof of the skill of its carver) a telescopic device for lifting. Formerly painted and gilded to its summit, this Suffolk wood-carver's masterpiece has been described, surely rightly, as 'the most beautiful cover in the world'.[75]

The font, traditionally placed within the body of the nave where the parishioners would view it as their responsibility, inevitably attracted their generosity. However, there was nothing on which they were more likely to be prodigal than on their own sepulchral monuments and effigies. When Sir John Say, knight, of Broxbourne in Hertfordshire, wished to provide for himself in 1476 an appropriate final resting-place in the parish church, nothing else would do for him but that he should extend the existing south aisle to make what was, in effect, a family chantry chapel adjoining the chancel on the south. In his directions to the mason, preserved in a contract of that date, he made it clear that the principal purpose of the extension was to house two tombs, one at the new east end of the aisle (sunk and overlain by a marble slab) and the other (rather grander and presumably for himself) under the new arch which was to be cut in the south chancel wall. Over a sunken stone-lined grave, the mason contracted to build there a 'Tombe of Fre Stone [freestone—an easily carved sandstone or limestone] vij fote in lenght at the lest and ij and an halff of brede and ij fote of height or more as it can be thought good by thadvyce of a marbler with moldyng therupon and a range of caters [quatrefoils] and scochyns [shields] to be made to ley a stone of marbyll therupon'. The whole was to cost, in workmanship alone without materials, £24 'of lawfull money of Englond'.[76]

114   The Wilcote Chapel at North Leigh Church, Oxfordshire, built in the early 1440s by Elizabeth Wilcote as a family chantry; the tomb under the canopy through to the chancel is of Sir William Wilcote (d. 1410) and of Elizabeth Wilcote (d. 1442), his widow

115 *Right* The late-fifteenth-century hammer-beam roof, one of the great masterpieces of medieval roof carpentry, at Needham Market Church, Suffolk, decorated with angel supporters bearing shields

116 The rood-screen, painted with the arms of the English episcopal sees, at Attleborough Church, Norfolk; *c.* 1500

117 Tomb of Alice, duchess of Suffolk (d. 1475), at Ewelme Church, Oxfordshire; the side of the tomb-chest is embellished with angels holding shields

Sir John Say's 'scochyns' were very much a piece with that emphasis on heraldry which affected everywhere the decoration of the late-medieval parish church. We have seen it already in the hangings of London churches, in memorial windows, and on bench-ends; it was there again on the shields held by the angel supporters of roofs such as those at Needham Market (Suffolk) or Swaffham and Knapton, both in Norfolk; and it might even feature on a parish church screen as, most magnificently, at Attleborough (Norfolk), or on such fonts as the John of Gaunt font at Fakenham (Norfolk) or the Archbishop Arundel font at the Kentish church of Sittingbourne. Particularly appropriately, it found a place on tombs. Reasonably enough, a prominent display of heraldry would characterize the tomb of a great lady like Alice, duchess of Suffolk, in the church that she and her over-ambitious husband, William de la Pole (murdered by sailors in 1450), rebuilt so lavishly at Ewelme (Oxfordshire). But it had long been a feature already of many of the more expensive gentry monuments in England, from the Blanche Mortimer tomb (1347) at Much Marcle (Herefordshire) to the handsome tomb-chest and paired alabaster figures of the fifteenth-century Thorpe monument at Ashwellthorpe, in Norfolk. On merchants' memorials, the same fashion was likely to be repeated. Already, at the very beginning of the fifteenth century, shields decorate the brass (1401) at Chipping Campden (Gloucestershire) of William Grevel, wool-merchant, and of Marion, his wife. The equally well-known Pounder brass (1525) from St Mary Quay, Ipswich, carries an escutcheon between the heads of Thomas Pounder and his wife on which is engraved the mark that Pounder used as a merchant (Fig. 120). Supporting this are the arms of the Company of Merchant Adventurers, to which Pounder belonged, and of the borough of Ipswich, which he had served, in his time, as bailiff.

118   *Right* The monument, decorated with heraldry, of Blanche Mortimer, Lady Grandison (d. 1347), at Much Marcle Church, Herefordshire; the wavy cresting and putti are a later insertion

119   Heraldic ornament on the Thorpe monument at Ashwellthorpe Church, Norfolk; first half of the fifteenth century

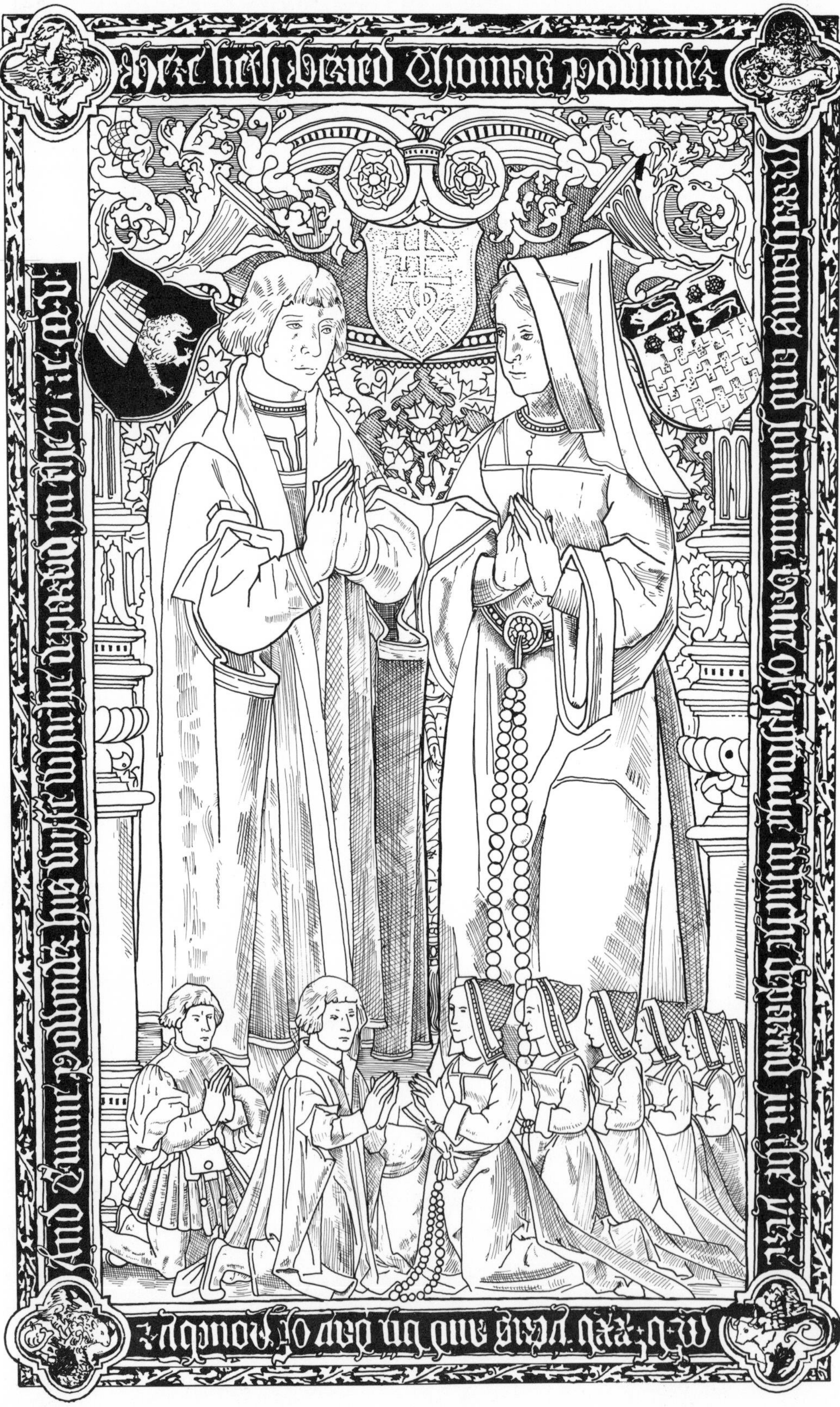
Here lieth beried Thomas Pownder

121 The tomb-chest and effigy of Richard Beauchamp, earl of Warwick (d. 1439), at the church of St Mary, Warwick

Thomas Pounder, his wife, and their eight children are shown fashionably dressed and in poses of conventional piety. And it was just these two characteristics—high fashion in dress and pious repose in bearing—which distinguished the whole class of late-medieval monuments in England. Gone was the high drama of the remarkable freestone knight effigies of the early fourteenth century (above, pp. 45–6). The knight was no longer ready, on the instant, to fight again, but had won—and had certainly paid for—his rest. It was some decades before Richard Beauchamp (d. 1439), earl of Warwick and hero of chivalry, was finally laid to rest in the chantry chapel built at St Mary's, Warwick, by his executors. However, the reason for the delay was not the niggardliness of his heirs but the high quality of the work they commissioned. Completed at a cost of over £2,000, the Beauchamp Chapel provided a magnificent setting for the tomb-chest and effigy of the warrior. It was John Bourde, marbler, of Corfe Castle (Dorset), who covenanted in the mid-1450s to 'make a tomb of as good and fine marble, as well coloured as may be had in England. The tomb to contain in length ix foot, in bredth iv foot, and in thickness vii inches, the tombe to bear in height iv foot and a half, and in and about the tombe to make xiv principal housings, and under each housing a goodly quarter for a scutcheon of copper and gilt to be set in, according to a portraiture delivered him'. The tomb was to be delivered and erected at Warwick where it would carry (as it still does today) the bronzes of William Austin, citizen and brass-founder of London, already contracted for as far back as March 1451. Austin had agreed—

> ... to cast of the finest latten to be gilded xiv images embossed of lords and ladyes in divers vestures, called weepers, to stand in housings made about the tombe; to be the bredth, length, and the thickness to xiv patterns of timber. Also, he shall make xviii lesse images of angells, as shall be appointed by patterns, whereof ix after one side and nine after another. And the executors shall pay for every weeper so made in latten, xiiis ivd and for every angel vs. And for every pound of latten that shall be in the herse xd. The said Will Austin doth covenant to cast and make an image of a man armed, of fine latten garnished with certain ornaments, viz.—with sword and dagger; with a garter; with a helme and crest under his head, and at his feet a

120 *Left* Brass to Thomas Pounder (d. 1525), his wife and family, formerly at the church of St Mary at the Quay, Ipswich, with escutcheons of Ipswich and the Merchant Adventurers, and with Pounder's own merchant's mark (Alan Burn)

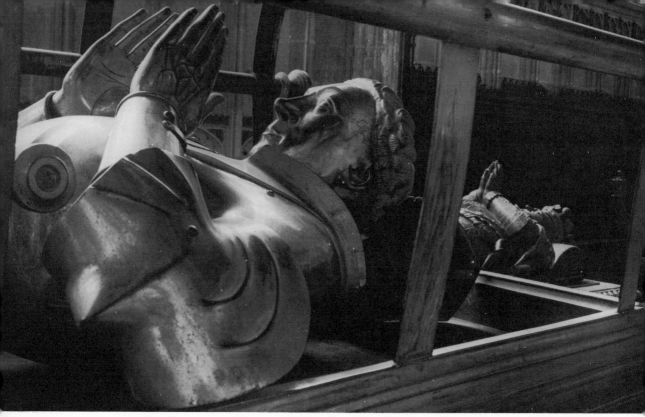

122 The effigy, cast by William Austin of London, of Richard, earl of Warwick, contracted for in 1451

bear musled, and a griffon, perfectly made of the finest latten, according to patterns, and to be layd on the tombe, at the perill of the said Austin, for the sum of xl li. [pounds].[77]

William Austin had no means of attempting a true portrait of the earl, who had died twelve years before. Nevertheless, the realism of Richard Beauchamp's effigy is particularly impressive, whether it is judged on the modelling of the veined hands raised in prayer or on the meticulous detailing of the armour. As a masterpiece of the tomb-maker's art, the Beauchamp monument readily stands comparison with the great contemporary series of Burgundian tombs with which it has so much in common.

The 'weepers' on the Beauchamp tomb, the heraldry of the tilting-helm and of the escutcheons at the base of the tomb-chest, and the fashionable up-to-the-minute plate-armour are all to be found on sepulchral monuments of lesser (but still remarkable) quality in parish churches up and down the length of the country. There are weepers, for example, on the Fitzherbert and Babyngton tombs at Norbury and Ashover, in Derbyshire; fine tilting-helms at Bottesford (Leicestershire) and Malpas (Cheshire), on the Roos and Brereton effigies respectively; and an extraordinary display of conspicuous consumption in the modish head-dresses and fashionable robes or armour of such paired husband-and-wife effigies as the Vernon tomb at Tong (Shropshire), the Greene monument at Lowick (Northamptonshire), or the Bardolf tomb in the parish church at Dennington, in Suffolk. This, among the gentry and wealthy burgesses of late-medieval England, was their final bid for remembrance. With the passage of the centuries, it has served them better than any of them could conceivably have anticipated.

123 The alabaster tomb-chest and effigies of Sir Ralph Fitzherbert (d. 1483) and his wife, at Norbury Church, Derbyshire

124 Effigy of John, Lord Roos (d. 1421), at Bottesford Church, Leicestershire, his head resting on his tilting-helm

125 A fashionable head-dress of the early fifteenth century, as worn by the wife of Sir Ralph Greene (d. 1417) and reproduced on their joint monument at Lowick Church, Northamptonshire

126 Monument, of high quality, to Sir Richard Vernon (d. 1451) and his wife, at Tong Church, Shropshire

Chapter 6

The Reformation

A man may call with the beck of a finger what he
cannot put away with both hands

The Reformation in England was no mere historical accident, and there are now many acceptable explanations for its coming, quite apart from the caprice of the king. Nevertheless, at parochial level its incidence and its consequences were frequently both arbitrary and unexpected. 'The Church is no hare,' they said, 'it will abide'. But few, in the 1530s, knew quite how.

One of the principal reasons for this uncertainty was that the new Continental heresies of Zwingli and Luther had scarcely touched England before the later 1520s, at least at a popular level, and that even then they had found comparatively little to take root on. Lollardy, as a heresy, was not insignificant. It had built up cells in rural Buckinghamshire and Oxfordshire, in Essex and south-west Kent, and had attracted considerable support among the artisan classes of such cities as Coventry, Bristol, and London. But its real achievement over the years had not been religious so much as political. Lollardy, in its continual attack on the wealth of the Church, played on the feelings of many contemporaries who, in the early sixteenth century, had come to believe themselves to be especially oppressed by their priests (above, p. 84). Those who in better times might have defended the Church and its institutions were kept silent by their memory of over-large probate fees, mortuaries, and tithes. They were uncertain of the jurisdiction of ecclesiastical courts, and resented any summons to attend them. What admitted the Reformation to Henry VIII's England was anticlericalism—the accumulation of many grudges. In exactly the same way, the first large-scale popular protests against the policies of Henry and his ministers arose among both priests and laymen whose economic interests, more than their beliefs, were at risk.[1]

In Lincolnshire certainly, where the local rebellion of October 1536 anticipated the politically much more dangerous Pilgrimage of Grace in the northern counties later that same year, the parish clergy had never felt less secure. For more than a decade, they had suffered the inquisitions of a busy, reforming prelate in John Longland, bishop of Lincoln from 1521 to 1547. And although Longland, through these early years of his office, had won the praise of Archbishop Warham—'of truthe I thynke veryly if all bysshoppes hadde doon ther duetyes as ye have in settyng forthe christes doctryne and repressing of vice by preching and otherwise, the dignytye of the church hadd nott bene soo cold and almost extencte in mennes hertes'—there is no doubt that his activity in this early Catholic 'reformation' left the clergy of his diocese especially reluctant to tolerate similar assaults from the Protestants.[2] Knowing their bishop of old, the Lincolnshire parish clergy had particular reason to fear deprivation when Thomas Cromwell's new definitions and instructions of 1536 (the Ten Articles and Injunctions) brought the threat of a fresh round of visitations. At just that time, too, the Crown had set in train another assault on clerical incomes. The priest of Croston (Lancashire) who, as early as 1533, had predicted that the king would 'put down the order of priests and destroy the sacrament',[3] would have found many more to agree with him three years later. In 1534, the Act of First Fruits and Tenths had empowered the king, as supreme head of the English Church in place of the pope, to take a full year's income from the new incumbent of every benefice, as well as to collect a tenth of any annual receipts thereafter. Moreover, this was immediately followed by a great new survey of clerical revenues (resulting in the *Valor Ecclesiasticus* of 1535) which was enough to convince many of the more timorous clergy that wholesale appropriation was on the way. Others foresaw the advantage, in the collection of first fruits, that the Crown was sure to gain from a policy of wholesale deprivation and re-appointment, while still more predicted, as a result of the survey, the closing and demolition of surplus churches as clerical incomes were rationalized. Very little of this, in point of fact, took place. However, both in Lincoln diocese and elsewhere, there was a significant drop in the number of candidates presenting themselves for ordination, beginning in 1536. The anticipated overplus of clergy never occurred for the very good reason that the 'career of priest' no longer held many obvious attractions.[4]

In 1536, the clergy were not alone in their anxieties. The first suppression in that year of the smaller religious houses, closely following Cromwell's survey and valuation of 1535, had persuaded the churchwardens as well as their parish priests of the danger to Church property of all kinds. There were rumours abroad, before the Lincolnshire rising, of an approaching confiscation of church 'jewels', no doubt fanned by such dissidents as the rector of Farforth who is said to have reported to his parishioners that 'churche goodis shuld be taken from them and he said ther was dyvers challyces made of tyne which sholdbe delyvered to them in exchange for ther sylver chalices and the sayd silver chalices to be had to the kinges visitors'.[5] And many, in any event, would have had reason to fear the image-breaking zeal that was beginning to infect some of the more doctrinaire reformers. Already, in 1532, images had been pulled down in some Essex churches and the rood had been smashed at Dovercourt in the same county.[6] Even in such a conservative region as Lancashire, hostile throughout the sixteenth century to reform, there were incidents like the breaking of his sword, in 1536, over the head of the image of St George at Hawkshead, in Dalton parish, followed by the taunt—'Let me see how now thou canst fight again'.[7] To the mounting concern of the majority of ordinary men and women who, over the years, had invested so much in the fabric and the ornaments of their parish churches, the desecrators grew bolder and more scandalous every day. When Matthew Price, of Staunton in Gloucestershire, had spoken out against penance—'hit was as goode to confesse hym to a tree, as to a prest'—and had denied the real presence at the Eucharist—'it was bredde & wyne, and not made by God but by manes hands, for Christ toke his owne bodye with hym up in to heven, and left it not behynde hym'—he had done nothing, when brought before the bishop's court in 1541 to account for his opinions, that was not already common form among the Lollards. But he had been guilty also of an irreverent obscenity which it would have

127 Upleadon Church, Gloucestershire, with its unusual timber-framed tower of *c.* 1500: the scene of Matthew Price's disreputable prank

been difficult for any Christian to forgive. At Upleadon Church, on the Worcestershire and Gloucestershire border, near which he and his associates had held their conventicles, he had indulged in a prank with William Baker during which he had 'spryncled & cast holy water upon the saide William Bakers ars', then calling on him to 'remember thy baptysm'. It was in this and in other ways that men of like boldness and advanced opinions 'dispised' the old rituals of 'holy water, holy bred, matence, evensonge and buryinge'.[8]

So long as the old king lived, they despised the sacraments still at their peril. However, the direction that the reformers were taking was clear already, even to the least able churchwardens, some years before the accession, on 28 January 1547, of Edward VI to the throne. Baptism and the Eucharist would survive all assaults, although stripped of much ritual and significance. The other five sacraments— confirmation and marriage, ordination, penance, and extreme unction—were progressively reduced or discarded. Simultaneously, the attack on images and church lights became official. The Articles and Injunctions of 1536 had made the distinction between 'feyned' images—images that were sacrificed to and that were therefore idolatrous—and commemorative images, recalling the lives and holy works of Christ, of the Virgin, and of the saints. Only the former were to be taken down 'forthwith', while the latter (especially images of Christ and Our Lady) might 'stand' in the churches, to be esteemed 'none otherwise' than as 'representers of vertue and good example . . . kindlers and stirrers of mens minds'. It was this distinction that survived in practice until the more comprehensive Act 'for the abolishing and putting away of divers books and images' published in 1550. As for church lights, the progress of reform was more rapid. In 1536, three lights had still been allowed to burn: on the altar, by the sepulchre, and before the rood. Five years later, in 1541, this had been reduced to an altar light alone.[9]

128 Paintings of angels on the screen at Southwold Church, Suffolk, deliberately defaced by Edwardian or later reformers

With these measures already, much church furniture had been rendered surplus, and if churchwardens had any remnant doubts about the need to dispose of their unwanted pieces as soon as possible, the king's exactions soon resolved them. In 1545, only six years after the last of the monastic houses had been dissolved, Henry's expensive wars against France and Scotland led him to appropriate, although initially only for the term of his life, the chantries and colleges, hospitals, gilds, and frater-nities which had escaped the earlier purge. With the survey of these and the outright seizure of some of them, the possibility of a similar confiscation of parish church plate and other furnishings could no longer be ignored by their guardians. Edward VI's accession in 1547 was followed immediately by a new Chantries Act, condemn-ing the superstitious errors and 'vain opinions' of Purgatory and the memorial mass. And the fresh surveys of chantry and gild possessions set in train by the govern-ment triggered off, understandably enough, a great flood of anticipatory sales. There were those, particularly in the greater towns, who fought with tenacity and some success for their gilds. Nevertheless, a more common response to the pressure of the times would probably have been that of the officers ('maisters') of the Gild of Our Lady, at Ulting Church (Essex), who before 1548 had sold 'all the Juells and goodes of the same for the Somme of xviij*li* and hathe the same Somme yet remayninge in theyre handes'. Like other gild officials and churchwardens in the county, they had thought it wise to move quickly to forestall outright confiscation by the king.[10]

129 A silver-gilt chalice, hall-marked 1525, from Wylye Church, Wiltshire: one of the rare survivors of the Edwardian collections

Most took advantage of the sales at this time to repair, re-roof, or even extend their churches. Thus the churchwardens of Woodham Ferrers had disposed of £5 worth of church plate 'abowte three yeres agoo' for the 'makinge of a newe fframe in the steple [tower] for the bells and for the shingling of the churche'; those at Chingford, also in Essex, had pawned a chalice and a silver-gilt cross for the 'makinge of a newe roofe and repayring the same churche'; at West Ham, likewise, the churchwardens had gone ahead 'without the consent of the hole parryshe' in a major sale of church plate which had included the disposal of five silver chalices, four cruets, a cross, a chrismatory, a pyx, a great censer (or thurible), and other equipment, to be 'bestowed', with other church moneys and with the proceeds of a sale of church lands and a lease, 'in makinge a newe yle in the saide churche'.[11] At a number of these Essex churches, the blame for the sale of church furnishings was placed, not unfairly, on the king, his wars, and his taxes. The men of South Benfleet had used the proceeds from the sale of a chalice partly on repairs to their church and 'partelie in settinge forthe souldyers towards the Kingis maiesties warres'; at Aldham, six shillings had been 'layed owte towarde the setting forthe of one Souldyr'; at Leigh, the comparatively large sum of £17 10s had been 'layed owte and gyven for redemyng of certayne men of the same parryshe which were taken prysoners in ffraunce'. The king's taxes had been met at Newport from the price of a great bell, broken and sold for scrap, and from 'certayne latten Candlestyckis that stood before thaulter and the roodloft'; at Manuden, 'abowte twoo yeres paste', the parishioners had had to pawn a chalice and a silver pax 'to help the vicar to pay the Kingis Subsydies'; at Braintree and at Colchester (St Rumbold's), the churchwardens, while using the surplus from the sales of plate, 'juells' and 'brasse' for repairs and new equipment, had also found considerable sums for Henry's subsidies and (at Colchester) for the arrears 'which the parson there dyd leave the said churche in to the King's majestie'.

It had been the opinion of one London militant 'that a sermon preached is better than the sacrament of the altar, and that he had rather go to hear a sermon than to hear a mass'.[12] And this characteristically Protestant taste is reflected in the expenditure of the Essex churchwardens as they attempted to bring themselves and their churches up to date. A broken cross and a chalice had been sold at Clacton before 1548, raising £14 10s, part of which had already been spent 'in makinge of stooles and a pulpytt in the Churche'; at Alresford, Frating, and Tendring, pulpits had been made, and at Elmstead another was intended. The full severity of the Edwardian reforms had yet to come, but the churchwardens of St James's, Colchester, as had others in their deanery, had anticipated some of these measures by white-washing out the existing wall-paintings, replacing them with texts, and by substituting plain glass for stained. It was probably with some satisfaction that the churchwardens of Bradwell reported that they had sold 'as moche olde baggage in theyre churche as came to xs. viijd.', and that those at Haseley 'doo presente that they have solde all the ymages in the churche for xxd. which was gyven to poore people'.[13]

When the Edwardian commissioners compiled their lists of what was still left at the parish churches by the early 1550s, they frequently found little remaining of real value there. Once richly furnished, the churches of St Paul's, for example, had by this time been stripped of their contents. At Chiswick (Middlesex), still one of the better equipped, the commissioners reported in 1552—'all the lynnynge [linen] of the Churche as albes, sorplesses, aulter clothes, and all other lynnynge, stowln owt of the Church and the Churche brokyn'. Later that same year, the churchwardens of Tillingham (Essex) were to certify that 'there ys remaynynge within oure seid Church of Tillingham' two old vestments and an old silk cope, two brass candlesticks, an old cross cloth, two albs, a surplice, a communion cloth, a 'lector' (reader's) cloth, four bells, and a glass which was used for the communion cup. Yet the contents of that same church, when listed for the dean and chapter of St Paul's almost a century before, had then been more than adequate. There had been seven vestments at Tillingham in 1458, among them at least three full sets. The church images had included a 'beautiful' alabaster carving of the miracles of St Nicholas, patron saint of the parish, with another alabaster of the Resurrection. There had been three crosses, one of them silver gilt with a gilded copper base, three silver-gilt chalices, and a pax, two cruets, and a thurible also of silver. Other church furnishings had included four more cruets and another thurible, two candlesticks, and a chrismatory, all of pewter ('tyn'), with painted altar-hangings and cloths, towels, a Lenten veil, banners, and bells. In books, too, the parish priest had had everything that—and more than—he needed. He had had three missals, three antiphoners and three processionals, two manuals, a gradual, a troper, a hymnal, an ordinal, a portable breviary (*portiforium*), and a calendar of saints and benefactors (*martilogium*).[14] It was to be against these that the root-and-branch Act of 1550 would be directed by Dudley (duke of Northumberland from October 1551) and his sympathizers. By the terms of this Act—

> . . . all books called antiphoners, missals, scrails, processionals, manuals, legends, pies, portuises, primers in Latin or English, couchers, journals, ordinals, or other books or writings whatsoever heretofore used for service of the church, written or printed in the English or Latin tongue, other than such as are or shall be set forth by the king's majesty [i.e. the Book of Common Prayer and its successors], shall be . . . clearly and utterly abolished, extinguished, and forbidden for ever to be used or kept in this realm or elsewhere within any the king's dominions.

Before the 'last day of June next ensuing', all such books were to be delivered up to the authorities 'to be openly burnt or otherways defaced and destroyed', the same defacement and destruction to apply also to every one of 'any images of stone, timber, alabaster, or earth (ceramics), graven, carved, or painted, which heretofore have been taken out of any church or chapel, or yet stand in any church or chapel'. Failure to comply with the terms of the statute would be met with heavy fines or, on a third conviction, imprisonment 'at the king's will'.[15]

130 A rood-screen, with its original parapet, as preserved at Flamborough, Yorkshire; the paintings in the niches have been lost, probably defaced

The rapidity with which individual churchwardens responded to such changes naturally varied widely. In Lancashire, home of the Pilgrimage of Grace, and Cornwall, of the Prayer Book Rebellion, the pace of reform fell far behind that set by the city parishes, as traditionally responsive to new ideas as the deep country had always been conservative. While the rural churches kept to the old ways as long as the law would allow them, the parish authorities of a city church like St Ewen's, Bristol, moved swiftly with the currents of the new reign. The 'booke of the Accompte of the Parish of St Ewens' for the year 1547–8, the first of Edward VI's reign, includes entries already for the 'takeinge down the tabernacles with the Images', the 'takeinge downe the Roode and the reste of the Images', the whiteliming of the chancel and the making good of the walls where the images had been ripped out, and the sale of church goods, among them candlesticks and wax, 'old pewter' and 'old iron', with the veil and the coverings of the rood. That same year, a bible was bought, to be bound in leather at the churchwardens' expense and provided with a lock and a chain.[16] At another city church, St Margaret Moses (London), four pence were paid to the parish clerk during 1547–8 for 'ripping of the images of the altar'.[17] At a third, St Mary the Great (Cambridge), the great silver cross was sold 'by the assent of the parysheners' on 13 October 1547, along with two valuable silver censers; the church was whitelimed, a bible was bought, and there was a general sale of 'sartyn old ympylmentes of the chyrche as paynted clothes lattyn candyllstykes wood ymages & tabarnakylles', the twenty-two shillings raised being given, by general consent, to the poor.[18]

Some churches, whether in these ways or others, anticipated the full drive of the reforms. However, for most the major impact of the Edwardian Reformation was not to be felt until later in 1548 or even well into 1549. At St Nicholas, Bristol, although the rood-loft was taken down during 1547–8, obits were kept as they always had been in the past, Lady Day and the feast of Corpus Christi were observed, the Easter Sepulchre was set up, dressed, and watched. When the next reckoning was made, in the spring of 1549, nothing was said of obits any more, and the 'formys & bordes & Ymages' of the church had been consigned permanently to store.[19] In just the same way, the traditional observances still maintained at Holy Trinity, Chester, in 1547–8 had gone by 1549; it was then that the altars and the tabernacle were taken down, and that a new movable altar was purchased.[20] When, in 1549–50, the churchwardens of St Mary the Great, in Cambridge, met together 'for the weyinge of the chyrch playte & vewynge the other goodes of the chyrch to put them in to the invytory accordyng to the kyngs commawndement' they treated themselves to a small feast of 'met & drynke' which cost them six shillings in all.[21] Yet it cannot have been a merry occasion even for the hardest of heart. 'Butt only thatt Christ mercy is so myche,' wrote Robert Parkyn, a Yorkshire curate, from the security of Mary's reign, 'it was marvell that the earth did nott oppen & swalow upp suche vilanus persons [the Edwardian reformers and image-breakers], as it dyd Dathan and Abiron.'[22]

The church plate of St Mary (Cambridge) was delivered to the king's officers at London in 1552, but only a year later, when Queen Mary's accession on 19 July 1553 brought a reversion to Catholicism, the wardens were buying in church furnishings again. Some of these had remained in the possession of the two churchwardens holding office at the time of the inventory. Mr John Rust sold back to his church two

131 *Left* St Mary the Great, Cambridge: rebuilt with considerable magnificence in the late fifteenth and early sixteenth centuries, but stripped shortly afterwards of its ornaments

candlesticks (6s), and a vestment, alb, cope, and three books (28s in all), while Dr John Blythe was able to return two blue velvet altar-cloths for a price of fifty shillings. Simon Watson, another leading parishioner, re-sold to St Mary's a 'fair' mass-book and a legend (a collection of readings from the scriptures), priced together at 14s, and Peter Sheres contributed a manual (5s). Other purchases included a girdle for the alb, a corporal case, a chrismatory, candles, and holy oil.[23] As Robert Parkyn reported it:

> . . . then [from August 1553] in many places of York shire preastes unmariede was veray glade to celebratt & say masse in Lattin withe mattings & evin songe therto, accordynge for veray ferventt zealle and luffe that thai had unto God & his lawes. . . . Holly breade and holly watter was gyven, alteres was reedefide, pictures or ymages sett upp, the cross with the crucifixe theron redye to be borne in procession, and with the same wentt procession.

With the formal reunion with Rome, agreed by Mary's third parliament in the last months of 1554, 'began wholly churche to reioce in God, synginge bothe with hertt & townge (Te Deum laudamus), butt hereticall persons (as ther was many) reiocyde nothinge theratt.'[24]

Mary Tudor died on 17 November 1558, and the Marian Reaction, for better or for worse, was over. Like Edward's reign, Mary's brief interlude of power had both given the extremists their head and, in so doing, had destroyed them. The Anglican Church, as it began to take final shape under Elizabeth I, was not without its tensions. But its middle-of-the-road conservatism and surely deliberate ambiguities suited all of a moderate and hopeful temper. They still do.

132 A post-Reformation communion table in the north aisle at Carleton Rode Church, Norfolk

133 The font at Westbury-upon-Severn Church, Gloucestershire: a medieval bowl has been re-set on a post-Reformation pedestal bearing the royal arms and date 1583

Once again, the city churches reacted quicker than most to the changes. In 1559, the churchwardens of the London church of St Mary at Hill had already found the funds for the purchase of a new communion table; they had supervised the taking down of the Great Rood and had arranged for the burning of the images; the altar-slab, built into a wall (probably for its safe-keeping) in Edward's reign, and restored to the high altar while Mary ruled, was finally wrenched out with all the other altars,

134 A rood-screen and loft, possibly not original to the building, surviving at Atherington Church,
Devonshire; early sixteenth century

135 *Right* The arms of Elizabeth in the chancel arch at Ludham Church, Norfolk, now facing eastwards
into the chancel but painted originally to face west

NON·ME·PVDET·EVANGELII·CHRISTI   VIVAT·REGINA·ELIZABETA·

136   A fifteenth-century Crucifixion painting at Ludham, turned towards the chancel when the arms of
     Elizabeth were painted on its back, but now restored to face the nave

and the 'rubbushe' carted away.[25] Only two years after they had made one of their more important investments in a fine new silver-gilt chalice and paten at the cost of over £6, the churchwardens of St Mary the Great (Cambridge) in 1559 were laying out other moneys, much smaller (but as significant of the mood of the times), in demolitions: 2s 8d to Thomas Swyngges 'for takyn downe the Alteres', 10d to John Bell and William Chapman 'for takyng downe the tabernacle'. A new communion table, that same year, cost them 6s, and it was then that they bought themselves a register.[26] In the more conservative north-west—those 'northe parttes' which Robert Parkyn had found 'grettlie reiocide' on the accession of Mary, 'makynge grett fyers, drynkinge wyne and aylle, prayssing God'—the Great Rood and its images (Mary and John) at Holy Trinity (Chester) were still being repaired and painted in 1559; while with banners and lights, processions and vigils, the whole ancient ritual of Holy Week and Easter was being observed. It was only in 1560, at the head of that year's account, that Thomas Wedrall and Thomas Wever, churchwardens since the reign of Mary, noted 'Q. Eliz. began'. It was then that they too, like their equivalents at Cambridge the year before, bought paper 'to make a boke to write buryings & kristnings in', that they took down the images and demolished the stone altars, that they paid a painter to 'black' the altar-cloth, whitelimed the church, and delivered the best suit of vestments and other church goods to the mayor.[27]

Superficially, what was happening at London, Cambridge, and Chester at the opening of Queen Elizabeth's reign may have seemed like a repetition, all over again, of the worst excesses of Edwardian iconoclasm. Yet the emphasis was subtly different. Both Henry VIII and Edward VI had called themselves, and acted as, 'Supreme Head of the Church'. Elizabeth, more susceptible to the finer feelings of her subjects, preferred the title by which the churchwardens of St Margaret Moses (London) described her in the heading of their 1561–2 account—'our sovereign Lady Elizabeth defender of the faith and supreme governor of the Church of England and Ireland next immediately under God'.[28] Elizabeth's own actions were frequently confusing. In a celebrated exchange with the dean of St Paul's on New Year's Day 1562, she was to ask him pointedly—'Have you forgotten our proclamations against images, pictures, and Romish relics in the churches? Was it not read in your deanery?', only to choke him off with a 'To your text, Mr Dean' when, three years later, he preached before her against images.[29] However, it was at least in part this very flexibility that made compromise at last more possible. There was no more talk, as there had been under Edward, of the removal of screens or, failing that, the shutting off altogether of the chancel. Nobody, even in this age of experiment in architecture, built one of those round churches that Martin Bucer, the German reformer in exile in England from 1549, had considered best adapted to corporate worship. Nor were Nicholas Ridley's views on the permanent migration of the altar

137 The Jacobean chancel screen and royal arms at Lydiard Tregoze Church, Wiltshire, with the remains of a medieval rood-painting over the arch itself and some fragmentary post-Reformation texts on the same wall

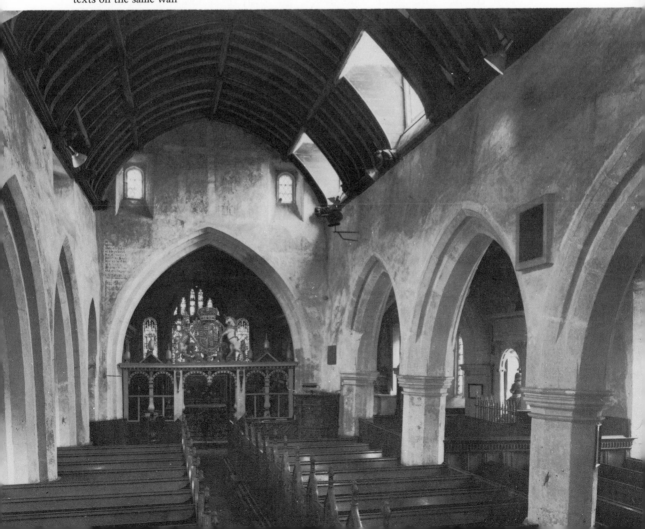

away from the east end of the church to a more central position in the chancel accepted without qualification by his successors. To be sure, the Elizabethan parish church, whitewashed and stripped of its ornaments, could look very unlike its pre-Reformation equivalent. But as a frame for worship, whether traditional or reformed, it continued essentially the same.

The elements of this frame, as they had been before, were the two distinct cells—nave and chancel. Fully corporate worship was a principle firmly established by the reformers. No priest, from now onwards, was to conduct divine service from behind the chancel screen, and it became usual for him to be supplied with a reading desk and seat either next to or in the midst of his congregation. But the chancel, for all that, preserved its special quality. At the east end, in its traditional place, stood 'God's board'—in Bishop Thomas Bentham's words, 'a decent and simple table upon a frame covered with a fair carpet, and a fine linen tablecloth upon it, in as beautiful a manner as it was being upon the altar'.[30] For the celebration of Holy Communion, this table would be moved to a more central position, 'as whereby the minister may be more conveniently heard of the communicants in his prayer and ministration, and the communicants also more conveniently and in more number communicate with the said minister'. However, when all was done, the table would go back against the east wall again, in rather the same way as the font, once thought by the reformers to be better placed by the altar, was restored under Elizabeth to the nave.[31]

Convenience and good order were the principles most emphasized by the Elizabethan Church authorities. Superstition and idolatry were still denounced as vigorously as they had been before, with the result that the rood and its images were invariably removed and the entire rood-loft usually demolished. Yet where these coincided, only the top of the chancel screen was removed, the rest being finished off decently with a suitable cornice perhaps crowned with a royal coat-of-arms. If the pre-Reformation screen were considered too dense, it might be taken down by the parishioners but would have to be replaced by some substitute.[32] And if idolatrous paintings were whitewashed over, there might still be a place for Time and Death figures, or for Moses and Aaron, supporting the Tables of the Law.[33] Improving texts, of course, as a form of church decoration, had been familiar since the reign of Edward VI. Shortly after his accession, the churchwardens of St Mary at Hill (London) had paid as much as £4 for the 'scriptures' on the rood-loft which were scrubbed off again under Mary, and at St Mary the Great (Cambridge), only a little later, even more had been found for the 'wryghtynge of the chyrch walles with scryptures' at a total cost of £4 3s 4d.[34] Usually, what these scriptures included would have been the Lord's Prayer, the Ten Commandments, and the Creed, frequently replacing the Doom over the chancel arch, or either flanking or over 'God's table'. Among the improvements completed at Holy Trinity (Chester) before 1566 was a fine 'table of commandemants', painted by Thomas Poole for a charge of 20s and clearly more important than the other 'scriptures in plaster in church' which the same painter 'did write' for a mere 1s 4d.[35] The purpose of these writings, as Elizabeth herself made clear, was chiefly the edification of the parishioners. But they had also, in her view, a decorative role—'to give some comlye ornament and demonstration, that the same is a place of religion and prayer'.[36]

For the clergy who lived through the events of the mid-sixteenth century the

138 The arms of Elizabeth, with a remarkably complete 'table of commandments', filling the chancel
     arch at Tivetshall Church, Norfolk

underlying conservatism of the Tudor Reformation was both good and bad in turn. Its happiest result, certainly, was that very few of the parish clergy, at least before the reign of Mary, faced any serious risk of deprivation. Its worst consequence was that no attempt was made, despite all the well-rehearsed arguments in favour of it, to improve or even to alter the funding of the ministry in the parishes.

Significantly, the deprivations which began in Mary's reign and which continued in some measure under Elizabeth, only exceptionally had anything to do with religious dissent. They were disciplinary, that is to say, not controversial, and although they included (as always) a small number of deprivations for non-residence, their usual cause was the issue of matrimony. 'Hoo,' cried the celibate Robert Parkyn, 'it was joye to here and see how thes carnall preastes (whiche had ledde ther lyffes in fornication with ther whores & harlotts) dyd lowre and looke downe, when thay were commandyde to leave & forsayke the concubyns and harlotts and to do oppen penance accordynge to the Canon Law, whiche then [after the formal reunion with Rome] toyke effectt.'[37] As a part of such penance, John Fisher, a priest of Norwich, was required to read a formal statement which began:

Derelye beloved. Forasmoche as I have taken to wyffe one Cecylie Harward, and
therbye (using her as my wyff) have offended bothe God and all faithfull and
catholik people, I do here, from the botomp of my harte, confesse that this my
doinge was evell and detestable before the face of God, contrarye to Gode's lawes,
the decrees of auncient fathers, and the King and Quene's graces [Philip's and
Mary's] lawes, and therfor I am hartelye sorye.[38]

One of those who was not so sorry was John Ponet, bishop of Winchester (1551–3),
whose loss of his see had a good deal to do with his own tangled matrimonial affairs.
As he warned from his exile, those who took over the confiscated benefices under the
new queen did so at their peril, for 'like as princes and rulers be subject to changes, so
a poor man's right dieth not. What is extortion if this be not? To put out of goods and
living one without a cause and to thrust in another without a just title?'[39]

In the final event, the Marian deprivations were to prove no more than an episode.
Serious enough in their time, they had resulted in the expulsion of over three
hundred clergy in the diocese of Norwich, the great majority of these for matrimonial
causes.[40] However, to take a smaller unit, of the eighty-eight Essex clergy deprived
for matrimony during Mary's reign, thirty were back in their benefices within two
years of Elizabeth's accession; nine had died in the meantime, and at least twelve had
found benefices elsewhere.[41] Characteristically, the expulsion of the 'usurpers' to
make way for the returning married clergy was not itself to result in much hardship.
Thirty such priests were removed in Essex, but so great was the shortage of qualified
clergy in England that eighteen of these, and probably more, were granted benefices
again very quickly.[42]

The many vacant cures at the beginning of Elizabeth's reign had resulted from a
number of causes. The Church, like everybody else, had experienced severe losses in
the high mortalities of the influenza epidemics of the late 1550s, and these would
have had to be made up. But the short-fall, estimated at between 10 and 15 per cent of
the benefices of England, was more obviously the result of a crisis of confidence and
of a profound and very general insecurity. Through the comings and goings of the
previous reigns, every priest in the realm, whatever his standing, had experienced
some challenge to the beliefs he held most dear. Yet as important an agent in the
contemporary destruction of clerical morale was a major change that had come about
in what was popularly expected of the parish clergy. In the pre-Reformation Church,
the quality of the individual priest, although still important, had mattered less in the
final event than the due performance of his formal round of services in the church—it
was the office that counted, not the priest, and a bad pastor might still sing a good
mass. However, the Protestant view of the role of the clergy placed much greater
emphasis on pastoral care and on preaching in the localities. What was required now
by popular demand was both a literate and an articulate priesthood. The old lady of
Bottesford (Leicestershire) who, in Oliver Cromwell's day, was 'preached to death' in
her pew, had stayed there so long for the very good reason that it was preaching that
she had come to church to hear.[43] The fumbling and demoralized divines of a century
earlier could only exceptionally have provided what she and her kind had become
accustomed to.

One solution to these difficulties in the early years of the Reformation in England had been to employ itinerant preachers in such rural churches as might otherwise have been starved of the word. But when, in 1575, Archbishop Grindal of York ordered an examination of his clergy, it was noted that although Robert Dande, curate of Newton (deanery of Bulmer) for the last eighteen months, was 'moderately learned', had taught the Catechism, had started a parish register, and seemed 'an honest young man as it appears', his congregation had had no sermons yet in the first four months of 1575 and only one the year before. John Rysdale, curate of Kneeby in the same deanery, was reported to be 'zealous'—'he holds the reason of the Faith; he has many sermons; he has observed the order of the register and similarly teaches the Catechism'. But his case was certainly exceptional. In the archdeaconry of Cleveland, Hugh Nixon, curate of Farlington, although he 'seems religious', had had no sermons. The rector of Balby 'seems pious and religious' but 'he has had no sermons because he can have no preachers who have the faculty of preaching'. In Craven, the rector of Bolton by Bowland, aged sixty-eight, 'keeps hospitality' and 'reads Latin moderately' but 'has not performed his due sermons'. Another pastor in the same deanery, aged seventy-five and a veteran survivor of the many religious skirmishes of his day, 'understands fairly well and reads indistinctly; altogether lacking in sound doctrine; vehemently contends that he has always abominated idols; does not perform his sermons'.[44]

Essentially, the problem had been one of recruitment. In Archbishop Grindal's time, the situation was beginning to improve, and young men of ability were again being attracted to the Church. But these, at least initially, soon won their promotion out of the parishes, and it was not to be until towards the end of Elizabeth's reign that the great majority of the rural churches would at last come in out of the cold. When they did so, the medieval Church, in country and town, had decisively come to an end. However, it should be the cause of no surprise that it had taken so long over its dying. For the Church as a whole, the Henrician Reformation, with its punishing regime of first-fruits and tenths, had proved a 'fiscal catastrophe'.[45] Moreover, lay hostility to the priesthood was strong. Heavy taxation elicited no sympathy, and no serious thought was given before the Civil War to the problem of maintaining a salaried clergy on stipends unchanged since the late Middle Ages, despite the erosion of these by inflation.[46] In some measure, the conservatism of the reformers, preserving tithes and the profits of the glebe as the principal basis of the parish-church economy, protected the revenues of the more fortunate clergy, which could now be expected to grow with inflation. But this protection was reserved for the beneficed clergy, privileged of old, and stipendiary chaplains, parochial assistants, and all those who had exchanged a monastic appropriator for a layman, were rarely better off—indeed, frequently suffered very badly. So long as graduates remained in short supply, as the prestige of the clergy persisted low, and as other professions like the law offered a more promising alternative, the more able and ambitious a man might be, the less he was drawn to the Church.

'Except,' it was said, 'the preacher himself lives well, his predication helps never a deal'. And Elizabeth's bishops, including Edmund Grindal as bishop of London and archbishop of York and of Canterbury in succession, did what they could to improve the quality and the status of their clergy. Elizabeth herself, early in her reign, diverted the income from Crown prebends to support students of theology at the universities. Sidney Sussex (Cambridge) was one of the colleges established specifically to serve as an Anglican seminary, while the statutes of Emmanuel, at the same university, declared the college's 'one aim' to be 'rendering as many persons as possible fit for the sacred ministry of the word and the sacraments; so that from this seminary the Church of England might have men whom it may call forth to instruct the people and undertake the duty of pastors'.[47]

Gradually, the manuals and other liturgical works that had formed the whole libraries of even the better-off pre-Reformation parish clergy were replaced by works of theology and up-to-date commentaries presenting more of an intellectual challenge. The vicar of Mattersey, on the Nottinghamshire-Yorkshire border, was not unique in possessing at his death in 1580 a small personal library that included 'Christstome works, two Geneva Testaments, Mizolius worke, a Greeke dictionarye, Mr Dr Arvinus Expositions in English upon the Episles and Gospelles'. At Burtor. Agnes (Yorkshire), six years before, Robert Pala, the vicar there, had left 'all my bookes of my owne written annotations and collections', with a number of commentaries and 'both my volumes of Mr Juells workes', being Bishop John Jewel's popular defence of the English Church—the *Apologia Ecclesiae Anglicanae* of 1562.[48] Many parish libraries from that time on would possess a copy of John Foxe's *Acts and Monuments*, the first of its numerous English editions being published in 1563. And there might also have been the works of Calvin and Bullinger, Erasmus and Arvinus, at last made available at comparatively low cost by the still recent technological breakthrough of mass printing.

The transformation of the parish clergy had taken its time, but by the end of the sixteenth century it was everywhere virtually complete. Although still not exclusively the preserve of the universities, the Anglican priesthood by 1600 was increasingly a graduate profession. The improved learning of the parish priest had recommended him to the society of the gentry, and if he continued to have problems, they were those he shared with every family, high and low, in the locality. 'He has care,' it was said, 'that keeps children'; and the clergy of Leicester, by the early seventeenth century, were undoubtedly finding it so. 'My livinge is verie small,' complained the vicar of Cosby, 'my charge verie great, xiii children livinge, and I live in debt'. From Enderby-with-Whetstone a colleague wrote, 'my estate very poor, my children are tenne'.[49] Women, as the medieval manual-writers and homilists had repeatedly emphasized (above, p. 52), are indeed 'the devil's mousetraps', and for all the warmth and humanity of the post-Reformation Church, there were undoubtedly those among its husbands and fathers who looked back to the past with nostalgia. John Foxe had suggested of the Marian suspended clergy that some at least, over-hasty in matrimony, were not unhappy 'of their own inconstant accord to be separated from their wives'.[50] But married or not, there was something to be said for the simplicities of an earlier unreformed Church in which the rules had been so very much clearer. In the rich proverbial wisdom of the fifteenth century, one piece of advice (as valid today) may serve as an epitaph to its teaching:

> Misspend not five [the five senses],
> Flee seven [the Seven Deadly Sins],
> Keep well ten [the Ten Commandments],
> And come to heaven.

Abbreviations

Antiq.	Antiquarian, antiquaries
Antiq. J.	*Antiquaries Journal*
Arch.	Archaeology, archaeological
Arch. J.	*Archaeological Journal*
Archit.	Architecture, architectural
Assoc.	Association
Bodleian	Bodleian Library, Oxford
Bul.	Bulletin
Bul. Inst. Hist. Res.	*Bulletin of the Institute of Historical Research*
Coll.	Collections
E.H.R.	*English Historical Review*
Ec.H.R.	*Economic History Review*
Hist.	History, historic, historical
Inst.	Institute
J.	Journal
J. Brit. Arch. Assoc.	*Journal of the British Archaeological Association*
J. Eccl. H.	*Journal of Ecclesiastical History*
Med. Arch.	*Medieval Archaeology*
N.M.R.	National Monuments Record
Proc.	Proceedings
Rev.	Review
Soc.	Society
Trans	Transactions
T.R.H.S.	*Transactions of the Royal Historical Society*
V.C.H.	*Victoria History of the Counties of England*

Notes and References

Chapter 1   Origins

1   For this and other proverbs quoted later in this book, see Bartlett Jere Whiting's invaluable *Proverbs, Sentences, and Proverbial Phrases from English Writings mainly before 1500*, 1968.
2   John Godfrey, *The English Parish 600–1300*, 1969, p. 44.
3   Ibid., p. 44.
4   G. W. O. Addleshaw, *The Development of the Parochial System from Charlemagne (768–814) to Urban II (1088–1099)*, St Anthony's Hall Publications, 6 (1954), p. 13; for another useful account of parish formation, see the same author's *The Beginnings of the Parochial System*, St Anthony's Hall Publications, 3 (1953).
5   G. W. O. Addleshaw, op. cit. (1954), p. 14.
6   Brian K. Roberts, *Rural Settlement in Britain*, 1977, p. 94; for a fuller discussion of the Lincolnshire evidence, see Dorothy M. Owen, *Church and Society in Medieval Lincolnshire*, 1971, pp. 2–12.
7   H. C. Darby, *Domesday England*, 1977, pp. 52–6.
8   David C. Douglas (ed.), *The Domesday Monachorum of Christ Church Canterbury*, 1944, pp. 8–13.
9   Frank Barlow, *The English Church 1000–1066*, 1963, p. 207.
10 H. C. Darby, op. cit., pp. 53–4.
11 For quotations from the chroniclers, see Reginald Lennard, *Rural England 1086–1135*, 1959, p. 297 (note 1).
12 *V. C. H. Sussex*, ii: 4–5.
13 G. H. Tupling, 'The pre-Reformation parishes and chapelries of Lancashire', *Trans Lancashire and Cheshire Antiquarian Soc.*, 67 (1957), pp. 1–16; S. A. Jeavons, 'The pattern of ecclesiastical building in Staffordshire during the Norman period', *Trans Lichfield and South Staffordshire Arch. and Hist. Soc.*, 4 (1962–3), pp. 5–22; Dorothy Sylvester, 'Parish and township in Cheshire and north-east Wales', *J. Chester Arch. Soc.*, 54 (1967), pp. 23–35; Christopher Brooke and Gillian Keir, *London 800–1216: the Shaping of a City*, 1975, p. 129.
14 D. C. Douglas and G. W. Greenaway (eds), *English Historical Documents 1042–1189*, 1953, pp. 953–6; B. W. Kissan, 'An early list of London properties', *Trans London and Middlesex Arch. Soc.*, new series, 8 (1938), pp. 57–69.
15 J. W. F. Hill, *Medieval Lincoln*, 1948, pp. 144–5.
16 J.-P. Migne (ed.), *Patrologiae Latinae*, cxlii: 651.
17 Francis Bond, *Dedications and Patron Saints of English Churches*, 1914, p. 17. Among many regional studies of church dedications, the more recent include the Rev. C. L. S. Linnell's *Norfolk Church Dedications*, St Anthony's Hall Publications, 21 (1962), William Addison's 'Parish church dedications in Essex', *Trans Essex Arch. Soc.*, 2 (1966–70), pp. 34–46, R. V. H. Burne's 'Church dedications in Dorset', *Proc. Dorset Nat. Hist. and Arch. Soc.*, 90, (1968), pp. 269–81, and J. E. Oxley's 'the medieval church dedications of the city of London', *Trans London and Middlesex Arch. Soc.*, 29 (1978), pp. 117–25.
18 D. J. Freke, 'Excavations in the parish church of St Thomas à Beckett, Pagham, West Sussex', *Bul. Inst. Arch.*, 14 (1977), pp. 62–3.
19 Dorothy M. Owen, op. cit., p. 13; Reginald Lennard, 'Two peasant contributions to church endowment', *E.H.R.*, 67 (1952), pp. 230–33.
20 For the king's churches, see J. H. Denton, 'Royal supremacy in ancient demesne churches', *J. Eccl. H.*, 22 (1971), pp. 289–302.
21 Edward Miller, 'Some twelfth-century documents concerning St Peter's Church at Babraham', *Proc. Cambridge Antiquarian Soc.*, 59 (1966), pp. 113–23.
22 Brian R. Kemp, 'The churches of Berkeley Hernesse', *Trans Bristol and Gloucestershire Arch. Soc.*, 87 (1968), pp. 96–110; also Arthur Sabin, 'St Augustine's Abbey and the Berkeley churches', ibid., 89 (1970), pp. 90–98.

23 F. R. H. Du Boulay, 'Bexley Church: some early documents', *Archaeologia Cantiana*, 72 (1958), pp. 41–53.

24 Ibid., pp. 42–3; for a useful survey of these practices, see G. W. O. Addleshaw, *Rectors, Vicars and Patrons in Twelfth and Early Thirteenth Century Canon Law*, St Anthony's Hall Publications, 9 (1956).

25 Barbara Harvey, *Westminster Abbey and its Estates in the Middle Ages*, 1977, p. 48.

Chapter 2   Buildings and Church Furnishings before 1350

1 For recently excavated examples of these, at Aismunderby (Yorkshire) and Broadfield (Hertfordshire), both attributed to the thirteenth and fourteenth centuries, see *Med. Arch.*, 9 (1965), pp. 187–8, and Eric C. Klingelhöfer, *Broadfield Deserted Medieval Village*, British Arch. Reports 2, 1974, pp. 16–23.

2 Some comment on the problems of status is included in Bridget Cherry's useful 'Ecclesiastical architecture', in *The Archaeology of Anglo-Saxon England* (ed. D. M. Wilson), 1976, pp. 151–200, especially p. 181.

3 The classification and listing is H. M. Taylor's, as published in his *Anglo-Saxon Architecture*, vol. 3, 1978, chapter 15 (Anglo-Saxon church plans).

4 Ibid., p. 997.

5 Warwick and Kirsty Rodwell, 'Excavations at Rivenhall Church, Essex', *Antiq. J.*, 53 (1973), pp. 220–25; J. G. Hurst, 'Wharram Percy: St Martin's Church', in *The Archaeological Study of Churches* (eds Peter Addyman and Richard Morris), pp. 36–9.

6 Warwick Rodwell, 'The archaeological investigation of Hadstock Church, Essex. An interim report', *Antiq. J.*, 56 (1976), pp. 55–71.

7 Martin Biddle, 'Excavations at Winchester, 1970. Ninth interim report', *Antiq. J.*, 52 (1972), pp. 104–7, 111–15; Christina Colyer and Brian Gilmour, 'St Paul-in-the-Bail, Lincoln', *Current Arch.*, 63 (1978), pp. 102–5; Alan Thompson, 'St Nicholas-in-the-Shambles', ibid., 65 (1979), pp. 176–9.

8 P. J. Drury and W. J. Rodwell, 'Investigations at Asheldham, Essex. An interim report on the church and the historic landscape', *Antiq. J.*, 58 (1978), pp. 133–51.

9 Dorothy M. Owen, *Church and Society in Medieval Lincolnshire*, 1971, p. 5. The date given by Mrs Owen is 'before 1180'.

10 J. G. Hurst, op. cit., pp. 36–9; also *Current Arch.*, 49 (1975), pp. 44–5.

11 Warwick and Kirsty Rodwell, op. cit., pp. 225–7.

12 Owen Bedwin. 'The excavation of the church of Saint Nicholas, Angmering, West Sussex', *Bul. Inst. Arch.*, 12 (1975), pp. 46–8.

13 Barry Cunliffe, *Winchester Excavations 1949–1960*, 1964, pp. 25, 44.

14 *Lincoln Archaeological Trust, 4th annual report 1975–6*, pp. 17–21; *Med. Arch.*, 21 (1977), pp. 231–2.

15 *Med. Arch.*, 16 (1972), p. 177.

16 Ibid., 18 (1974), p. 194.

17 For stone-building, ecclesiastical and lay, in the twelfth and thirteenth centuries, see my own *Medieval England. A Social History and Archaeology from the Conquest to 1600 A.D.*, 1978, especially chapter 2 (Economic Growth).

18 Warwick Rodwell, op. cit. (1976), pp. 64–5; *Med. Arch.*, 22 (1978), p. 165 (St Paul-in-the-Bail); Dorothy M. Owen, op. cit., p. 113. The Wyberton failure may not have occurred before the early fifteenth century, for it was only then, in 1419–20, that the church at Wyberton was substantially rebuilt, probably following the collapse of the tower over the crossing (*Lincolnshire Notes & Queries*, 14 (1917), pp. 225–35).

19 T. R. Thomson and H. M. Taylor, 'St Mary's Church, Cricklade: part II', *Wiltshire Arch. and Nat. Hist. Mag.*, 61 (1966), pp. 38–42.

20 Owen Bedwin, op. cit., p. 46; J. G. Hurst, op. et loc. cit.

21 *Med. Arch.*, 16 (1972), p. 177 (Thurleigh); P. J. Drury and W. J. Rodwell, op. cit., p. 141 (Asheldham).

22 L. F. Salzman, *Building in England down to 1540*, 1967, pp. 437–8.

23 W. Sparrow Simpson (ed.), *Visitations of Churches belonging to St Paul's Cathedral in 1297 and in 1458*, Camden Society, new series, 55 (1895), pp. 48–9, 102.

24 F. M. Powicke and C. R. Cheney (eds), *Councils and Synods, with other Documents relating to the English Church, II. A.D. 1205–1313. (Part II, 1265–1313)*, 1964, pp. 1005–6; H. Michell Whitley, 'Visitations of Devonshire churches', *Report and Trans Devonshire Assoc.*, 42 (1910), pp. 449–51.

25 W. Sparrow Simpson, op. cit., pp. 48–9.

26 H. Michell Whitley, op. cit., pp. 452–3.

27 G. G. Coulton, 'A visitation of the archdeaconry of Totnes in 1342', *E.H.R.*, 26 (1911), p. 109.

28 F. M. Powicke and C. R. Cheney (eds), op. cit., p. 1003.

29 Harry Rothwell (ed.), *English Historical Documents 1189–1327*, 1975, p. 695.

30 C. Eveleigh Woodruff, 'Some early visitation rolls preserved at Canterbury. II', *Archaeologia Cantiana*, 33 (1918), p. 85. For other sets of useful early visitation records, see W. Sparrow Simpson's *Visitations of Churches belonging to St Paul's Cathedral 1249–1252*, Camden Society, new series, 53 (1895), and the same author's 'Visitations of certain churches in the City of London in the patronage of St Paul's Cathedral Church, between the years 1138 and 1250', *Archaeologia*, 55 (1897), pp. 283–300; and see also Dom Aelred Watkin's *Inventory of Church Goods temp. Edward III (Archdeaconry of Norwich)*, Norfolk Record Society, 19 (1947).

31 Eve Baker, 'East Shefford Church, Berkshire', *Trans Ancient Monuments Soc.*, new series, 19 (1972), pp. 37–45.

32 Audrey M. Baker, 'The wall paintings in the church of St John the Baptist, Clayton', *Sussex Arch. Coll.*, 108 (1970), pp. 58–81.

33 Tancred Borenius and E. W. Tristram, *English Medieval Painting*, 1927, p. 4.

34 E. Clive Rouse and Audrey Baker, 'Wall paintings in Stoke Orchard Church, Gloucestershire, with particular reference to the cycle of the life of St James the Great', *Arch. J.*, 123 (1966), pp. 79–119.

35 E. W. Tristram, *English Medieval Wall Painting. The Thirteenth Century*, 1950, pp. 349–53, 626–9, and plates 177–90.

36 Ibid., pp. 275–81, 510–15, and plates 123–8.

37 Tancred Borenius and E. W. Tristram, op. cit., p. 21 and plate 52.

38 L. A. S. Butler, 'Minor medieval monumental sculpture in the East Midlands', *Arch. J.*, 121 (1964), pp. 111–53; and see also the same author's 'Medieval cross-slabs in Nottinghamshire', *Trans Thoroton Soc.*, 56 (1952), pp. 25–40, and 'Medieval gravestones of Cambridgeshire, Huntingdonshire and the Soke of Peterborough', *Proc. Cambridge Antiquarian Soc.*, 50 (1956), pp. 89–100.

39 For a useful discussion, with illustrations, of these effigies, see Edward S. Prior and Arthur Gardner, *An Account of Medieval Figure-Sculpture in England*, 1912, pp. 646–51.

40 Early-fourteenth-century tiled floors have been recorded, for example, at the parish churches of Meesden (Hertfordshire), Northill (Bedfordshire), and Helpston (Northamptonshire); for these, see Laurence Keen, 'A fourteenth-century tile pavement at Meesden, Hertfordshire', *Hertfordshire Arch.*, 2 (1970), pp. 75–81, J. M. Bailey, 'Decorated 14th-century tiles at Northill Church, Bedfordshire', *Med. Arch.*, 19 (1975), pp. 209–13, and Laurence Keen and David Thackray, 'Helpston Parish Church, Northamptonshire: the remains of a medieval tile pavement', *J. Brit. Arch. Assoc.*, 129 (1976), pp. 87–92.

41 J. G. Davies, *The Secular Use of Church Buildings*, 1968, passim.

42 Thomas Bruce Dilks (ed.), *Bridgwater Borough Archives 1200–1377*, Somerset Record Society, 48 (1933), pp. 65–7.

Chapter 3   The Clergy

1 The words are from John Mirk's *Festiall*, a work of the early fifteenth century (Karl Young, 'Instructions for parish priests', *Speculum*, 11 (1936), p. 225).

2 W. A. Pantin, *The English Church in the Fourteenth Century*, 1955, pp. 193–4.

3 F. M. Powicke and C. R. Cheney (eds), *Councils and Synods, with other documents relating to the English Church A.D. 1205–1313*, 1964, ii: 1078–80.

4 The passage is from the *Penitential* of Bartholomew Iscanus, bishop of Exeter (1161–84), being a part of the section headed 'Of Magic' (John T. McNeill and Helena M. Gamer, *Medieval Handbooks*

of Penance, 1938 (reprinted 1965), p. 350).

5   W. A. Pantin, op. cit., pp. 195–202. Much, of course, even of William of Pagula's social advice was not original to his manual. For the warning against the smothering of babies, for example, see the Worcester statutes of 1240, chapter 27 (F. M. Powicke and C. R. Cheney (eds), op. cit., i: 302). The proverbs are from Bartlett Jere Whiting's *Proverbs, Sentences and Proverbial Phrases*, 1968.

6   W. A. Pantin, op. cit., p. 209.

7   Ibid., p. 208.

8   C. N. L. Brooke, 'Gregorian reform in action: clerical marriage in England, 1050–1200', *Cambridge Hist. J.*, 12 (1956), pp. 1–21, 187–8.

9   Colin Morris, 'Letheringsett: the early history of a parish church', *Bul. Inst. Hist. Res.*, 44 (1971), pp. 116–20.

10   Brian R. Kemp, 'Hereditary benefices in the medieval English church: a Herefordshire example', *Bul. Inst. Hist. Res.*, 43 (1970), pp. 1–15.

11   Glanmor Williams, *The Welsh Church from Conquest to Reformation*, 1962, pp. 337–44.

12   Marion Gibbs and Jane Lang, *Bishops and Reform 1215–1272, with special reference to the Lateran Council of 1215*, 1934, pp. 158–60; F. M. Powicke and C. R. Cheney (eds), op. cit., i: 98–9.

13   Harry Rothwell (ed.), *English Historical Documents 1189–1327*, 1975, p. 696.

14   C. Eveleigh Woodruff, 'Some early visitation rolls preserved at Canterbury', *Archaeologia Cantiana*, 32 (1917), pp. 161, 164, 177.

15   Harry Rothwell (ed.), op. cit., p. 719. Professor Rothwell has here translated a passage left in the original Latin in Woodruff's earlier edition.

16   Ibid., p. 696.

17   For the very general dying-out of the practice, see C. N. L. Brooke, op. cit., pp. 18–19; also C. R. Cheney, *From Becket to Langton, English Church Government 1170–1213*, 1956, pp. 128–9, and, at a local level, J. E. Newman, 'Greater and lesser landowners and parochial patronage: Yorkshire in the thirteenth century', *E.H.R.*, 92 (1977), pp. 281–2.

18   Marion Gibbs and Jane Lang, op. cit., p. 162.

19   F. M. Powicke and C. R. Cheney (eds), op. cit., i: 268, and see also Roy M. Haines, 'Education in English ecclesiastical legislation of the later Middle Ages', in *Studies in Church History* (eds G. J. Cuming and Derek Baker), 7 (1971), pp. 162–3.

20   H. S. Bennett, 'Medieval ordination lists in the English episcopal registers', in *Studies presented to Sir Hilary Jenkinson* (ed. J. Conway Davies), 1957, pp. 31–4.

21   Harry Rothwell (ed.), op. cit., p. 703.

22   Roy M. Haines, op. cit., p. 166.

23   Rosalind M. T. Hill (ed.), *The Rolls and Register of Bishop Oliver Sutton 1280–1299* (vol. 1), Lincoln Record Society, 39 (1942), p. xx. For a useful discussion of the working of *Cum ex eo*, see Roy M. Haines, 'The education of the English clergy during the later Middle Ages: some observations on the operation of Pope Boniface VIII's constitution *Cum ex eo* (1298)', *Canadian J. Hist.*, 4 (1969), pp. 1–22.

24   David Robinson, *Beneficed Clergy in Cleveland and the East Riding 1306–1340*, Borthwick Papers 37, 1969, pp. 14–15, 37, 43.

25   W. A. Pantin, op. cit., pp. 195–6.

26   Norma Adams, 'The judicial conflict over tithes', *E.H.R.*, 52 (1937), pp. 1–22.

27   C. R. Cheney, *Medieval Texts and Studies*, 1973, p. 197.

28   For these, see C. R. Cheney, op. cit. (1973), pp. 198–9, and the very comprehensive discussion of clerical incomes in John R. H. Moorman's *Church Life in England in the Thirteenth Century*, 1945, chapters IX and X.

29   W. A. Pantin, op. cit., pp. 203–4.

30   John R. H. Moorman, op. cit., pp. 126–32; G. W. O. Addleshaw, *Rectors, Vicars and Patrons in Twelfth and Early Thirteenth Century Canon Law*, St Anthony's Hall Publications, 9 (1956), pp. 4–5.

31   Harry Rothwell (ed.), op. cit., p. 705.

32   C. R. Cheney, op. cit. (1973), p. 196.

33   For a properly cautious discussion of this, see Marjorie Chibnall, 'Monks and pastoral work: a problem in Anglo-Norman history', *J. Eccl. H.*, 18 (1967), pp. 165–72.

34   For an example of this at Tavistock Abbey (Devonshire), still the case in the late fourteenth

century, see R. A. R. Hartridge, *A History of Vicarages in the Middle Ages*, 1930 (reprinted 1968), p. 150.

35   Ibid., loc. cit.; also cited by W. A. Pantin, 'Medieval priests' houses in south-west England', *Med. Arch.*, 1 (1957), p. 120.

36   A. R. Myers (ed.), *English Historical Documents 1327–1485*, 1969, p. 726.

37   W. A. Pantin, op. cit. (1957), pp. 121–4 and plate XVII.

38   *Med. Arch.*, 11 (1967), pp. 314–15.

39   F. M. Powicke and C. R. Cheney (eds), op. cit., i: 273.

40   R. A. R. Hartridge, op. cit., pp. 130–33; W. A. Pantin, op. cit. (1957), pp. 120–21.

41   S. E. Rigold, 'The demesne of Christ Church at Brook', *Arch. J.*, 126 (1969), pp. 270–72; for Ashleworth, see my own *The Monastic Grange in Medieval England*, 1969, especially pp. 187–8.

42   E. G. Cuthbert F. Atchley, 'Medieval parish-clerks in Bristol', *Trans St Paul's Ecclesiological Soc.*, 5 (1901–5), pp. 107–116; for the festival of the boy-bishop on St Nicholas's Day, see C. H. Evelyn-White, 'The boy bishop (*episcopus puerorum*) of mediaeval England', *J. Brit. Arch. Assoc.*, 11 (1905), pp. 30–48, 231–56.

43   A. R. Myers (ed.), op. cit., pp. 726–8.

44   R. A. R. Hartridge, op. cit., p. 154.

45   John R. H. Moorman, op. cit., p. 122.

Chapter 4   A Crisis of Faith

1   For the difficulties experienced by the abbots of Meaux (Yorkshire) at this time, especially at their Humberside granges, see my *The Monastic Grange in Medieval England*, 1969, pp. 63–5.

2   Dorothy M. Owen, *Church and Society in Medieval Lincolnshire*, 1971, p. 141.

3   Colin Platt, *Medieval England. A Social History and Archaeology from the Conquest to 1600 A.D.*, 1978, pp. 111–15.

4   J. G. Bellamy, *Crime and Public Order in England in the Later Middle Ages*, 1973, p. 79.

5   Colin Platt, op. cit. (1978), p. 100.

6   Ian Kershaw, 'The Great Famine and agrarian crisis in England 1315–1322', *Past and Present*, 59 (1973), pp. 3–50.

7   A. Hamilton Thompson, 'Registers of John Gynewell, bishop of Lincoln, for the years 1347–1350', *Arch. J.*, 68 (1911), pp. 309–10. Bishop Gynewell's preoccupation with the wars is probably to be explained by the part he had taken in 1344 in peace negotiations between England and France (ibid., p. 306).

8   Ibid., pp. 313–14.

9   A. R. Myers (ed.), *English Historical Documents 1327–1485*, 1969, p. 90.

10   R. M. Haines (ed.), *A Calendar of the Register of Wolstan de Bransford, bishop of Worcester 1339–49*, Worcestershire Historical Society, 4 (1966), pp. li–lii.

11   A. Hamilton Thompson, op. cit., pp. 315, 319, 321.

12   Ibid., p. 329.

13   Claude Jenkins, 'Sudbury's London register', *Church Quarterly Rev.*, 107 (1928–9), pp. 232–4.

14   Nevill Coghill (trans.), *Visions from Piers Plowman taken from the poem of William Langland*, 1949 (reprinted 1953), p. 16.

15   R. C. Fowler and C. Jenkins, *Registrum Simonis de Sudbiria Diocesis Londoniensis A.D. 1362–1375*, Canterbury and York Society, 38 (1938), p. xxix.

16   A. R. Myers (ed.), op. cit., pp. 728–9.

17   R. A. R. Hartridge, *A History of Vicarages in the Middle Ages*, 1930 (reprinted 1968), p. 114.

18   R. B. Dobson, *Durham Priory 1400–1450*, 1973, p. 165; Julian Cornwall, 'The people of Rutland in 1522', *Trans Leicestershire Arch. and Hist. Soc.*, 37 (1961–2), p. 21.

19   Harry Rothwell (ed.), *English Historical Documents 1189–1327*, 1975, p. 704.

20   For a useful discussion of these ambiguities, see Keith Thomas, *Religion and the Decline of Magic*, 1971, chapter 2 (The Magic of the Medieval Church).

21   For this passage and a full discussion of both incidents, see Dorothy M. Owen, 'Bacon and eggs:

Bishop Buckingham and superstition in Lincolnshire', *Studies in Church History*, 8 (1972), pp. 139–42.

22 Harry Rothwell (ed.), op. cit., p. 731.

23 For the cult of Archbishop Scrope, see Richard Marks, 'The glazing of Fotheringhay Church and College', *J. Brit. Arch. Assoc.*, 131 (1978), pp. 96–7; and for Henry VI, see Brian Spencer, 'King Henry of Windsor and the London pilgrim', *Collectanea Londiniensia* (eds Joanna Bird, Hugh Chapman and John Clark), 1978, pp. 235–64. Another contemporary cult, that of Bishop Edmund Lacey of Exeter (d. 1455), is discussed by U. M. Radford, 'The wax images found in Exeter Cathedral', *Antiq. J.*, 29 (1949), pp. 164–8.

24 G. G. Coulton, *Five Centuries of Religion*, 1936, iii: 196.

25 R. A. R. Hartridge, op. cit., p. 109.

26 R. B. Dobson, op. cit., pp. 269–71; for Pershore, see R. A. R. Hartridge, op. cit., p. 110.

27 R. B. Dobson, op. cit., p. 251.

28 G. G. Coulton, op. cit., iii: 182.

29 Ibid., p. 181.

30 A. Hamilton Thompson, *The English Clergy and their Organization in the Later Middle Ages*, 1947, pp. 114–15.

31 I. Keil, 'Impropriator and benefice in the later Middle Ages', *Wiltshire Arch. and Nat. Hist. Mag.*, 58 (1961–3), pp. 351–61.

32 R. A. R. Hartridge, op. cit., p. 78.

33 G. G. Coulton, op. cit., iii: 173.

34 Ibid., p. 169.

35 Ernest Harold Pearce, *Thomas de Cobham, bishop of Worcester 1317–1327. Some studies drawn from his register with an account of his life*, 1923, pp. 125–6.

36 R. M. Haines, *The Administration of the Diocese of Worcester in the First Half of the Fourteenth Century*, 1965, p. 254.

37 A. Hamilton Thompson, op. cit. (1947), p. 115.

38 K. L. Wood-Legh, *Studies in Church Life in England under Edward III*, 1934, pp. 134–5.

39 P. A. Bill, *The Warwickshire Parish Clergy in the later Middle Ages*, Dugdale Society Occasional Papers 17, 1967, p. 10.

40 Barbara Harvey, *Westminster Abbey and its Estates in the Middle Ages*, 1977, p. 51.

41 A. Hamilton Thompson, op. cit. (1947), p. 112.

42 G. G. Coulton, op. cit., iii: 209.

43 K. L. Wood-Legh, op. cit., p. 152.

44 G. G. Coulton, op. cit., iii: 175.

45 Ibid., iii: 176 (Commons petition of 1432).

46 Ibid., iii: 199.

47 Christopher Harper-Bill, 'A late medieval visitation—the diocese of Norwich in 1499', *Proc. Suffolk Inst. Arch.*, 34 (1977), p. 44.

48 R. A. R. Hartridge, op. cit., p. 78.

49 P. A. Bill, op. cit., p. 14.

50 M. J. Bennett, 'The Lancashire and Cheshire clergy 1379', *Trans Hist. Soc. Lancashire and Cheshire*, 124 (1972), p. 7; J. T. Driver, *Cheshire in the Later Middle Ages 1399–1540*, 1971, p. 130.

51 Peter Heath, *The English Parish Clergy on the Eve of the Reformation*, 1969, p. 137.

52 M. J. Bennett, op. cit., pp. 11–17.

53 Peter Heath, op. et loc. cit.

54 J. E. Newman, 'Greater and lesser landowners and parochial patronage: Yorkshire in the thirteenth century', *E.H.R.*, 92 (1977), pp. 280–308.

55 Joel Thomas Rosenthal, *The Training of an Elite Group: English Bishops in the Fifteenth Century*, Trans American Philosophical Soc., new series, vol. 60, part 5, 1970, p. 21.

56 P. A. Bill, 'Five aspects of the medieval parochial clergy of Warwickshire', *University of Birmingham Hist. J.*, 10 (1966), p. 106.

57 Margaret Aston, *Thomas Arundel. A Study of Church Life in the Reign of Richard II*, 1967, pp. 312–13.

58 Ibid., pp. 309–10; A. R. Myers (ed.), op. cit., pp. 699–703.

59   A. R. Myers (ed.), op. cit., p. 731; for the Durham churches, see R. B. Dobson, op. cit., chapter 5 (Monastic Patronage); also Elizabeth M. Halcrow, 'The social position and influence of the priors of Durham, as illustrated by their correspondence', *Archaeologia Aeliana*, 4th series, 33 (1955), pp. 70–86, and Robert Donaldson, 'Sponsors, patrons and presentations to benefices—particularly those in the gift of the priors of Durham—during the later Middle Ages', ibid., 38 (1960), pp. 169–77.

60   A. Hamilton Thompson, 'Pluralism in the mediaeval Church; with notes on pluralists in the diocese of Lincoln', *Assoc. Architectural Soc. Reports and Papers*, 33 (1915), pp. 41–3.

61   Ibid., pp. 70–71.

62   Christopher Harper-Bill, op. cit., p. 41.

63   Margaret Bowker, *The Secular Clergy in the Diocese of Lincoln 1495–1520*, 1968, pp. 90–92.

64   Ibid., p. 97.

65   C. H. Williams (ed.), *English Historical Documents 1485–1558*, 1967, pp. 653–4, 657.

66   Margaret Bowker, op. cit., p. 109; and see also, for a similar defence of the clergy, J. F. Fuggles, 'The parish clergy in the archdeaconry of Leicester 1520–1540', *Trans Leicestershire Arch. and Hist. Soc.*, 46 (1970–71), pp. 25–44, and Peter Heath, op. cit., passim.

67   Peter Heath, *Medieval Clerical Accounts*, St Anthony's Hall Publications 26, 1964, p. 10.

68   Ibid., p. 24.

69   A. C. Chibnall (ed.), *The Certificate of Musters for Buckinghamshire in 1522*, Buckinghamshire Record Society, 17 (1974), p. 13.

70   Margaret Bowker, op. cit., p. 141.

71   W. G. Hoskins, *Essays in Leicestershire History*, 1950, pp. 3–4.

72   F. R. H. Du Boulay, 'Charitable subsidies granted to the archbishop of Canterbury, 1300–1489', *Bul. Inst. Hist. Res.*, 23 (1950), pp. 147–64.

73   Peter Heath, op. cit. (1969), p. 146.

74   For a comment on this, see R. B. Outhwaite, *Inflation in Tudor and Early Stuart England*, 1969, pp. 13–14, and Peter H. Ramsey, *The Price Revolution in Sixteenth-Century England*, 1971, p. 4.

75   C. H. Williams (ed.), op. cit., p. 654.

76   Christopher Harper-Bill, 'Archbishop John Morton and the Province of Canterbury, 1486–1500', *J. Eccl. H.*, 29 (1978), pp. 1–21.

77   Margaret Bowker, 'The Commons Supplication against the Ordinaries in the light of some archidiaconal *acta*', *T.R.H.S.*, 5th series, 21 (1971), pp. 61–77.

78   C. H. Williams (ed.), op. cit., pp. 669–70.

Chapter 5   The Community of the Parish

1   Charles Drew, *Early Parochial Organisation in England. The Origins of the Office of Churchwarden*, St Anthony's Hall Publications 7, 1954, passim; Emma Mason, 'The role of the English parishioner, 1100–1500', *J. Eccl. H.*, 27 (1976), particularly pp. 24–6.

2   Charles Drew, op. cit., pp. 16–17.

3   Jean Scammell, 'The rural chapter in England from the eleventh to the fourteenth century', *E.H.R.*, 86 (1971), pp. 1–21.

4   For these titles, see Dorothy M. Owen, *Church and Society in Medieval Lincolnshire*, 1971, pp. 116–17.

5   A. R. Myers (ed.), *English Historical Documents 1327–1485*, 1969, pp. 726–8.

6   W. O. Ault, 'Manor court and parish church in fifteenth-century England: a study of village by-laws', *Speculum*, 42 (1967), p. 65.

7   Charles Drew, op. cit., p. 19.

8   C. Trice Martin, 'Clerical life in the fifteenth century, as illustrated by proceedings of the court of Chancery', *Archaeologia*, 60 (1907), p. 369. I have here modernized the spelling.

9   W. O. Ault, op. cit., pp. 58–9.

10 Ibid., pp. 62–3.

11 A. T. Bannister, 'Visitation returns of the diocese of Hereford in 1397', *E.H.R.*, 44 (1929), pp. 279–89, 444–53, and 45 (1930), pp. 92–101, 444–63.

12   L. F. Salzman, *Building in England down to 1540*, 1967, pp. 499–500.

13   Ibid., pp. 547–9. The churches are illustrated together in my *Medieval England*, 1978, fig. 93.

14   Thomas Bruce Dilks (ed.), *Bridgwater Borough Archives 1200–1377*, Somerset Record Society, 48 (1933), pp. 159–64.

15   A. R. Myers (ed.), op. cit., pp. 741–4.

16   J. F. Williams, 'The Black Book of Swaffham', *Norfolk Archaeology*, 33 (1962–5), pp. 243–53.

17   L. F. Salzman, op. cit., pp. 496–7.

18   Margaret Bowker, *The Secular Clergy in the Diocese of Lincoln 1495–1520*, 1968, pp. 127–9.

19   W. M. Palmer, 'Fifteenth-century visitation records of the deanery of Wisbech', *Proc. Cambridge Antiq. Soc.*, 39 (1940), pp. 69–75.

20   A. R. Myers (ed.), op. cit., pp. 722–4.

21   For this characteristic contemporary opinion, see K. L. Wood-Legh, 'Some aspects of the history of chantries in the later Middle Ages', *T.R.H.S.*, 4th series, 28 (1946), p. 48.

22   W. Sparrow Simpson (ed.), *Visitations of Churches belonging to St Paul's Cathedral in 1297 and in 1458*, Camden Society, 55 (1895), p. lxviii.

23   D. A. Johnson, 'Dean Bate's statutes for St Edith's, Tamworth, Staffordshire, 1442', *Trans South Staffordshire Arch. and Hist. Soc.*, 10 (1968–9), p. 59.

24   Brian S. Smith, 'Little Waltham church goods, c. 1400', *Trans Essex Arch. Soc.*, 1 (1961–5), pp. 111–13.

25   Leland L. Duncan, 'The parish churches of West Kent, their dedications, altars, images, and lights', *Trans St Paul's Ecclesiological Soc.*, 3 (1890–5), pp. 268, 272, 273.

26   R. Garraway Rice, 'Notes relating to the parish church of St Mary Pulborough, Sussex, derived from 15th and 16th century wills', *Trans St Paul's Ecclesiological Soc.*, 4 (1895–1900), p. 136.

27   E. G. Cuthbert F. Atchley, 'Some inventories of the parish church of St Stephen, Bristol', *Trans St Paul's Ecclesiological Soc.*, 6 (1906–10), pp. 161–84. For similar entries in the records of other Bristol churches, see the same author's 'On the mediaeval parish records of the church of St Nicholas, Bristol', ibid., 6 (1906–10), pp. 35–67, and Betty R. Masters and Elizabeth Ralph, *The Church Book of St Ewen's, Bristol, 1454–1584*, Publications of the Bristol and Gloucestershire Archaeological Society, Records Section, 6 (1967), passim.

28   W. Sparrow Simpson, 'Inventory of the vestments, plate, and books, belonging to the church of St Peter Cheap, in the city of London, in the year 1431', *J. Brit. Arch. Assoc.*, 24 (1868), pp. 150–60.

29   T. F. Reddaway, 'The London Goldsmiths, circa 1500', *T.R.H.S.*, 5th series, 12 (1962), p. 57.

30   W. H. St John Hope, 'Ancient inventories of goods belonging to the parish church of St Margaret Pattens in the city of London', *Arch. J.*, 42 (1885), in particular pp. 320–23.

31   Ibid., p. 330 and passim.

32   Ibid., p. 329.

33   H. F. Westlake, 'The parish gilds of the later fourteenth century', *Trans St Paul's Ecclesiological Soc.*, 8 (1917–20), p. 105.

34   W. H. St John Hope, op. cit., p. 326.

35   A. Hamilton Thompson, *The English Clergy and their Organization in the Later Middle Ages*, 1947, p. 141.

36   R. M. Haines (ed.), *A Calendar of the Register of Wolstan de Bransford, Bishop of Worcester 1339–49*, Worcestershire Historical Society, 4 (1966), pp. xxxviii–ix; also the same author's *The Administration of the Diocese of Worcester in the First Half of the Fourteenth Century*, 1965, pp. 233–4.

37   William St John Hope, 'The colour-rule of Pleshy College, 1394–5', *Trans St Paul's Ecclesiological Soc.*, 8 (1917–20), pp. 41–8. For liturgical colours in general, see the same author's 'On the English liturgical colours', ibid., 2 (1886–90), pp. 233–72.

38   William St John Hope and Cuthbert Atchley, 'An inventory of Pleshy College, 1527', *Trans St Paul's Ecclesiological Soc.*, 8 (1917–20), pp. 160–72.

39   For the diocese of Worcester figures, see R. M. Haines, op. cit. (1965), p. 231.

40   Anthony G. Dyson, 'A calendar of the cartulary of the parish church of St Margaret, Bridge Street (Guildhall Library MS. 1174)', *Guildhall Studies in London History*, 1: 3 (1974), pp. 177, 179–80.

41   Rosalind Hill, ' "A Chaunterie for Soules": London chantries in the reign of Richard II', in *The Reign of Richard II* (eds F. R. H. Du Boulay and Caroline M. Barron), 1971, p. 244.

42 R. B. Dobson, 'The foundation of perpetual chantries by the citizens of medieval York', *Studies in Church History*, 4 (1967), p. 31.

43 Colin Platt, *Medieval Southampton. The Port and Trading Community, A.D. 1000–1600*, 1973, pp. 188–9.

44 E. G. Cuthbert F. Atchley, op. cit., pp. 176–7.

45 R. B. Dobson, op. cit., p. 35.

46 Ibid., p. 36.

47 For a full discussion of these duties, see K. L. Wood-Legh, *Perpetual Chantries in Britain*, 1965, chapter XI.

48 H. F. Westlake, *The Parish Gilds of Mediaeval England*, 1919, pp. 32–3, and the same author's 'The parish gilds of the later fourteenth century', *Trans St Paul's Ecclesiological Soc.*, 8 (1917–20), pp. 102–3.

49 H. F. Westlake, op. cit. (1917–20), p. 104.

50 Alexandra F. Johnston, 'The guild of Corpus Christi and the procession of Corpus Christi in York', *Mediaeval Studies*, 38 (1976), pp. 372–403.

51 L. V. D. Owen (ed.), *The Account Books of the Gilds of St George and of St Mary in the Church of St Peter, Nottingham*, 1939, pp. 48–9.

52 J. F. Williams, 'The Gild of St John the Baptist at Swaffham', *Norfolk Arch.*, 33 (1962–5), pp. 2–5.

53 W. G. Hoskins, *Old Devon*, 1971, p. 184.

54 *V.C.H. City of Kingston upon Hull*, pp. 288–9.

55 L. F. Salzman, op. cit., p. 503.

56 E. G. Cuthbert F. Atchley, 'Some more Bristol inventories', *Trans St Paul's Ecclesiological Soc.*, 9 (1922–8), pp. 48–9.

57 J. E. Jackson, 'Wiltshire chantry furniture', *Wiltshire Arch. and Nat. Hist. Mag.*, 22 (1885), pp. 318–29.

58 This passage from John Mirk's *Festial* is quoted by A. Caiger-Smith, *English Medieval Mural Paintings*, 1963, p. 42.

59 Wilfrid Puddephat, 'The mural paintings of the Dance of Death in the guild chapel of Stratford-upon-Avon', *Trans and Proc. Birmingham Arch. Soc.*, 76 (1958), pp. 29–35.

60 Ethel Carleton Williams, 'The Dance of Death in painting and sculpture in the Middle Ages', *J. Brit. Arch. Assoc.*, 3rd series, 1 (1937), pp. 230, 238.

61 For Widford, see E. T. Long, 'Medieval wall paintings in Oxfordshire churches', *Oxoniensia*, 37 (1972), pp. 89, 105–6; for Peakirk, see E. Clive Rouse, 'Wall paintings in the church of St Pega, Peakirk, Northamptonshire', *Arch. J.*, 110 (1953), pp. 144–7. For the legend, see A. Caiger-Smith, op. cit., pp. 45–9, and E. Carleton Williams, 'Mural paintings of the Three Living and the Three Dead in England', *J. Brit. Arch. Assoc.*, 3rd series, 7 (1942), pp. 31–40.

62 Gillis Kristensson (ed.), *John Mirk's Instructions for Parish Priests*, 1974, p. 67.

63 Ibid., p. 81.

64 A. Caiger-Smith, op. cit., pp. 58–63.

65 Ibid., pp. 55–8; for the earlier interpretation, see E. W. Tristram, '*Piers Plowman* in English wall-painting', *Burlington Magazine*, 31 (July–December 1917), pp. 135–40.

66 Barbara Harvey, 'Work and *festa ferianda* in medieval England', *J. Eccl. H.*, 23 (1972), pp. 289–308; also C. R. Cheney, 'Rules for the observance of feast-days in medieval England', *Bul. Inst. Hist. Res.*, 34 (1961), pp. 117–47.

67 Christopher Woodforde, *English Stained and Painted Glass*, 1954, p. 26; E. A. Gee, 'The painted glass of All Saints' Church, North Street, York', *Archaeologia*, 102 (1969), pp. 158–62 and plate xxiii.

68 Richard Marks, 'The glazing of Fotheringhay Church and College', *J. Brit. Arch. Assoc.*, 131 (1978), pp. 79–109.

69 John A. Knowles, *Essays in the History of the York School of Glass-Painting*, 1936, pp. 169–70.

70 Richard Marks, 'Henry Williams and his "Ymage of Deth" roundel at Stanford on Avon, Northamptonshire', *Antiq. J.*, 54 (1974), pp. 272–4 and plate liv.

71 W. Sparrow Simpson (ed.), *Visitations of Churches belonging to St Paul's Cathedral in 1297 and in 1458*, Camden Society, new series, 55 (1895), p. lxiii.

72 Arthur Gardner, *Minor English Wood Sculpture 1400–1550*, 1958, pp. 20–38; and see also the same author's almost identical 'The East Anglian bench-end menagerie', *J. Brit. Arch. Assoc.*, 3rd series, 18 (1955), pp. 33–41.

73 H. Munro Cautley, *Norfolk Churches*, 1949, pp. 218, 270. For church screens in general, see Aymer Vallance's *English Church Screens*, 1936, and Francis Bond's *Screens and Galleries in English Churches*, 1908.

74 H. Munro Cautley, op. cit., p. 240.

75 H. Munro Cautley, *Suffolk Churches and their Treasures*, 1937, p. 82.

76 L. F. Salzman, op. cit., pp. 537–8.

77 Fred H. Crossley, *English Church Monuments A.D. 1150–1550*, 1921, p. 31.

Chapter 6   The Reformation

1 A. G. Dickens, 'Heresy and the origins of English Protestantism', in *Britain and the Netherlands* (eds J. S. Bromley and E. H. Kossman), 1964, pp. 47–66.

2 Margaret Bowker, 'The Henrician Reformation and the parish clergy', *Bul. Inst. Hist. Res.*, 50 (1977), pp. 32–3.

3 Christopher Haigh, *Reformation and Resistance in Tudor Lancashire*, 1975, p. 86.

4 Margaret Bowker, op. cit., passim; also the same author's 'Lincolnshire 1536: heresy, schism or religious discontent?', *Studies in Church History*, 9 (1972), pp. 195–212.

5 Margaret Bowker, op. cit. (1972), p. 206.

6 Claire Cross, *Church and People 1450–1660*, 1976, p. 77.

7 Christopher Haigh, op. cit., p. 83.

8 K. G. Powell, 'The beginnings of Protestantism in Gloucestershire', *Trans Bristol and Gloucestershire Arch. Soc.*, 90 (1971), pp. 146–7.

9 Leland L. Duncan, 'The parish churches of West Kent, their dedications, altars, images, and lights', *Trans St Paul's Ecclesiological Soc.*, 3 (1890–5), p. 251.

10 Edward Percival Dickin, 'Embezzled church goods of Essex', *Trans Essex Arch. Soc.*, 13 (1915), p. 170.

11 Ibid., pp. 157–8, 161.

12 Claire Cross, op. cit., p. 72.

13 Edward Percival Dickin, op. cit., passim.

14 W. Sparrow Simpson, *Visitations of Churches belonging to St Paul's Cathedral in 1297 and in 1458*, Camden Society, 55 (1895), pp. 76–7, 118, 121.

15 C. H. Williams (ed.), *English Historical Documents 1485–1558*, 1967, p. 853.

16 Betty R. Masters and Elizabeth Ralph, *The Church Book of St Ewen's, Bristol, 1454–1584*, 1967, pp. xxxvi, 182–5.

17 Gordon Huelin, 'A sixteenth-century churchwardens' account book of St Margaret Moses', *Guildhall Studies in London History*, 1: 1 (1973), p. 2.

18 J. E. Foster (ed.), *Churchwardens' Accounts of St Mary the Great, Cambridge, from 1504 to 1635*, Publications of the Cambridge Antiquarian Society, 35 (1905), pp. 116–17.

19 E. G. Cuthbert F. Atchley, 'On the mediaeval parish records of the church of St Nicholas, Bristol', *Trans St Paul's Ecclesiological Soc.*, 6 (1906–10), p. 63.

20 J. R. Beresford, 'The churchwardens' accounts of Holy Trinity, Chester, 1532 to 1633', *J. Chester and North Wales Archit., Arch. and Hist. Soc.*, 38 (1951), p. 97.

21 J. E. Foster (ed.), op. cit., p. 120.

22 A. G. Dickens, 'Robert Parkyn's narrative of the Reformation', *E.H.R.*, 62 (1947), p. 68.

23 J. E. Foster (ed.), op. cit., pp. 129–30.

24 A. G. Dickens, op. cit. (1947), pp. 80, 82.

25 Henry Littlehales (ed.), *The Medieval Records of a London City Church (St Mary at Hill), A.D. 1420–1559*, Early English Text Society, 128 (1905), p. lxxii.

26 J. E. Foster (ed.), op. cit., pp. 146–7.

27 J. R. Beresford, op. cit., p. 123.

28 Gordon Huelin, op. cit., p. 4.

29   John Phillips, *The Reformation of Images: Destruction of Art in England, 1535–1660*, 1973, pp. 127–8.
30   G. W. O. Addleshaw and Frederick Etchells, *The Architectural Setting of Anglican Worship*, 1948, p. 34.
31   Ibid., p. 24.
32   Ibid., pp. 30–31.
33   E. Clive Rouse, 'Post-Reformation mural paintings in parish churches', *The Lincolnshire Historian*, 1 (1947), p. 11.
34   Henry Littlehales (ed.), op. cit., p. lxxii; J. E. Foster (ed.), op. cit., p. 119.
35   J. R. Beresford, op. cit., p. 124.
36   John Phillips, op. cit., p. 129; G. W. O. Addleshaw and Frederick Etchells, op. cit., p. 35.
37   A. G. Dickens, op. cit. (1947), p. 82.
38   J. F. Williams, 'The married clergy of the Marian period', *Norfolk Arch.*, 32 (1958–61), p. 93.
39   Hilda E. P. Grieve, 'The deprived married clergy in Essex, 1553–1561', *T.R.H.S.*, 4th series, 22 (1940), p. 161.
40   J. F. Williams, op. cit., p. 88.
41   Hilda E. P. Grieve, op. cit., pp. 165–6.
42   Ibid., p. 168.
43   W. G. Hoskins, *Essays in Leicestershire History*, 1950, p. 23.
44   J. S. Purvis, 'The literacy of the later Tudor clergy in Yorkshire', *Studies in Church History*, 5 (1969), pp. 158–60.
45   J. J. Scarisbrick, 'Clerical taxation in England, 1485 to 1547', *J. Eccl. H.*, 11 (1960), p. 53.
46   Felicity Heal, 'Economic problems of the clergy', in *Church and Society in England: Henry VIII to James I* (eds Felicity Heal and Rosemary O'Day), 1977, pp. 99–118.
47   Rosemary O'Day, 'The reformation of the ministry, 1558–1642', in *Continuity and Change. Personnel and Administration of the Church in England 1500–1642* (eds Rosemary O'Day and Felicity Heal), 1976, pp. 62–3.
48   J. S. Purvis, op. cit., p. 155.
49   W. G. Hoskins, op. cit., p. 18.
50   Quoted by Hilda E. P. Grieve, op. cit., p. 153.

Index